Paths to Prayer

FINDING YOUR OWN WAY
TO THE PRESENCE OF GOD

Patricia D. Brown

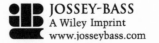

JOSSEY-BASS
A Wiley Imprint
www.josseybass.com

Jossey-Bass books and products are available through most bookstores. To contact Jossey-Bass directly
call our Customer Care Department within the U.S. at 800-956-7739, outside the U.S. at 317-572-
3986, or fax 317-572-4002.

Jossey-Bass also publishes its books in a variety of electronic formats. Some content that appears in
print may not be available in electronic books.

Library of Congress Cataloging-in-Publication Data
Brown, Patricia D., date.
Paths to prayer: finding your own way to the presence of God /
    Patricia D. Brown.—1st ed.
      p. cm.
    Includes bibliographical references.
    ISBN 0–7879–6565–0 (alk. paper)
    1. Prayer.   I. Title.
BV210.3.B76 2003
248.3'2—dc21   2003007628

Printed in the United States of America
FIRST EDITION
HB Printing 10 9 8 7 6 5 4 3 2 1

Contents

To Ken Cowles
and
pilgrims on the Christ Path

Though one may be overpowered,
two can defend themselves
A cord of three strands is
not quickly broken.
—BASED ON ECCLESIASTES 4:12

For where two or three are gathered
together in my name
there I am in their midst.
—BASED ON MATTHEW 18:20

Introduction

*T*eresa of Avila wrote:

> Mental prayer in my opinion is nothing else than an intimate sharing between friends; it means taking time frequently to be alone with him who we know loves us. The important thing is not to think much but to love much and so do that which best stirs you to love. Love is not great delight but desire to please God in everything.

It is this thought of Teresa's, paired with a loving desire to teach a deep and lasting love of prayer to others, that is at the heart of this text. My whole life, in one sense, has been an experiment in how to be honest—before God and with myself—

in prayer. For honest prayer arises in an attitude of humility—a humility that opens the mind and heart, our whole being, to God. In humility I renounce my own power and acknowledge my poverty and dependence on God. I leave behind all the illusions about myself and am grounded in the truth of my life. It is in this truth that I learn to practice the presence of God in the midst of my daily life.

I created this collection of prayer practices for people who want to join me on a journey of discovery to look for ways to mature and move into a practice-centered life of prayer. I have drawn on the wealth of faith-based practices from Christian tradition, across centuries and communities, to present prayer practices and rituals that can speak to each of us, wherever we are in our journey of faith. As you explore these ways of praying, I hope you will find the integrity that helps you to be humble and honest in your prayer life.

Teresa's guidebook on prayer, *The Way of Perfection*, was written during a controversial time of reform in the saint's religious community, the Carmelite Order. Intended to serve as a guide in the practice of prayer, it sets forth directives for growing into the image of Christ through prayer. Like Teresa, my aim in writing this guidebook is to do justice to the needs of the present turbulent age within religious institutions and our culture.

Sage words from Teresa's prologue offer further guidance for me: "I shall speak of nothing of which I have no experience, either in my own life or in observation of others, or which the Lord has not taught me in prayer." Many wise men and women past and present have experienced God through prayer; we could spend a lifetime learning from them. In creating this book, I've consulted the teachings of both traditional and contemporary theologians, and in the workshops and prayer retreats I lead I've listened to the experience of people who faithfully practice prayer. I have drawn on their wisdom to supplement my own knowledge and experience.

Yet experience remains my best teacher. I try to be open to what my own prayerful encounters, along with common sense, have to teach me. In this book, I share practices and methods that have changed my life since I began to create an "inner room" for God. These writings contain some of the understandings that have come to light as I struggled to put prayer into practice, both in my own life and in my work with others who also seek a prayerful relationship with God.

I believe that an authentic Christian life is one that binds us to Christ and leads us each moment, through the power of God's Spirit, as we continue to enter the daily struggle of accepting the gift and responsibility that the Holy Spirit gives. My end desire remains the same: that I draw closer to God and dwell in the Holy. I hold fast to the promise that "the one who began a good work among you will bring it to completion by the day of Jesus Christ" (Phil. 1:6). This desire has in turn fed my intention in writing this book: to provide a resource of prayer practices for thinking believers that integrates heart and head, faith and reason, and holy living with active compassion. My prayer is that you will find ways of praying that make you attentive to the needs of the world around you, and that create a sacred space in which you move past your differences with others of faith, to find commonality and community.

We are in the midst of an awakening that underscores the breakdown of isolation among all the spiritual traditions. In fact, a recent study showed that 85 percent of those Americans who responded who identify with Christianity do not exclude from their lives wisdom and teachings from other great world religions. They understand that other faiths have something to share with us; their writings, teachings, and practices help us understand our own faith in a fresh way.

My hope is that Christians are healthily moving past the walls of prejudice to become part of a greater universal community, but without negating their own rich

4

faith tradition. We are gaining a deep, evolving experience of community between and among faiths and a growing receptivity to the inner treasures of the world's religions. Catholic Brother Wayne Teasdale, author of *The Mystic Heart,* explains that openness to other faiths does not mean that one submerges the differences; instead, this spirituality sees traditions in relationship to one another, opening the door to a broader truth.

My further hope, therefore, is that by encouraging exploration of prayers and practices used in different cultures throughout the two thousand years of Christian history, you will discover new ways to encounter the divine that deepen both your faith and your understanding of God.

I have attempted to create an easy-to-read, user-friendly handbook that you can apply on your own or in a group. *Paths to Prayer* leads you through step-by-step instructions for more than forty ways to pray. These gentle introductions to a variety of prayer styles encourage even the most hesitant of spirit to find ways of praying that are comfortable for them. This hands-on approach is intended for those who want to learn to pray, those who already pray but want to deepen their practice of prayer, and those who want to know how prayer "works." Using illustration and instruction, the book balances intellectual knowledge of prayer along with heart-centered practices that can be applied to our lives and transform us.

Obviously, each practice in this book has had to be simplified, abridged, and shortened to make it manageable for a first-time introduction. One colleague, a Jesuit with an intimate knowledge of Ignatius's *Spiritual Exercises,* was amazed that I would try to reduce Ignatian prayer to such a short order, thereby leaving out important nuances. This is the reason I list so many other resources you can turn to for further instruction. This book is meant to whet your appetite, not serve the full course.

Before we set out on this journey together, I would like to clarify my approach to writing a book about prayer. First, no single book could hold all the ways of praying, for there are as many ways to pray as there are souls who walk the earth. I don't have the definitive word on prayer, but my hope is that in the variety of prayers included in this book you may find some prayer practices that speak to you. Whether you choose to develop one practice or many, my end desire remains the same: that you grow closer to God and reside in the Holy.

Second, I have very little patience with prepackaged answers or categorizations that make prayer sound easy and manageable. Prayer is not something to be managed. Nor is it always easy. I'm skeptical of aggressive efforts by some religious individuals and groups who push shortcut methods to a comfortable prayer life and do not struggle with the whole person. I favor a slower, but sturdier and more humbling, development of one's prayer life that builds an all-embracing spiritual foundation for the sometimes-difficult soul searching that prayer requires.

I find little validity in romanticized prayer, idealized in sweetness and light, an approach that sees the rose while denying the thorn. It bypasses the reality of searching and the hard work of self-surrender that comes as we open our mind and heart—our whole being—to God. This is not a recipe book or an invitation to escape. Rather, it is an invitation to wrestle with the responsibility that prayer entails, both within our own souls and also in the world around us. Theologian Karl Barth is said to have observed that the Christian of today should have a Bible in one hand and a newspaper in the other. I agree. A life of prayer doesn't turn its back on the concerns of the world. Instead, it helps us discover the felt presence of God amid the nitty-gritty of everyday living.

HOW TO USE THIS BOOK

This book is structured so that the practices of prayer can be taught in a variety of settings and circumstances. Along with some basics of prayer to get you started,

I have included a prayer styles self-assessment, which invites you to reflect on your life, your beliefs, and your way of interacting with the world. Your responses on the self-assessment will guide you toward one of four styles of prayer—innovative, searching, relational, and experiential—that can serve as a comfortable starting point for the growth of your prayer life. Try a prayer, allow it to touch you, and then stop to reflect and absorb the prayer and mull it over for some time after experiencing it, before moving on to the next. Allow the experience to live and grow, just as your prayer life grows. You will discover that the experience of a particular prayer becomes more meaningful as you practice it on your own. You may find yourself jumping around in this book, scanning back to a previous chapter or exercise to reconsider a certain prayer with understanding and clarity you might have gleaned from a different practice altogether. Most of these practices can be used by an individual, but some do require a partner.

If you are more brave-hearted and have adventurous friends, gather a group to join you in this informal experiment. People who want to learn how to pray appreciate giving and receiving assistance from like-minded individuals. You'll find that there are lots of people who want to expand their spiritual life or learn how to pray.

Each practice begins with basic teachings and is laid out in an easy-to-follow manner for use by an individual or a group. If you are in a group, it is not necessary to have one appointed facilitator. Instead, the group members may want to rotate the responsibility. Through God's spirit, participants become teachers as well as the light of discovery for one another. Check beforehand to make sure you have any required props, such as beads for the rosary or a floor mat for the body prayer. Choose a space or room where you won't be interrupted. You might want to dim the lights, or burn a candle to give your space a more intimate atmosphere.

The first section common to most of the chapters, "Thoughts Before You Begin," helps you understand the history and background of a particular prayer practice. Be careful not to spend so much time in preparing that you don't leave sufficient time for the most important element, the practice itself.

The "Now Begin" section gives the step-by-step instructions. Take a few moments to center or quiet yourself before taking the first step. Then allow ample time for the prayer practice itself. Don't rush the experience.

"Some Things to Think About" and "Questions for Reflection" help you debrief your experience. If you are in a group, remember to pause for a few minutes of silence and reflection before opening a group discussion. Thinking about your experience of a prayer following the prayer itself is extremely important. Reflecting on your experience and putting it into words helps you come to thoughtful conclusions about your spiritual growth and development. If you are working through this book alone, you might seek the guidance of a spiritual companion, director, or mentor. When we tell our stories in the context of our faith, we become more aware of how God is speaking to us. When we listen carefully with our hearts as well as our heads, God touches us in a greater way than we ever imagined possible.

If you are in a group, share your experience in ways that honor each person's uniqueness. Sometimes it may be appropriate for you to respond to others in your group verbally, but most often listening is the best response. As you allow one another to share freely and as you learn to refrain from responding when it is unnecessary or unhelpful, you may experience what it means to serve as the compassionate presence of Christ to one another. Warmth and mutual support are present, but they are not the focus. Instead, the focus is the working of the Holy Spirit helping each individual to grow in faithfulness.

"Other Resources to Continue Your Journey," in most of the chapters, lists additional books and resources for study and practice. Between meetings, members of the group may choose to continue to explore the same practice until the next meeting, when they can set aside a period of time to share insights and reflections together.

MY OWN PATH TO PRAYER

My most recent study of prayer has been as an academic theological discipline, and I frequently lead seminars and retreats for people who also seek to nurture their spiritual growth. But my experience of Jesus began long ago, with dim awareness of the stirring of the Spirit in my heart as a young girl in the mountains of Pennsylvania. I was raised in a Christian home and an orthodox "Bible believing" congregation. It is from their faithful example that I continue to participate in the Church, the body of Christ, and God's mission.

As a young adult, I joined with the Evangelical United Brethren, who merged into the United Methodist Church, where I was ushered into the orthodox teachings and historic creeds of the Church. I continue to celebrate the gifts I received from my Wesleyan heritage, which gives me spiritual practices that have deepened my faith. In keeping with Wesley's "catholic spirit," I embrace the gifts Christians of past ages have conferred to us, which hold a vast storehouse of experience from which we can extract ways of being with God.

◊   ◊   ◊

My prayer life took a drastic turn at the death of my young husband, Richard. I was twenty-five, with a three-year-old son. As Richard underwent a series of surgeries, and through the final one, I prayed consistently for his recovery. But as his condition worsened, my prayers changed too. After four weeks, I no longer demanded God's cure, but rather God's compassion. I saw my husband's body for what it was: unable to sustain his life as God intended it. How did my prayer change? Richard was facing more surgical procedures, which would only prolong his suffering. His life had become a grueling struggle, each day worse than the last. What sort of lover would I be to make such a totally selfish request?

For Richard, my deepest desire was not that he live, but that he no longer suffer. In that moment, God's will and my desire became one. My prayer was answered with a yes. Death came six weeks after surgery. To some, this may seem like defeat after so much praying. But I believe his death was as much an answer to prayer as his recovery would have been. Now, my life of prayer is more open to the will of God than to my own limited human understanding.

Today, my "second" family and I are members of First United Methodist Church in downtown Orlando. Tonight, my husband, Dale, and I will join our Sunday school class, "The Parent's Forum," for our yearly Christmas dinner as our son Stephen goes to his weekly youth meeting at the *Skylight.* My son Christian, who was three when Richard died, now lives across the country and is always near to my heart and my thoughts. I have been richly blessed.

So, with roots deep and convictions strong, I offer a vision of prayer that is shaped by an ecumenical and interreligious sensibility and enriched by insights from psychology and related disciplines. Although I am well schooled in the variety of methods and approaches to prayer and the spiritual life, this work does not cling to any one of them. The concept of prayer presented here is at once broad and deep. What I share in this book has taken me a long time to experience and will take even longer to deepen into its purest promise. Therefore, I offer this book with humility and deference.

*An Invitation
to Prayer*

*T*his is an invitation to join in with the "cloud of witnesses," the "communion of the saint." You are one link in the continuous chain. We are carried by the prayer of others and by the prayer of the community of the faithful. People have prayed and are praying in different places, at different times, and even in different centuries. In collective prayer we place our lives within a broader context. Prayer rolls on without ceasing—someplace, somehow, someone is always praying. We then tend to act in accordance from this interior place of prayer in all aspects of our daily living.

Foundations of Prayer: One Size Doesn't Fit All
How Do You Pray? Finding Your Prayer Type

Foundations
of Prayer

ONE SIZE DOESN'T FIT ALL

*T*here is a common assumption that individuals who want to pray can simply pray. Or that people of faith automatically know how to pray—that somehow, talking with God comes naturally. There is also a misconception that people learn how to pray in private and then bring those practices of prayer with them into the community. In reality, I have found that for the most part people first learn how to pray in the context of community, and then they are able to carry the practice into their private lives.

Prayer is learned in much the same way that we learn how to drive. We watch and learn from others. We observe those who know what they are doing and imitate their actions. In the same way, we create opportunities for the inexperienced to observe how the community prays in common. Prayer is both gift and task. Spiritual writer Pat Collins explains: "When we pray unceasingly, we listen long and lovingly to the beating of the heart of God in human life, in history, in the world, and in the church. Every inch and ounce of life, the whole of creation, becomes a precinct of God's constant coming. If only we would have ears to hear and eyes to see!"

Prayer is not one-size-fits-all. The author of the fourteenth-century spiritual classic *The Cloud of Unknowing* seemed to understand that there is no single right way to pray, no one method that works for everybody all the time: "Do not pray with words unless you are really drawn to this; or if you do pray with words, pay no attention to whether they are many or few. Do not weigh them in their meaning. Do not be concerned about what kind of prayers you use, for it is unimportant whether or not they are official liturgical prayers, psalms, hymns, or anthems; whether they are for particular or general intentions; or whether you formulate them interiorly by thoughts, or express them aloud, in words."

To follow the apostle Paul's call to the Church to "pray without ceasing," we strive to find the right variety of *prayer rhythms* in our lives that address every level of our being, while at the same time remaining true to our deepest self.

What Is Prayer?

Let's start with a bit of background about the word *prayer.* The English word means "petition" or "request." *Precari,* the Latin word for prayer, means, "to beg." The Hebrew word for prayer, *palal,* means "to meditate," and a related Hebrew word-concept, *tsela,* means to bow down. In New Testament Greek, the word for prayer, *euchomai,* means to "wish" or "vow." So prayer is to petition, to request, to beg, to meditate, to bow down, to wish. Prayer is all that and more.

When we pray, we use words (spoken out loud or silently) and gestures to express what we believe about God and how we think about our relationship to God and to one another. In prayer, we communicate how God is active and present to us. In faith we pray, believing that God is concerned about and responsive to human need. Prayer expresses our personal relationship to God—a relationship that God intends and initiates and that we accept through the intercession of the Holy Spirit.

Prayer is not a technique or "gospel technology" that enables us to live a better life or reach a higher status; prayer is not a mechanism to save ourselves or a conversation with an exalted spiritual version of ourselves. If our higher self is all we have to pray to, then we are in big trouble. Christ-centered theology negates this thinking. The truth is that we cannot save ourselves; it is through God's grace that we are rescued. In the end, prayer is about a relationship in which we see God face to face as God loves us, with unflinching mercy, and gives God's self as a gift to each and every one of us. We give ourselves to God in return.

Prayer practices further a God-centered identity, as individuals and communities of faith. From age to age, the question of Christians is "How can I be more perfectly Christlike?" We don't achieve this likeness to the compassionate Christ by means of our own personal resources, self-actualization, superhuman effort, or sheer force of will. Rather, the power of the Holy Spirit conforms our lives to the ideal of the all-loving Christ (Rom. 5:5). We foster prayer disciplines such as fasting, acts of service, worship, and study to help ourselves cooperate with the Holy Spirit in transforming our lives. The work of the Holy Spirit leads us to a more authentic, vibrant walk with Christ.

Those who take the apostle Paul's words to heart know that unceasing prayer requires openness to prayer as a gift. They also realize that what Collins (the author of *Prayer and Practice: A Biblical Approach*) writes is true: "Prayer is, above all else,

16   a response to God's initiative. We can lift our mind and heart and voice to God in
prayer because of the life and love that have first been given to us."

PRAYER: OUR SPIRITUAL LEGACY

Prayer is our Christian heritage, developed over centuries of faithfulness. Therefore,
consider this book a voice of the community. It is not only the voice of the first
Christians but also a reflection of the prayer practices that developed over time as
the Christian Church grew larger and spread to new cultures. The approaches to
prayer that have come down to us from the many streams of Christian spiritual tradition tell us a great deal about how these early Christians understood God, themselves, and the world they lived in. Understanding these prayer forms that have been
developed over the years can also help us deepen our relationship with God.

Many Christian spiritual communities, such as the Dominicans of the late
twelfth century, the Franciscans of the late twelfth and early thirteenth centuries,
and the Beguines of the thirteenth century, originated during the Middle Ages,
when the printing press had not yet been invented and texts were scarce and hard to
come by. The prayer life of these groups revolved around community-based repetition and memorization. Other streams of Christian tradition, notably the Byzantine and Eastern Orthodox, emphasized special pictures and symbols to remind the
faithful to draw closer to God. Still others, such as the Celtic and, much later, the
Wesleyan tradition, gave prominence to poetry and hymns, forms that were easily
committed to memory.

As a product of the Reformation and the first printing press, books became ac-
cessible, and Anglican Christians used such works as the Bible and the *Book of Common Prayer* in their communion with God. Later, other groups, such as the
Methodists of the early eighteenth century, emphasized a variety of "felt" experi-

ences—spiritual practices such as prayer, reading scripture, observing the Lord's Supper, fasting, and Christian "conferencing" (meeting with others).

By claiming the Reformation Church—its history, tradition, and saints—as a significant part of their spiritual legacy, Protestants can gain new understanding of the foundational building blocks of their own traditions. I can only offer a brief historical sketch here. For about fifteen hundred years—this is before the Reformation that brought about the division of the Western Church—most Christians were part of either the Eastern Church of Constantinople or the Western Church of Rome. Before Martin Luther became a reformer, his faith was fueled by his life as an Augustinian monk; John Wesley, who lived and died an Anglican priest, studied at Oxford, where he was influenced by the lives of early church leaders such as Origen. Learning about the time period in which the prayer practices were created and used, and focusing on the life-giving truth they give, facilitates the development of a richer spiritual life. Each generation learns from those who have gone before them.

On the flip side of the same coin are members of the present Roman Catholic Church and Orthodox Churches who are missing out on the rich contribution that Protestant spirituality offers. Joseph Driskill, in his book *Protestant Spiritual Exercises: Theology, History and Practice,* asserts that within the Protestant heritage (especially the spiritual life of the early movements and leaders) they have a spiritual legacy that affirms the post-Reformation tradition and provides spiritual practices that integrate reason and faith, head and heart, prayer and social action to deepen faith. "Mainline Protestants need to celebrate the spiritual gifts they have received from their Protestant heritage: the mandate for ethical reflection and prophetic social action; the critical and analytical sensibilities that have committed Protestants to an understanding of modern worldviews and the Word of God; and the Protestant commitment to a transcendent God whose mysterious nature makes one suspicious of all authorities who claim to 'know God's will' or 'speak for God.'"

Christians of past ages have conferred to us a vast storehouse of experience from which we can extract ways of being with the divine. In writing about these prayer practices, it is not my attempt to impose on you outmoded and outdated forms of spiritual practices in the interest of nostalgia or in the hope of restoring some ancient order. Instead, I believe it is essential to study how our brothers and sisters attended to God in the past so that we might attend to and not miss the present-day "signs of the time" with which the same God beckons us. As we re-shape the old practices and combine them with the dynamism of constantly new forms of prayer, we remain faithful to the deepest sense of our calling.

Another benefit of examining past spiritualities is the wisdom that you can gain for your own prayer life. By reclaiming these early practices, you open yourself to an experience of God that gives meaning and hope to life. Visiting the Church of the past is not so much taking a new road as returning to the same worn path that contains guideposts and landmarks from long ago. Christianity, Eastern and Western, has given birth to an immense range of spiritual wisdom. We who are seeking God do not have to constantly blaze new trails; thank goodness, the paths are already marked. Brother Wayne Teasdale reminds us those spiritual traditions "are our common heritage; they belong to each one of us. . . . These great treasures are part of a universal mystical tradition, and our growth in the future depends on our willingness to integrate them into our own experience." Using a variety of practices is a way for us to get more deeply in touch with God and our sense of self.

Many of us have been trained to enter into religious actions with somber, inner control. Practicing new forms of prayer gives us an outlet for emotional expression—our feelings, needs, and yearnings—with an emphasis on sensory experience. We amaze even ourselves when we discover that laughter is not hostile to prayer, and that play can have profound power.

Lifting the cup and breaking the bread, waving palm branches on Palm Sunday, and lighting candles at the Easter Vigil: all of these are significant prayer rituals and practices that take the ordinary and recognize it as sacred. Rituals move us out of the temporal and into a sacred reality.

When prayer rituals and ceremonies are authentic, they kindle the imagination, evoke insight, and touch the heart.

- Rituals—community-based and personal—weave past, present, and future into life's ongoing tapestry. They help us face and mark the shocks, triumphs, and mysteries of everyday life by giving us tangible memories that we can hold onto.
- Prayer helps us experience the unseen webs of meaning, purpose, and passion that tie us together with others in community by offering symbols, words, and gestures that give expression to what is beyond understanding or explanation.
- Prayer helps us look at life in a new way, and make sense of it in the process.
- Prayer rituals elicit and reinforce faith within the Christian community. If feelings fail, we can rely upon the ritual and thus find strength.
- Living prayer rituals emphasize action, informality, and spontaneity even as they uphold the theological integrity of the written text, actions, and form.

Some Protestant expressions of the Christian faith balk at using prayer practices or rituals that introduce nonbiblical characters, stories, or incidents attributed to biblical people but not found in the Bible. They omit some of the ancient historical traditions and expressions of Christian faith, and in doing so they limit their opportunities to experience God afresh. The faithful Christian men and women of centuries past lived in a different culture and historical time period than we do, and their spiritual expression was colored by their experiences of their world. Their symbols, myths, stories, and traditions are part of the rich Christian history we have inherited. Their mythology and stories should not be viewed as "untruth," but rather an attempt to speak the truth in a symbolic way that points to a reality beyond words.

A nonbiblical story you'll encounter in this book is the legend of Veronica's aid to Jesus on the way to his crucifixion, which is part of the stations of the cross. Mary's assumption into heaven and her enthronement, used in the rosary, is understood as evidence of the "first fruits" of the mystery of bodily resurrection found in I Corinthians 15. You won't find a physical prayer labyrinth in the scriptures, but neither will you find pews or collection plates, which also assist us in our worship of God, nor the Christmas stories of the little drummer boy or the *three* kings. Yes, there were magi from the East, but their number is never stipulated.

We can draw on these practices and traditions from earlier generations of Christians as if they are gifts. With each prayer practice included in the book, I explain where the stories and traditions came from and how they came to be accepted into Church practice and belief. I encourage you to be open to a variety of prayers, even if they feel unusual at first.

A PRACTICE-CENTERED SPIRITUALITY

The foundation for practice-centered spirituality is in relationship: *with ourselves,* where we are attentive to our own journey; *with others,* as we treat each person with civility and respect that is rightfully theirs as a person of sacred worth; and *with God,* the author of our life and to whom we are intricately connected. The task of loving ourselves and others is achievable as we join ourselves in God's love.

Anyone who has ever been in any kind of relationship—as a spouse, sibling, parent, child, or friend—knows that it takes hard work and stick-to-it commitment to sustain relationships. Relationships take root and grow when lived lovingly with discipline and perseverance. These consistent, persistent actions that sustain us are what I introduce in my book *Learning to Lead from Your Spiritual Center* as "holy habits."

Through the daily living of these holy habits, we express our deep and innate desire to live intimately in God's presence. In this new relational reality, the disquieted and frenzied voices, the craziness of the world that would try to make us deaf, are stifled. In the stillness, we hear the soft, gentle call of the Spirit. In that space we hear God's voice, feel God's presence, and taste fully the joy of all that a life of prayer can be.

These holy habits include "prayer practices," intentional activities that deepen our relationship to God. When I say that spirituality and prayer are to be practiced, I mean that you will consciously exercise the spiritual activities of prayer in your life. As you coauthor your life with God, you devote time to various practices of prayer, including those found in public and private worship, in reading sacred and inspirational texts, and in service to others.

Be careful that you don't try to make this spirit work of holy habits into just another form of self-improvement. We are not after self-improvement, but the unfolding of the Spirit. What I call spirit work is revealed as the Spirit at work within you, helping you to become more fully the person God intends (and you pray) to be. It is God's work, not yours.

The work of the Spirit calls you, not to a destination but to a journey. In my experience, this journey is not taken at a fast pace. The Spirit seems to travel at an unhurried pace. I've had to learn to move with patience and remain constant and faithful. The experience of God within is not something one can make happen, but one can prepare to receive the gift when it is given.

The Latin word *habitus* means "practice" or "habit," and creating a practice of prayer is very much about making prayer a habitual part of your routine. As I work with people in workshops and prayer retreats, I see that when people create the habit, the heart follows. It rarely works the other way around. Spiritual discipline is one person saying to another, "Here is how I experience God and the way I do it."

Practices of prayer always involve a certain degree of technical knowledge. When we first begin to pray, we think about and examine each step of our process and intention. Learning a practice also involves hearing the wisdom that holy people past and present have to offer. Through personal trial and error, we discover for ourselves the truth of these practices—and that we deprive ourselves by taking short cuts. Prayer practices require integrity and a commitment to the wisdom, the ways, and the work of the practice itself.

There is a distinction between practicing and merely following techniques. We may strive to use all the best prayer techniques, but it is not the techniques that are important. It is immersion in prayer—individual personal encounter with the living God—that transforms our life and the lives of those around us, and changes the world.

To begin your practice of prayer, however, you need to consciously set aside time to experience the presence and inspiration of God in your life. Seek a regular place for solitude, one free from distraction and interruption. Take time to quiet yourself into a place of stillness. Silence in your speech, thoughts, and entire being is extremely important in developing intimacy with God.

Remember that your body is also a party to your prayer life. This isn't like any other appointment on your calendar; you can't run in, sit down, and begin. As the Quakers say, you have to "center down." Relax and become still; set aside your mental to-do list. I find that first doing some stretching, flexing, and back-bends help me to bring my body into prayer. Next, I find a comfortable posture so I'll be relaxed but attentive. Then I simply trust the Spirit to guide me.

Be patient with your practice as you develop new ways of praying that allow God to speak transformationally to the deepest levels of your being. In these set-aside moments, don't worry if your mind wanders or about the quality of your prayer. Simply know that your time is well spent, for prayer truly is a gift that allows us to sort out life's complications and enables us to strengthen our connections to God and to other people.

Over time, practice becomes covenantal, and this covenant distinguishes practice from mere development of technical skill. Prayer becomes a natural part of our day, as natural as eating and sleeping. Prayer becomes not something we *do*, but who we *are*. We internalize the wisdom and enlightenment that come from a life of prayer, and we are reshaped. A practiced prayer life lets go of the daily chaos and the whims of our mood to gain a deeper order, discipline, and focus. We settle into a routine that permits us to cultivate a deep understanding of who we are, and who God is.

How Do You Pray?

FINDING YOUR PRAYER TYPE

*I*gnatius of Loyola, founder of the Society of Jesus, wrote a book of prayer exercises to introduce prayer to people who wanted to pray but had little idea how to go about it. He tells his sixteenth-century audience that his step-by-step guides are not an end in themselves but are meant to free them to find the way of praying that suits them best. This is what I hope, that you will be freed to find new ways to pray.

As people who pray, we want to be connected to the mystery of God. Our hungry hearts long for a mystical link to God, a link that is creative and life-giving. We seek encounters with God that feed the soul. Individuals experience the spiritual dimension of prayer in their own way depending on their personalities and backgrounds. Some do this intellectually; as they gain more knowledge, they come to

HOW DO YOU PRAY?

know God. Others have a more intuitive approach to their relationship with God, taking into account their subjective experiences. For most, however, both the reasoning mind and the imaginative mind combine in their experience of God. The important thing is that God's spirit works individually with each one of us.

Christian mystic Evelyn Underhill noted that personality and prayer struggle with the spiritual dimensions of life, "and how people experience that same dimension in different ways. We shall find when we look into our souls or those with whom we have to deal that there is an immense variation among them, both in aptitude and in the method of approaching God. . . . The first thing we have to do is to find out the kind of practice that suits our souls; yours, not someone else's, and now at this stage of growth."

In the following pages, you will discover a brief, forty-item questionnaire on prayer styles. Read through it step-by-step, and follow the directions. It's easy and fun. This assessment helps you begin to think about the four styles of prayer (innovative, searching, relational, or experiential) in this book and which one(s) might best suit your personality and aptitude. Think of the questionnaire more as an opportunity to divide up the reading and get you started than as categories to keep you in only one dimension of prayer.

This assessment can steer you toward a starting point where you're likely to feel comfortable and inspired. But don't use the assessment as an excuse to limit yourself. The assessment examines only particular ingredients that make up the whole you. There are numerous variables that influence your prayer life: your family, education, geography, culture, experiences, current mental state, present living situation, skills, and abilities, to name a few. You may not like all the prayers in a category, and you may be drawn to prayers outside of a particular category. As you go along, you'll see that many of the individual prayer practices could easily fit into each of the four categories. Maintain a balanced stance on any way in which you pray easily and the stretching benefits of trying a new, perhaps less comfortable way.

So, why do the assessment at all? Whether you are taking it alone or participating in a group, this assessment helps to create an open forum to acknowledge, explore, and discuss your differences and similarities. In this way, you begin within a climate of acceptance, so that you can be open to others' experiences that might differ from your own. I hope that the results will also create tolerance of faith and religious differences, encouraging you to try some new prayers that you might not normally choose, in order to enter into your neighbors' experiences.

The Prayer Styles Self-Assessment Answer Sheet instructs you to place a numeral *1* in the numbered boxes that coincide with the numbered statements that are typical of you. After completing the answer sheet, add up the numerals in each column to discover the style of prayer that is most compatible with your personality and preferences. (It's possible that you fall into more than one category.) Then read the description of your prayer style(s) to gain a greater understanding of what a particular style means to you and your prayer life. Remember that this assessment is only one tool for discerning your prayer preferences; the best test is spending time with each prayer, and paying attention to how each one feels for you.

PRAYER STYLES SELF-ASSESSMENT

Learn your prayer preferences by taking the assessment given here. Discover if you gravitate toward a style that is searching, experiential, relational, or innovative—or a combination of two or more. Using the Prayer Styles Self-Assessment Answer Sheet after the questionnaire, place a numeral *1* in any numbered box that coincides with a numbered statement that is typical of you. Place a *0* in any box that does not apply. The statements are generalizations and are not explained in detail. If you do not understand a statement, give the best answer you can, according to what you think it means. You may choose not to respond to a particular statement, leave it blank, and move on to the next one.

1. You have knowledge and intellectual skills that help you live a spiritual life.
2. Celebrating traditions and significant occasions is important to you.
3. You are an emotional person who is in touch with the longings of your heart.
4. You are an optimistic and hopeful individual.
5. Spiritual insights come to you as you observe, study, and debate.
6. Your heart soars when you see the beauty of creation.
7. Close, harmonious relationships with friends and family are important to you.
8. You rejoice in new insights, the imagination, creativity, and novelty.
9. You evaluate new teachings in a logical way to determine if they mesh with your beliefs.
10. You look for opportunities to apply your faith in daily life.
11. Your motto is, "What you see is what you get."
12. You spend time contemplating the mysteries of the faith.
13. You appreciate wisdom that can be applied to concrete life circumstances.
14. You like instructions and plans to be orderly.
15. You are invested in helping others and your community grow spiritually.
16. You look beyond the nuts and bolts of what happens to see its deeper importance.
17. Accountability and fairness are important to you.

18. You have a deep appreciation of history.

19. You are inspired by the stories and examples of others.

20. You see beneath the event, story, or practice to find connections and the deeper meaning.

21. Structure and order are important to you.

22. You like to observe others to determine what might work for you.

23. You extend yourself to help others locate their spiritual center.

24. You are able to pull together ideas, occurrences, people, and scholarship to come up with a better idea.

25. You have a logical mind and humble intellect.

26. You are known as a person with a lot of common sense.

27. You hold strong core values and beliefs.

28. You are a creative free spirit.

29. You are a truth-teller with a discerning spirit.

30. You possess strong problem-solving abilities.

31. You are a person of compassion who is sensitive to the emotions of others.

32. You are an optimist.

33. You appreciate order and hold a linear viewpoint.

34. You like to focus on the present day and worry about tomorrow when it comes.

35. Spiritual companions and friends are important to you.

36. You have a great imagination.

37. You are known as a person with clear convictions.

38. You like to look at the practical side of a situation.

39. You have long friendships that connect you to others.

40. You are an independent person with a strong sense of self.

PRAYER STYLES SELF-ASSESSMENT ANSWER SHEET

Place a numeral *1* in any numbered box that coincides with a numbered statement that is typical of you. Place a *0* in any box that does not apply. Add the numbers in each of the four vertical columns, and enter the total count for each column separately in the spaces below. A blank space is counted as a zero.

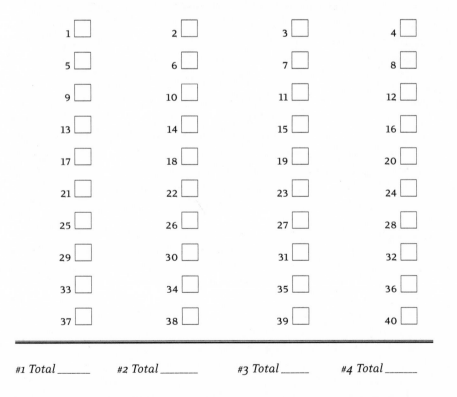

1 ☐	2 ☐	3 ☐	4 ☐
5 ☐	6 ☐	7 ☐	8 ☐
9 ☐	10 ☐	11 ☐	12 ☐
13 ☐	14 ☐	15 ☐	16 ☐
17 ☐	18 ☐	19 ☐	20 ☐
21 ☐	22 ☐	23 ☐	24 ☐
25 ☐	26 ☐	27 ☐	28 ☐
29 ☐	30 ☐	31 ☐	32 ☐
33 ☐	34 ☐	35 ☐	36 ☐
37 ☐	38 ☐	39 ☐	40 ☐

#1 Total _____   *#2 Total* _____   *#3 Total* _____   *#4 Total* _____

30 ## Prayer Styles Self-Assessment Preview

If you haven't already done so, take a moment now to look at the Table of Contents of this book and preview the various prayer practices we'll be covering. Check off any that you have practiced in the past.

Now look at the prayer types and descriptions, along with their corresponding prayer practices, on the next few pages to discover what styles of prayer you may be most naturally inclined toward, on the basis of your personality and preferences. Remember that this self-assessment is only one way of exploring your prayer life. Your results from the self-assessment should by no means limit your experience of prayer. Instead, I encourage you to use these prayers as a starting place, and eventually try all the prayers included in this book. Form your own opinion about what works for you and what doesn't seem to fit.

As you read through the descriptions, keep in mind that any of the forty statements could, to some degree, fit any of the four categories. What I am asserting, in the description under each category, is that together the statements tend to be characteristic of people who are similarly inclined.

Searching Prayer

If you scored high in column no. I, you may be inclined toward *searching prayer*.

As someone predisposed to searching prayer, you lean upon your knowledge and intellectual skills to help you live a spiritual life. Spiritual insights come to you through observation, study, and debate. As you learn and experience new prayer practices, you evaluate them in a logical way to determine if they mesh with your beliefs. You appreciate clear teachings and wisdom that can be applied to concrete life circumstances. Accountability and fairness are important to you, as are structure and order. You are an astute observer as you discern whether or not a particular prayer practice draws you closer to God.

Celebrate your

Logical mind

Truth telling

Linear viewpoint

Clear convictions

Humble intellect

Discerning spirit

Thirst for God

Searching prayer practices include

- Lord's Prayer
- Praying the scriptures
  - Lectio divina
- A journal of prayer
- Pilgrimage
- Praying with icons
- Novenas
- Prayers for the dead

Experiential Prayer

If you scored high in column no. 2, you may be inclined toward *experiential prayer.*

As someone who tends toward experiential prayer, you find commemorating traditions and significant occasions important. Your heart soars in thanksgiving for the gift of life and the beauty of creation. When you pray, you emphasize what is happening in the here-and-now, and you look for opportunities to apply your faith in daily life as you work, play, eat, and even sleep. You are drawn to ways of praying that can be done in an orderly, step-by-step fashion. You have a deep appreciation for the history and theology of particular practices and are therefore a keen observer of what has worked for others.

Celebrate your

Uncommon sense	Problem-solving abilities
Life experiences	Practical side
Focus in the present moment	Strong foundation
Established talents and skills	

Experiential prayer practices include

- Fasting
  - Abstinence from food
  - Fasting as prayerful solitude
- Breath prayer
  - The Jesus Prayer: prayer of the heart
- Benediction and blessing
- Tallith: the prayer shawl
- Centering prayer
- Meditation: mental prayer
- Anointing for healing

Relational Prayer

If you scored high in column no. 3, you may be inclined toward *relational prayer.*

As someone with an affinity for relational prayer, you look for personal meaning in your spiritual experience of prayer. You pay attention to your emotions and are in touch with the longings of your heart. Close, harmonious relationships with friends and family are important to you. You strive to live what you say you believe; you aim to be authentic in both your inner and outer life. You want to mature, and you are open to change. This openness allows you to invest yourself in the spiritual growth of other individuals and the greater community. You are inspired to learn new ways of prayer as you hear the stories and examples of others who have walked with God. You do the internal work to know what is of ultimate importance for your life, and you extend yourself to help others locate their spiritual center.

Celebrate your

Core values and beliefs Sensitivity to emotions

Spiritual companions and friends Compassion

Interconnectedness to others Long friendships

Authentic you, who is integrated
   and balanced

Relational prayer practices include
- Adoration prayer
- Affirmation prayer
- Prayers of confession
- Prayer of examen
- The daily office
- Tongsung kido
- Prayer walks
   - An Emmaus walk
   - Stations of the cross

34   *Innovative Prayer*

If you scored high in column no. 4, you may be inclined toward *innovative prayer.*

As someone who gravitates toward innovative prayer, you are an optimistic and hopeful individual. You rejoice in new insights, the imagination, creativity, and novelty. Contemplating the mysteries of the faith, you look beyond the nuts and bolts of spiritual ritual to see vast possibilities for meaning, growth, and change. You see beneath the event, story, or practice to find connections and the deeper meaning. You are able to synchronize ideas, occurrences, people, and scholarship, allowing you to adapt and adopt traditions and rituals for prayer.

Celebrate your

Creativity	Optimism
Free spirit	Insights
Imagination	Visionary side
Independence and sense of self	

Innovative prayer practices include

- Praying with our bodies
  - Palms up, palms down prayer
  - Body prayer
  - Body prayer with music
- Prayer labyrinth
- Home prayer altars
- Ignatian prayer: guided imagination
- Prayer beads
  - Praying the rosary
  - Chaplet of seven: covenant chaplet

- Praying with mandalas
- Prayer dance
  - Dancing the Lord's Prayer
  - Hava Nagila circle prayer dance
  - Dance of Jesus

○   ○   ○

A life of prayer is a journey about change and being stretched in constructive, God-centered ways. You may find yourself at times being challenged, or even taken to the edge of your comfort zone. If this happens, please don't run. Keep your heart and mind open. Further practice of a particular prayer style may open a new door for you. If you determine that a certain prayer practice is not for you, remember that it still may be helpful to another.

The prayers presented here are intended to serve as a doorway to spiritual growth, to help those who long after God to become deep people who commit the whole of their lives to the transforming work of the Spirit of Christ. Remember that you have the assurance of a divine guide, the Holy Spirit, who is your faithful companion and counselor through every experience along the way (Gal. 5:22–25 and John 14:25–27). The most important aspect of using this book is therefore not simply determination to do the practices so you can check them off a list, but willingness to surrender your own agenda and be responsive to the leading of the Spirit within as you continue to grow in a committed relationship with God. These prayers are the means by which we give our attention to God. The contemplative attitudes of surrender and commitment are formed and sustained, in a deepening commitment to finding and doing the will of God.

I invite you to enter into this book of prayer practices deliberately, with your heart and mind, body and soul. There is no best way to use this book; adjust it to enhance your own spiritual journey. Much depends on your needs and circumstances.

But even as you adjust, try to keep the integrity of these practices, which have been used for many years to help people grow closer to God. Sometimes using a cut-and-paste approach undermines the integrity and original intention of the practice. Other times, although you respect the original intent, you may decide to adapt or alter a practice in a way that increases your sensitivity to the presence of God. There are suggestions on procedure throughout the book, but listen to any thoughts, feelings, and desires that arise in your heart, attuning you more closely to the leading of the Spirit. Do not doubt your own spiritual experience; you may have insights and feelings very different from those I have studied or expressed.

Let me pause here to share a word of caution that I received from a wise friend. The catchy phrase "Pray as you can, not as you can't," attributed to any number of authors, has been misused by individuals who are resistant to trying new ways of praying. Kent Ira Groff, author of *Active Spirituality*, teaches a correction to that phrase: "Until I try some ways that I think I can not pray, I don't know fully how I can pray." Indeed, it may be the prayer practice that is most opposed to who you are and what you think you need—and where you are the most uncomfortable—that the Spirit will use to take you to new stages of understanding and surrender.

Now I invite you to take a deep breath and jump right in—either by yourself or with a community—with this prayer to send you on your way. I pray that the Holy Spirit may be at work in your life.

From the cowardice that dare not face new truth,
From the laziness that is contented with half truth,
From the arrogance that thinks it knows all truth,
Good Lord, deliver us.

—PRAYER FROM KENYA

Questions for Reflection

1. What is your definition of prayer?
2. Why do you pray?
3. How many varieties of prayer have you used in your prayer practices?
4. Which styles would you like to explore and why?

Searching Prayer

*T*he prayer practices in this section lift up the searching part of you. Get ready to nurture that part of your soul that appreciates your intellectual skills of observation, study, and debate to glean new knowledge for your prayer life. The logical side of you will be rejuvenated by the structured, clear teachings and wisdom that can then be applied to your current life circumstances.

Lord's Prayer
Praying the Scriptures
   Lectio Divina
A Journal of Prayer
Pilgrimage
Praying with Icons
Novenas
Prayers for the Dead

Lord's Prayer

This is the nature of prayer, that it raises one from earth to heaven, higher than every heavenly name and dignity, and brings one before the very God of all.

—GREGORY PALAMAS, 1296–1359, MT. ATHOS

Thoughts Before You Begin

A good place to begin to learn how to pray is with the Lord's Prayer, also known as the Our Father. For many of us, it is the first prayer we memorized as children. In times of stress, it feels like home—the original chicken soup for the soul. The Lord's Prayer shapes the prayers of all who share Jesus' desire to know and do the will of God and is at the heart of both formal community prayer of the Church and informal personal prayer. We pray the Our Father in the communion liturgy, the rosary, and the daily office, at times alone and frequently with others. It is tearfully recited in unison at funerals and beautifully sung at weddings.

This prayer of thirty-eight words, give or take a few depending on the rendition, offers as much comfort quality as the Twenty-Third Psalm but is even better well known. Although we appreciate the simplicity of the petitions, we can plumb their deeper significance as we pray. We understand, for instance, that when we ask for "our daily bread" we are requesting more than just the sustaining morsel that comes out of the oven; we ask for bread because it symbolizes basic needs such as a bed to sleep in and a hug from our mother.

In New Testament times, it was common for religious teachers, such as rabbis, to teach using model prayers. Jesus was in the middle of a lesson on giving and fasting when followers asked him to teach them to pray: "Lord, teach us to pray, as John taught his disciples" (Luke 11:1). (From this we learn that John, whom the book of Luke suggests is Jesus' cousin and who was also a Jewish teacher, apparently did so with his followers as well.) Jesus responded by giving John's disciples the Lord's Prayer, which these same men and women later passed down to subsequent generations.

There are two versions of this prayer in the Gospels. The longer version is in Matthew 6:9–13, and the shorter, which is believed by some to be the older version and thought by some to be more authentic, is found in Luke 11:1–4: "He was praying in a certain place, and after he had finished, one of his disciples said to him, 'Lord, teach us to pray, as John taught his disciples.' He said to them, 'When you pray, say: Father, hallowed be your name. Your kingdom come. Give us each day our daily bread. And forgive us our sins, for we ourselves forgive everyone indebted to us. And do not bring us to the time of trial.'"

I grew up listening to sermons about how original the prayer was, how Jesus was the first to address God in such an intimate manner: Abba, Daddy. I was told that this prayer was revolutionary, setting the world on its ear. In truth, I discovered in my research that most of the phrases used by Jesus were drawn directly from Jewish prayers in circulation in his day. The Lord's Prayer is a compilation of excerpts from prayers that are part of the traditional Jewish prayer book. All four Gospels have Jesus addressing God as "Abba," or "father," emphasizing that Jesus—like Moses before him—prayed to God confidently and that he thought it was OK for others to pray to God with the same expectation. "Hallowed be thy name" is an Aramaic line that is familiar to Jews, for it is the first line of the *Kaddish*, a traditional mourner's prayer. It is also a refrain used throughout the Jewish Orthodox prayer service. "Thy kingdom come, thy will be done, on earth as it is in heaven" comes from the *aleinu* prayer used at the conclusion of each prayer service and in the observance of Yom Kippur (the Jewish Day of Atonement). "Give us this day our daily bread" comes from the first paragraph of the Jewish grace after meals. "Forgive us our sins" is repeated many times in the Yom Kippur prayers. "For thine is the kingdom and the power and the glory" is recited in the synagogue, during the Sabbath morning prayer, just before the reading of the Torah. "Forever and ever," is our adaptation of the Hebrew phrase that literally means "from generation to generation." Finally, "Amen" is a Hebrew word drawn from the verb "to believe." In Jewish prayer, to say "Amen" means "I believe this."

44   What is original to the Lord's Prayer, and what isn't, is interesting speculation. Learning that the Lord's Prayer was anything but original disappointed me—at first. But in researching this book, I've been pleased to learn that so much of our Christian prayer inheritance comes from a rich Jewish background. Since Jesus was a rabbi, this should not be a surprise. It makes me feel good to know that his wisdom was tried, true, and tested.

So, what if the Hebrew "father" for God has been used for millennia to begin prayer? The question is, what image does the metaphor represent when we use it in our prayer? Is it the prayer of a child to a heavenly daddy, as I was taught? That is one interpretation. But the meaning is more expansive; other understandings of the metaphor have substantial reasoning behind them.

Father, in Jewish antiquity, designates one with *sovereign power over lives* and therefore as the people's *protector*. In Deuteronomy 32:6, father God refers to the *creator*. In Isaiah 63:16, the word infers *long-time redeemer* and *liberator*. In the Hebrew story of Joseph, father God is the *rescuer* and *one who forgives*. In Jewish prayers that date from Jesus' time, the word is used in regard to one who shows *mercy, compassion,* and *pity*—father as *teacher, sustainer,* and *deliverer*. Broadening the meaning of the salutation Jesus used in addressing Abba Father allows us to share in the richness of a metaphor that encompasses all these dimensions.

C. S. Lewis wrote of a practice that he thought was his original idea: taking a familiar prayer, such as the Lord's Prayer, and embellishing it with one's own intentions until this elaboration becomes an act of prayer itself. He even gave it a name: "festooning." If you were to festoon the line "forgive us our sins," you might ramble on to say, "like on Monday when I became angry at that bus driver, and I didn't keep my word to my daughter." As you festoon, let these ideas about God shape the attitude you carry into the prayer.

Now that you know the background on Abba, imagine that you are asking a merciful protector (to use two of the metaphors just listed) about your life. What do you say to God? What is the response? Now transfer that attitude to the Lord's Prayer. God is compassionate, ready to respond as any good governor would. When we strive to understand and accept the real presence of God we begin to ask what will happen as the result of our prayers. Instead of reciting the words of the Lord's Prayer vaguely like pious sentiments or amorphous wishes, this prayer reveals who God is and teaches us to submit our will to that of the Divine. Praying this prayer is a way to understand who we are in relation to our loving God and our community of faith.

Now Begin

In this outline of the prayer (from Luke 11:2–4), following the address to the father, the first two petitions are about God and the remaining three are about us, the petitioners.

Salutation:	Father,
God-directed petition:	hallowed be your name.
	Your kingdom come
Us-directed petitions:	Give us each day our daily bread.
	And forgive us our sins,
	for we ourselves forgive everyone
	indebted to us.
	And do not bring us to the time of trial.

Pray the prayer slowly and thoughtfully, as prayed by the apostle Luke's community of the first century. First, weigh the implications of the salutation, then of the two God-directed petitions, and finally the three us-directed petitions. To help you pray the Lord's Prayer in a deeper manner, I have attached quotes to each phrase as well as questions for you to reflect upon.

Father, . . .

> To call God "Father," then, is not to claim something about God but to claim something from God. It is to claim God's promises, to call God to be near even though he seems far away.
>
> —THEODORE JENNINGS, UNITED STATES, 1982

What other names and metaphors for God come to mind as you pray? The word *father* can have many meanings. For some people, it conjures up a loving hug; for others it brings to mind hurtful abuse. What does it mean to you when you call God "Father"? If the image of God as father is painful for you, how might you reclaim its strength and comfort? To begin, look to the story of the welcoming father found in Luke chapter 15, verses 11–32.

hallowed be your name . . .

> Jesus' prayer teaches us that God is holy. It helps us to discover the holiness of the Being that creates, provides, judges, chooses and abounds in generosity, welcomes and rejects, rewards and punishes equally. This is what characterizes the quality that belongs to God, the quality that the scriptures call by the name of God.
>
> —ORIGEN, THIRD CENTURY, EGYPT

Hallowed is God's nature. When and where does God's holiness become reality for you? Do you see God in the "least of these"—the poor, the stranger, and the prisoner—as Jesus instructed? (Matt. 25: 40). "Truly I tell you, just as you did it to one of the least of these who are members of my family, you did it to me." Do you experience God's presence in the outdoors as the psalmist did? "Praise the Lord from the earth, you sea monsters and all deeps, fire and hail, snow and frost, stormy wind fulfilling his command! Mountains and all hills, fruit trees and all cedars! Wild animals and all cattle, creeping things and flying birds!" (Ps. 148:7–10). Can you sense God in religious ceremonies such as weddings or funerals, Sunday worship or prayer meetings?

Your kingdom come . . .

> Just so, nondirected prayer does not require us to wipe the slate of the mind totally clean. We may still experience feelings, emotions, and images, but not as specific goals or preferred outcomes.
>
> —LARRY DOSSEY, 1993, NEW MEXICO

In his book *Healing Words,* Dr. Larry Dossey describes a study on what he calls "nondirect prayer," or the "thy will be done approach," which was taught by Jesus and lived by mystics. He cites studies indicating that nondirect prayer produces better results than directed prayer with a specific outcome in mind.

When we say, "Your will be done on earth as it is in heaven," we are saying that we conform our deepest desires to God's will rather than the other way around. Do you believe that God has a better vision of what is best for you? Are you able to trust and surrender to God, rather than employ your own self-control, allowing that this produces the best outcome?

Give us each day our daily bread.

> Make us worthy, Lord, to serve those throughout the world who live and die in poverty and hunger. Give them, through our hands, this day their daily bread; and by our understanding love, give peace and joy. Amen.
>
> —MOTHER TERESA OF CALCUTTA, INDIA

What do you understand by "bread"? What physical need, or bread, will you ask God for? What spiritual bread do you need today? The prayer uses the word *us,* not *me.* How do you understand God's will for community and communal bread?

And forgive us our sins, for we ourselves forgive everyone indebted to us . . .

The work of purging the soul neither can nor should end except with our life itself. We must not be disturbed at our imperfections, since for us perfection consists in fighting against them. How can we fight against them unless we see them, or overcome them unless we face them?

—FRANCIS DE SALES, 1567–1622, SWITZERLAND

When we pray "Forgive us our sins as we forgive those who sin against us," we ask that God also work in our hearts to allow us to be bearers of grace and forgiveness. What sins do you carry to God today? Who do you need to forgive? How does being forgiven help you live differently?

And do not bring us to the time of trial.

Blessed Jesus, you are always near in times of stress.
Although we cannot feel your presence you are close.
You are always there to help and watch over us.
Nothing in heaven or on earth can separate you from us.

—MARGERY KEMPE, NORFOLK, FIFTEENTH CENTURY

Hopefully, in times of trial you feel God's presence and watchful eye. Trials come upon each of us at some time. What stresses have you experienced lately? What trials have come upon your community? What was your prayer in these times of hardship? Did you ask God for protection, endurance, patience, or health?

Some Things to Think About

Although many synagogue prayers today are said in Hebrew, Jesus' prayer may have been scribed in Targum. This means when he taught the Lord's Prayer to the disciples he taught it to them in their indigenous language. In doing this, he made a strong statement: that prayer was not just for the religious professionals of the temple, but for the ordinary people of the street. We take his lesson to heart; the prayer is for us.

It's probable, from the form of the Our Father found in the "Didache" (also known as "the teaching of the Twelve Apostles"), a text written sometime in the first three centuries of the Church, that the version of the Lord's Prayer in the book of Matthew was the original one adopted in the early centuries of the Church.

In the fourth-century Church, outsiders were not allowed to learn the words of this most sacred prayer. To protect it, the prayer was ceremoniously handed over to catechumens (candidates) who were preparing for baptism and to take the vows of the Christian faith. At that time, candidates were also instructed in its meaning. We can still read the lessons taught by Cyril in Jerusalem (315–386) and Ambrose, Bishop of Milan (339–397), where the prayer was not taught until after baptism.

During the Middle Ages, the Our Father was prayed in Latin, even by the uneducated. Therefore it was commonly known as the *Pater noster.*

The phrase "Lord's Prayer" became familiar in England at the Reformation, whereas Rome continued to call the prayer the "Our Father." The English text used both by Catholics and Protestants was derived from a version imposed upon England by a 1541 ordinance of Henry VIII and employed in the 1549 and 1552 editions of the *Book of Common Prayer.* The Church wanted a uniform English translation of the Latin *Pater noster,* as well as the Apostles' Creed, that could be learned and recited in unison by all. The text differs in two ways: "which art" is now "who art," and "in earth" is "on earth." As a result, the version continues to be universally familiar in the English-speaking world.

The 1581 Rheims Testament Bible and 1611 King James Bible translators provided different renderings of Matthew 6:9–13, but the older form, which is pretty close to the 1525 Tyndale New Testament Bible translation, was retained by Protestants and Catholics alike. The final line of the prayer is used by some churches to end the prayer while others omit it. Here it is:

Our Father, who art in heaven,
hallowed be thy name.
Thy kingdom come,
thy will be done on earth as it is in heaven.
Give us this day our daily bread.
And forgive us our trespasses,
as we forgive those who trespass against us.
And lead us not into temptation,
but deliver us from evil.
For thine is the kingdom, and the power, and the glory,
forever. Amen.

Questions for Reflection

1. Recall the first time you remember hearing or saying the Lord's Prayer. When was it? Where were you? What were the circumstances?
2. What version of the Lord's Prayer do you employ?

Other Resources to Continue Your Journey

James R. Mulholland, *Praying Like Jesus: The Lord's Prayer in a Culture of Prosperity* (San Francisco: HarperSanFrancisco, 2001). Mulholland doesn't mince words. He points out that the recently popular prayer of Jabez uses all *me* language; it says more about the person praying than about God. The Lord's Prayer uses *us* language, pointing to concern for the community. You'll appreciate Mulholland's clear insights.

Roberta C. Bondi, *A Place to Pray: Reflections on the Lord's Prayer* (Nashville, Tenn.: Abingdon Press, 1998). This book has an accompanying video series that opens up new meaning to the Lord's Prayer. Bondi offers a biblical treatment of the prayer. An excellent scholar, Bondi is also a warm speaker who presents in an engaging manner.

Praying the Scriptures

Do not allow me to judge according to the sight of my eyes, nor to pass sentence according to the ears of ignorant men; but to discern with a true judgment between things visible and spiritual, and above all things, always to inquire what is the good pleasure of your will.

—THOMAS À KEMPIS, 1380–1471, COLOGNE

Thoughts Before You Begin

When we read the Bible, we are reading the Word of God. Being attentive to God means spending time with the sacred stories of our faith traditions. When we listen carefully with our hearts as well as our heads, the Word touches us, moving our hearts to live God's will in a greater way than we ever imagined possible.

Read the wise words of Madame Guyon, a woman of faith who lived in France from 1648 to 1717: "Taste it and digest it as you read. . . . 'Praying the Scripture' is not judged by how much you read but by the way you read. If you read quickly, it will benefit you little. You will be like a bee that merely skims the surface of a flower. Instead, in this new way of reading with prayer, you become as the bee who penetrates into the depths of the flower. You plunge deeply within to remove its deepest nectar."

As you can discern, this practice of praying the scriptures is more than just *reading* the scriptures as one normally does. The four R's—reading, reflecting, responding, and resting—are the basic rhythm of this approach. Reading in this way leads you to prayer that cuts to the heart and makes room for the Spirit to do the inner work. Move slowly from verse to verse, and idea to idea, rather than trying to consume whole passages at once as you do when you're reading for comprehension. In the practice outlined here, you write key verses and phrases as is helpful to you. Sometimes I receive an uncomfortable word from God. In those moments, when I recognize how sinful I am, I move quickly into prayers of confession and repentance, and then into prayer for the strength to desire God above all else. In the end, I rest in God's mercy.

Now Begin

When praying, limit the amount of scripture to approximately ten verses or lines. More than this becomes overwhelming. Passages from the psalms and stories from the Gospels are good to use. You'll need paper and pencil for this prayer.

STEP ONE: If you are in a large gathering, divide into smaller groups of three to five. Circle your chairs and sit knee to knee. Space the groups around the room.

STEP TWO: Choose a short passage from the "Suggested Lectionary Readings" at the back of this book. You can also start with one of the psalms, which you can find in a prayer book or Bible. The most well-known, of course, is the Twenty-Third Psalm:

The Lord is my shepherd, I shall not want.
He makes me lie down in green pastures;
he leads me beside the still waters; he restores my soul.
He leads me in right paths for his name's sake.
Even though I walk through the darkest valley,
I fear no evil; for you are with me;
Your rod and your staff—they comfort me.
You prepare a table before me in the presence of my enemies;
You anoint my head with oil; my cup overflows.
Surely goodness and mercy shall follow me all the days of my life,
and I shall dwell in the house of the Lord my whole life long.

STEP THREE: Read the passage aloud slowly. (If you are in a group, one person should read aloud while the others read along silently.) Take care to read it fully and with gentleness.

STEP FOUR: Remain in silence for at least two minutes, meditating on what you have heard and read.

STEP FIVE: Read the passage aloud again. (A group may choose to read it in unison.)

STEP SIX: Remain in silence for at least two minutes, again prayerfully contemplating the words and their meaning.

STEP SEVEN: Slowly reread the passage to yourself in silence. Stop at a portion of text that touches your heart, and copy this verse or phrase onto paper. In a group, allow two minutes for writing. Those who are finished writing before the time is up are to wait quietly.

STEP EIGHT: Finally, take the portion of the reading that stopped you and touched you, and write your response. You may also turn it into a simple prayer (of no more than ten to twelve words). If you wrote a prayer, repeatedly pray it quietly to yourself or in silence for several minutes.

STEP NINE: If you are in a group, you might choose to share your prayers, or pass and remain in silence.

Some Things to Think About

I statements are important in group prayer—not narcissistic, navel-gazing *I* statements, but *I* statements that lead to accountability for the choices we make in our lives. To say "We are people who need God's grace" is one thing, but to admit that "I am a sinner in need of God's grace" is quite something else. *I* statements remind us to be mindful of the plank in our own eye and to leave the speck in the other person's eye to God's care. Habit often leads us to use the general *we* when praying; consciously use *I* statements in prayer until you became accustomed to doing so.

When praying with a group, you may feel the need to explain your prayer statements for the benefit of other members of the group. You may fear that your meaning will be misinterpreted. But you need to be free to express your prayers in words that suit your meaning, without pressure to conform to some (probably imagined) norm. As you learn to hear others nonjudgmentally, your defensiveness will lessen.

Some people have difficulty listening. If you are one, work at stifling the urge to jump in and comment on what others say. You may find, however, that you benefit most by hearing and receiving each prayer, reflection, or insight silently, by sitting and observing. Listening with your whole heart enables you to extend your love to God and others. In this love, you grow to be a person who is healthy and whole— an individual with plenty to give others.

Questions for Reflection

1. What happened each time you read the passage? How did the meaning of the passage become more alive to you?
2. Did listening to the prayers and reflections of others give you new insight into this passage of scripture? What was fresh and new about your reading of the scripture today? Where did you gain new understanding?

Lectio Divina

Seek in reading
And you will find in meditation;
Knock in prayer
And it will be opened to you
In contemplation.

—ST. JOHN OF THE CROSS, 1542–1591, SPAIN

Thoughts Before You Begin

Reading in the quest for God (or reading for holiness) is what has traditionally been called *lectio divina.* John of the Cross, an ordained pastor and mystic, paraphrased this verse from Luke's gospel (11:9), which gives us an outline of the steps used in lectio. In Latin, *lectio divina* literally means "divine reading" or "sacred reading." The Bible is the primary source for the practice of lectio divina, but secondary sources include other texts recognized as sacred by the Christian community, such as the Apostles' Creed or the Interior Castle by Teresa of Avila.

The practice of lectio took root in the fourth and fifth centuries, a time when books were produced by hand and were therefore scarce and expensive. One individual—becoming both proclaimer and reader—was assigned to read for all those gathered. The text was therefore read more than once so that it could be absorbed by those in attendance, and even memorized by participants for later personal use.

Lectio divina was a staple of ninth-century Benedictine community life, which revolved around eight daily prayer services. This amounted to the monks spending four hours a day in community prayer. Since personal prayer books were not available, the psalms were memorized and the community prayed through them in their entirety each week. In this practice, each Benedictine monk chose a brief biblical phrase or petition to repeat over and over until it became a prayerful undercurrent to his entire day. An example from Psalm 70 is "Be pleased, O God to deliver me. O Lord, make haste to help me!"

Guigo II, a medieval Christian leader, systematized the lectio divina process into four stages: (1) *lectio,* (2) *meditatio,* (3) *oratio,* and (4) *contemplatio. Lectio* refers to the actual reading aloud of the sacred text. The reflective part, pondering upon the words of the sacred text, was called *meditatio,* or "meditation." The spontaneous movement of the will in response to these reflections was called *oratio,* or "affective prayer." As these reflections and acts of will became plainer and more transparent, one moved on to a state of resting in the presence of God, called *contemplatio,* or "contemplation."

During the initial sixteen centuries of Church history, this process of prayer was fundamental to Christian spirituality. After the Reformation, this heritage, at least as a living tradition, was virtually lost outside the monastery. Now, with the advent of cross-cultural dialogue and historical research, this prayer tradition is being recovered.

Practitioners of lectio divina pray it in a variety of ways. This is only one way to get you started.

Now Begin

Although the outline given here is written to be used by an individual, it can be adapted for group use.

Through lectio divina, the mingling of reading and prayer, the stories and texts of the Bible meet us in our own life story. Each text holds a personal message for us. Right now, in this moment and in this place, God has something to say to us.

LECTIO : (READING)	Turn to a scripture text of no more than ten to fifteen verses or a short portion of a spiritual reading taken from the Sunday scriptures. (See "Suggested Lectionary Readings" in the back of the book.) Read the passage aloud slowly.
MEDITATIO: (MEDITATION)	Linger over the text for as long as you wish. In silence, identify and recall the word, phrase, sentence, or idea that most caught your attention, and reflect on it for five minutes or longer. Ponder and rest in it.

60

LECTIO:	Read the passage aloud again.
MEDITATIO:	Ask yourself, *Where does this passage touch my life, my community, my nation, or my world today?* Pause again and reflect for five minutes or longer.
LECTIO:	Read the passage aloud for the third and final time.
CONTEMPLATIO: (CONTEMPLATION)	Ask yourself, *From the passage I have read and reflected upon, what does God want me to do or be? How does God invite me to change?* Pause for five minutes or longer to contemplate. What personal message is God sending you? Ruminate on it, and ponder and rest in it.
ORATIO: (PRAYER)	Lectio divina is a form of reading that leads to prayer. What begins as God addressing us—through the reading, and our response—leads eventually to our being drawn into the presence of God, into the heart of God, into perfect union with the divine will. Our hearts and minds move toward God, who is the great physician, and this movement of the heart is the beginning of prayer. Continue to pray to the divine healer as you are led.

Some Things to Think About

Ideally, lectio takes about thirty minutes. Of course, longer periods of lectio divina are also desirable. You will find yourself spending more time in oratio as you grow closer to God through your deepening life of prayer. Enter this prayer practice with an attitude of expectancy; it is your time with God. Particularly if you are going to attempt a more sustained period of lectio, find a quiet place and take some "attitude adjustment time." This can be accomplished by slow, quiet repetition of the name of Jesus, deep breathing, or invoking the aid of the Holy Spirit in your own way.

Once you are focused, begin to read aloud the text. When a word or phrase catches your attention, stop. Rhythmically repeat it over and over, allowing the text to sink deeply within you. When you are ready to move on, or your mind begins to wander with thoughts that are unconnected or unrelated, simply return to your reading. Continue to weave back and forth between the four motions of the method for the time you allotted or until you feel the prayer is completed.

Conclude with a prayer of thanksgiving to God for what you have received in your time of prayer.

Questions for Reflection

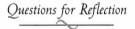

1. Lectio is a process that calls for you to surrender to God. During your practice of lectio divina, did you ever feel the need to be in control, wanting a certain outcome or answer (your answer) from your prayer? How did this feeling affect your practice of this style of prayer?

2. What challenges and obstacles did you face as you prayed in lectio divina? How do you intend to confront them?

3. The lectionary (a set, three-year read-through of the Bible, taken from liturgical traditions of the Christian Church) is a great resource for daily lectio (see the "Suggested Lectionary Readings" at the back of this book). Make a list of books and other texts that can be used. The resources listed here are a few to get you started.

Other Resources to Continue Your Journey

William P. McDonald, *Gracious Voices: Shouts and Whispers for God's Seekers* (Nashville, Tenn.: Discipleship Resources, 1996). Here is where I discovered Madame Guyon. The words of mystics and saints will offer you hope, challenge, and inspiration.

Norvene Vest, *Gathered in the Word: Praying the Scripture in Small Groups* (Nashville, Tenn.: Upper Room Books, 1996). Vest presents a history of divine reading, instructions, and suggested readings from the Bible and classic Christian writings.

Joan Chittister, *Illuminated Life: Monastic Wisdom for Seekers of Light* (Maryknoll, N.Y.: Orbis Books, 2000). In each chapter, Chittister illuminates a spiritual quality we need to cultivate, such as awareness, humility, and more.

Keith Beasley-Topliffe (ed.), *The Soul's Passion for God: Selected Writings of Teresa of Avila* (Nashville, Tenn.: Upper Room Books, 1997). This translation includes selections of the sixteenth-century nun's writings, including *The Book of Her Life*, *The Interior Castle*, and *The Way of Perfection*.

A Journal of Prayer

You yourselves are our letter, written on our hearts, to be known and read by all; and you show that you are a letter of Christ, prepared by us, written not with ink but with the Spirit of the living God, not on tablets of stone but on tablets of human hearts.

—2 CORINTHIANS 3:2–3

Thoughts Before You Begin

Keeping a journal is a meaningful prayer practice. In order to be authentic—not a carbon copy of someone else—you need to learn what you like, want, need, and desire. In this process, you may sort out what you believe too. Placing your thoughts on paper when you pray helps you step back from yourself and be more objective about what you truly feel and think. This then opens your mind and heart so that you can hear what God really wants and desires with you.

My prayer journal is a bit like the diary I kept in a secret place as a girl. Writing in my diary was a way of sorting out who I was before sharing what I was thinking with my family or friends. I could write secret thoughts and safely explore my most hidden, inner self. Now, my prayer journal also includes entries from conversations, scripture readings, dreams, meaningful quotes, and daily encounters and experiences.

Journal writing has been a standard practice throughout Judeo-Christian history. This form of spiritual autobiography is found in the writings of the prophets and the psalms, as well as many passages from the letters of Paul. These honest writings chronicle the writers' search for, and discovery of, how God acts in human life. Among early Church mothers and fathers, journaling was used as a discipline for spiritual growth. In his *Soliloquies,* Augustine (A.D. 354–430, North Africa), a great saint of the early Church, writes how a voice urged him to record his innermost thoughts and discoveries as he continued to seek God's truth. His eight-thousand-some pages attest to his "desire to know God and the soul."

Examples of spiritual diaries can also be drawn from the monastic and mystic (as well as Reformation) traditions. The journals of the Quakers and Pilgrims, especially George Fox, witness to the resurrection of this important prayer practice. It is even claimed by some that these spiritual treatises, a distinctive mark of Puritanism, were the Puritan substitute for the confessional. (To learn how to establish an examen journal, refer to the chapter "Prayer of Examen.")

Writing in a journal is a gift we give to ourselves as well as to those we care for. Writing about life challenges, past and present, helps us gain clarity in our relationships with God, ourselves, and others. Over time, our patterns of acting, relating, and thinking all emerge. This distinct literary form, used notably by Anne Frank and Thomas Merton, can be a channel for self-understanding. As we read and reread what we've written, we begin to see the choices we have made and how we have changed. We can see evidence of God's work in our lives, as well as times where we chose not to let God act. The pages can both remind us of our inner beauty and humble us as we confront our frailties.

Now Begin

Here are three activities to get you started:

1. *A letter from me to God:* Write a letter to God. Tell God what you think, feel, and need. As you write, remember that God is one who knows you through and through and cares deeply for you.

2. *A letter from God to me:* Write a letter that you imagine you might receive from God. What does God have to say to you? As you reflect and write, remember that God loves you and wants what is best for you.

3. *A letter to myself:* Write yourself a letter that comes from the depths of your heart. A wise friend once gave me a piece of spiritual advice: "It is important to know two things: what you want and what you'll settle for." Once you've written your letter, be aware of the difference as you give your prayer over to God's will. As I coauthor my days with God, I find that I can live in the peace of believing that life usually unfolds as it should.

Periodically review what you've written to find repeating patterns, to recapture past insights, or to see how and where you've changed. I usually do this on my birthday, although New Year's Day or an anniversary date also suffice.

Some Things to Think About

In my personal prayer journal, I reflect on my experiences—on the places in which I realize God is present to me. This invites me to express what is in my heart and explore my creativity. As I write, I remember I am not alone; I call upon God's Spirit for guidance, wisdom, and—above all—compassion and mercy. I remember that I am worthy of God's love. I find the peace that comes from being deeply connected to God and living in spiritual harmony with my mind, with my body, and in my relationships.

In light of the highly personal nature of the journal, privacy is important. Keep your journal where it will not be read by another, so that you never hold yourself back from writing what is really in your heart. The candor and honesty with which you approach your journal helps you find your voice and prepares you to share yourself with others. Remember, however, that you share your journal with others *only as you choose.*

Blank journals may be purchased from a discount or stationery store; bound journals may be found in bookstores. The style of journal you choose is completely a matter of personal preference. If you are intimidated by blank sheets of paper, you may prefer using a guided journal. A guided journal presents specific questions to answer and topics to think and write about. I like my journals to be special, and I have had journals of all sizes and styles. Since I use my computer constantly, I've found that I am better able to form my thoughts there.

Questions for Reflection

1. What thoughts came to mind that you consciously decided not to put on paper? Why did you bypass them?
2. What type of journal might you purchase?
3. Did your journal entries include relationships or physical and material needs? Did you write about hopes and dreams, your desires, shortcomings, concerns for another, a specific situation, or a difficulty you are facing?

Other Resources to Continue Your Journey

Patricia D. Brown, *How to Start and Sustain a Faith-Based Women's Spirituality Group: Circle of Hearts* (Nashville, Tenn.: Abingdon Press, 2003). This book contains a whole chapter on keeping a journal. Or if you want a ready-made journal that is fun and easy to use, see my book *From the Heart Journal: A Personal Prayer Journal for Women*, from the same publisher.

Rose Layton Offner, *Journal to the Soul: The Art of Sacred Journal Keeping* (Salt Lake City, Utah: Gibbs Smith, 1996). I love the cover, layout, big size, and everything about this book. It has writing prompts and plenty of room to write.

Carolyn Manzi, *Coloring Your Prayers: An Inspirational Coloring Book for Making Dreams Come True* (New York: Harmony Books, 2000). Here is a journal for the more creative and artistic among us. Manzi is a bit eclectic in her approach, so take what is helpful (and fun) and leave the rest.

Pilgrimage

Let us concern ourselves with things divine, and as pilgrims ever sigh for and desire our homeland; for the end of the road is ever the object of the traveler's hopes and desires, and thus, since we are travelers and pilgrims in the world, let us ever ponder on the end of the road, that is of our life, for the end of our roadway is our home.

—SANCTI COLOMBANI OPERA, 521–597, IONA, SCOTLAND

Thoughts Before You Begin

Two paths converge in making a pilgrimage: the physical and the spiritual, a specific destination and a perpetual journey. In pilgrimage, the spiritual and the physical are deeply interconnected; both reach for abundant fullness, not merely getting enough to satisfy. Both require the stretch of leaving our comfort zone behind and, literally or metaphorically, sleeping away from our familiar bed.

Every pilgrimage begins with a call from God. It is always personal, for it is an invitation to go deeper into the fullness of Christ. The word *pilgrimage* comes from the Latin *peregrinus,* which means "stranger," denoting a person who travels to a foreign place. In a sense, we all are pilgrims wandering here on earth, trying to find our way back home to God. Jesus was the pilgrim *par excellence.* His initial venture was from the heart of God into the heart of our human reality.

Sacred sites have long been the object of pilgrimage. In the middle of the third century, Origen wrote about the caves in Bethlehem where pilgrims would go to see the birthplace of Jesus: "There is shown at Bethlehem the caves [sic] where he was born . . . and this sign is greatly talked about of [sic] in the surrounding places." Fifth-century monks from Egypt took pilgrimages to Jerusalem. Many stayed, planting themselves in the Judaean wilderness outside the city and making the region a center of Christian monasticism. Pilgrimage was also a striking phenomenon in the Middle Ages. Great pilgrimage centers were established throughout Europe in the eleventh and twelfth centuries, when Muslim occupation deprived Christians of access to the Holy Land.

Santiago de Compostela, located in northwestern Spain, is the most famous of the medieval pilgrimage routes. The remains of Saint James, the first martyred apostle, were believed to have been brought to Spain from the Holy Land during the ninth century. After James's death, he was thrown into the sea, and when his body was recovered it was covered with barnacles and shells. The scallop became the symbol worn in his honor; because Compostela was such a prominent pilgrimage route, this shell eventually came to symbolize pilgrimage itself.

Two other popular pilgrimage sites where people still flock today are Rome and Canterbury. The former lands of the Celtic saints—Iona, Scotland, and Lindisfarne, on the northeast coast of Northumberland, England—also continue to grow in popularity.

In May 2001, in the great fifty days between Easter and Pentecost on the Christian calendar, I took a group to France on pilgrimage. We followed many of the ancient paths taken by medieval Christians. My understanding of pilgrimage took shape in my mind gradually (even now it continues to form). I was drawn to the construction of the cathedrals and to the monasteries for the holy and intellectual. I longed to walk where the people of the Middle Ages walked pilgrimages, great distances under arduous conditions, inspired by faith.

Although my pilgrimage was undertaken with a group, it was a very personal and singular act of devotion. I wanted to receive the blessing that pilgrimage would bring. Each person in the group had his or her own motivation, and each of us derived a particular result or benefit from it. I saw the pilgrimage as an opportunity to do something motivated by no other reason than my faith.

Now Begin

Even if you are not able to take a journey to a far-off place, with a little prayer and planning you still can be a pilgrim. In pilgrimage, we find a place where we belong, not on a map but in our hearts. We find the place where life really is as it should be. We know this deep in our bones and in our heart of hearts. We discover home. The journey is always home.

Plan to take a pilgrimage. If you are able to travel in the United States, you might choose the National Cathedral in Washington, D.C.; the monastery home of Thomas Merton in Gethsemane, Kentucky; or the mission churches of the Southwest. Traveling overseas, you can follow one of the actual medieval pilgrimage routes, such as to the still-popular Santiago de Compostela in Spain or to Chartres Cathedral and Notre Dame in France, or a visit to the Holy Land. If you stay close to home, your pilgrimage might include the grave of a loved one, a local religious retreat center or site, or a church you've never entered. Set aside a time—fifteen minutes, an hour, a day, perhaps more—and make a pilgrimage. You might just walk around your own neighborhood and notice the trees and flowers, rocks and sand. Give thanks. Stop and pray for specific homes and families that you pass. Remember that God resides in the ordinary, everyday places of your life too.

Why not practice by going on a pilgrimage right now? Get up and go for a walk. If you are alone, when you return write your thoughts in your journal about what you experienced. If you are in a group, share where you went, what you saw, and how you felt. Ask yourself these questions: Where was God in all that I saw, heard, and felt? How did God touch and change my life through the people and places I encountered? How is God now inviting me to live differently from what I've experienced?

Some Things to Think About

The church in Rome tried unsuccessfully to control the pilgrimage routes, offering indulgences and forgiveness for completion of certain journeys. But people took willingly to the road, imposing penance on themselves. Soon an entire industry grew up along pilgrimage routes. The abbeys gave lodging and organized pilgrimages from one place to another, and a number of organizations and hospices provided aid and protection for travelers.

Pilgrimage continues today, blessing us with its enduring worth. In its dramatic simplicity, it invites us to root ourselves imaginatively in the past, even as we search for the spiritual center of our being.

Questions for Reflection

1. If you were to take a pilgrimage to a far-off place, where would you like to go? Would you go with a companion, or would you go alone?
2. A pilgrimage, great or small, is a microcosm, a picture of your life. What would your trip reveal?
3. Where are your present places of pilgrimage, the places where you go to remember and meet your heart?

Other Resources to Continue Your Journey

Louise Collis, *Memoirs of a Medieval Woman: The Life and Times of Margery Kempe* (New York: HarperCollins, 1983). Born in Norfolk in 1373, Kempe wrote a single manuscript: her autobiography, which was first discovered in the twentieth century. Read her description of her pilgrimage to Compostela during the Middle Ages.

Jennifer Lash, *On Pilgrimage: A Time to Seek* (New York: Bloomsbury, 1999). Travel with this modern-day pilgrim to Lourdes, Lisieux, and Taizé as well as the numerous stops of the Vezelay pilgrimage, and of course Santiago de Compostela.

Sarah York, *Pilgrim Heart: The Inner Journey Home* (San Francisco: Jossey-Bass, 2001). The cover alone sells the book, and you won't be disappointed as York offers her firsthand account of her soul journey. Going on a pilgrimage demands willingness to face the unfamiliar and unexpected in order to change and grow.

Praying with Icons

We call them saints when what we really often mean to say is "icon," "star," "hero," ones so possessed by an internal vision of divine goodness that they give us a glimpse of the face of God in the center of the human. They give us a taste of the possibilities of greatness in ourselves.

—JOAN CHITTISTER, 1996, ERIE, PENNSYLVANIA

Thoughts Before You Begin

Many of us have trouble praying with our eyes closed. Our imagination races from one thing to another. It can be hard work to get off the speedway inside our heads. Attention to an icon can help overcome such distraction. As physical objects, icons invite us to pray with our eyes wide open, focusing our whole, undivided attention on images that point the way to God. Looking at images of the great heroes of the faith, or the holy Trinity, or Mary, or Jesus helps to still our mind's frantic pace and rein in our wandering thoughts. Icons help us get beyond words to connect with the holy by giving us a visual reminder of the mystery of God's love for us, when words lack power or cannot express the full complexity of God. This visual reminder of the holy is another way for us to ponder our faith and who God is.

Icons have long been a part of Christian tradition, for the Western and the Eastern Church. From Asia Minor to Spain, Christian icons are preserved in catacombs, monasteries, and burial houses. In the fourth and fifth centuries, icons were often created in mosaics located on the walls of a church and behind the main altar. They were used in monasteries during the sixth and seventh centuries. The evangelist Luke is even said to have created three icons of Jesus' mother, Mary.

Just as in the present time there has been controversy about icons, there were early critics of icons, including Tertullian and Clement of Alexandria. Some feared that iconography (the word used for the art of icons) stemmed from art of the pagan world, while others objected on the basis of the Old Testament restrictions on carved statues of foreign deity. Still others argued that images of Christ diminished his divinity by lifting up his humanity. In 787, the council of bishops affirmed that it is not the icon itself that is venerated but the prototype whose image is represented in the icon. With most reservations set aside, iconography reached its height in Russia from the mid-fourteenth to the mid-sixteenth centuries.

During the Protestant Reformation of the fifteenth century, the Western Church's physical demonstration of religious life eroded drastically. This occurred largely as a defense against the fanaticism of sects and the charge by the Roman Church that in their bias they were leaving behind essential beliefs of the faith. The Western Church emphasized prayer as an inwardly focused activity, thus leaving behind many of the visual tools of prayer, such as icons. Where icons remained, they were simply seen as artwork or decoration instead of the intended instrument for transmission of Christian tradition and faith, and as aids to worship.

But icons are far more than artwork or decoration. They are more than colorful teaching tools for the illiterate. Icons are visual tools that tell the Christian story in images and color. They erase the borders of time and space to help people feel a closeness to the events and people portrayed in the pictures. Even when there is no liturgy or worship service taking place in a church building, people stop at specific icons, using physical gestures such as kissing, bowing, and lighting candles as if greeting a dear friend. This movement is all part of their devotion and prayer.

Non-Orthodox Christians sometimes misunderstand the purpose of icons and view them as idolatrous, but this is far from the truth. Icons are not idols. Instead, they are visual symbols that aid our worship. These visual images create a community of memory through generations of the Church. By the time Jesus was born, painted portraits in the Greek and Roman worlds looked almost as real as today's camera-produced images. Icons were a reaction against the "photographic" realism of the pagan artists, and as a consequence they intentionally conveyed a fixed and stylized version of Jesus' features, as a way to impart theological truths and offer a window to God's presence. Through their painstaking efforts, these early iconographers, first-generation artists of religious portraiture, became the bearers of the Church's memory and experience, thereby passing on to succeeding generations what they witnessed, including the face of Jesus.

The cross is perhaps the earliest and most common icon shared by every branch of the Christian faith. The first Christians would have been amazed that the cross—which is, after all, the equivalent of the gallows or electric chair—would one day be a decorative object for sale in jewelry stores and gift shops.

The first known icons in the Eastern Church are said to have been made by Abgar of Osroene, a king who was dying of leprosy. Orthodox Church history relates that he sent a message from Edessa, begging Jesus to come to him and cure him. Instead of going, Christ pressed his face against a linen cloth that took on his image, and he sent this as his gift of healing. After the king's miraculous recovery, the icon remained in Edessa until the tenth century, when it was taken to Constantinople. It remained there until 1204, when it disappeared during the Crusades. In some parts of the Christian world, this icon is known as the Shroud of Turin.

The Western Church tells the story of Veronica, a woman who faithfully stood at the roadside as Jesus carried his cross down the Via Dolorosa. When he stumbled under the weight of the cross and fell in weariness, she offered him a cloth to wipe his face. His image is said to have been imprinted on the cloth.

Many of the first icons came into the Christian church by way of Jewish sources depicting Jewish history. The first icon shown here, of the Holy Trinity, was originally a Jewish painting that depicted the story of Sarah and Abraham providing hospitality to three strangers who turned out to be angels. The picture was adapted by the early synagogue-based Christian community to represent the Trinity of God: Father, Son, and Holy Spirit. In the middle of the three figures is an altar holding a gold chalice. Once representing the drink offered to the unknown visitors, and in still earlier depictions a sacrificial lamb, it now reminds practicing Christians of their communion with the Holy Trinity. The hand levitating above the cup is a gesture of blessing.

Steeped in tradition, iconographers adhere to strict rules and protocols for their lifestyle and craft. They consider making an icon a work of prayer, fasting, and

The Holy Trinity

meditation. Hundreds of years ago, the church commissioned these (always-male) artists to the work of iconography; to protect the holiness of the calling, the Russian church ruled that the iconographer be "meek, mild, pious, not given to idle talk or to laughter, not quarrelsome or envious, not a thief or a murderer." Many of these traditions still continue in the Eastern Church.

Today there are Western religious artists such as Robert Lentz, whose fresh approach breathes new life into icons. Some modern iconographers contend that in the past the Church's acceptable icons were religious figures who supported the reigning institution—those people who were theologically proper, did not question church leaders, and upheld the then-popular morals of the institutional church. As a result, an entire body of people, including laity, women, and Christians who may not be Roman Catholic, have been ignored or eliminated. Lentz's icons include modern-day saints such as Martin Luther King, Mother Jones, and Dorothy Stein.

Icons are said to be "written," not "painted." Just as the printed Bible tells us about God, an icon is written to recognize that it too conveys a story of faith. To be faithful in carrying on the church's tradition and history, an iconographer avoids stylistic innovations and does not create original works of art but instead makes faithful copies—exact duplicates—of earlier icons. There may be occasional changes in style, but the essence of the icon always remains the same. Yet authentic iconography is not merely slavish copying of work done by others; it is understood as a work inspired by God, in which the writer understands himself or herself as a coauthor and part of a collective endeavor. The artist never signs an icon, as modern artists do with their art forms, because the icon is not the work of an individual artist but the fruit of many generations of artists who are faithful in telling the salvation story in pictures.

The icon is not intended to force a calculated emotional response from the viewer. Scenes rarely express the artist's feelings, or, when a work is commissioned, the owner's intentions. Instead, the iconographer hopes to suggest virtues such as purity, forgiveness, compassion, love, and suffering. Icons are also meant to guard against overfamiliarity with the divine. An early iconographer would never paint our currently popular notions of Jesus kneeling in the Garden of Gethsemane or boisterous with laughter. The icon is silent. No mouths are open; there are no physical details that suggest sound.

Icons avoid the artistic techniques that create the illusion of three-dimensional space. This keeps the focus on the virtues, the symbolism, and the simple truths of faith, rather than getting carried away with flourishes and embellishments. The painting is built up from a dark base to lighter colors; the lighting, hard to identify, never comes from a single light source. There is a minimum of detail in the person being depicted and a minimal background scene, if any. The lines of the painting pull the person at prayer into the icon, inviting the pray-er to participate in the mystery that the icon depicts.

Now Begin

Begin by dimming the lights and lighting a candle. Place the book open with the lit candle in front of it to illuminate the icons. Sit in a comfortable position and still your mind as you prepare to contemplate the nature of God. Gaze with complete attention on each icon found in these pages. *Gaze* is probably the best word for how to touch the core of icon spirituality. (The Western Church has emphasized listening, but the Eastern Church has focused on gazing, which is evident in all of its spiritual practices and worship.) Hopefully, over time you will begin to *see* these icons for yourself, and uncover layers of symbolism that speak to you deeply and powerfully of the unique way God has chosen to love you.

Return to the icon of the Holy Trinity, which represents the Trinity of God: Father, Son, and Holy Spirit at a table supporting a chalice. This icon depicts a mystery of Christian faith that is hard to express in words alone: the Holy Trinity is a community of love so perfect that the Father, Son, and Holy Spirit are one. The Trinity invites us to enter into loving communion with the three and demonstrates for us how all Christians are to be one.

The second in our quick study of icons is "The Virgin of Vladimir." This is one of the most frequently painted, and according to legend it was originally painted by Luke, the disciple and evangelist. The picture shows the baby Jesus in his mother's arms, with their faces pressed together. One of her hands holds him in tenderness and the other hand draws our attention to him, a motion reinforced by the tilt of her head. There is a subtle sense of apprehension in Mary's face. Her eyes look past the baby as if she can already see his suffering and death. The baby gazes at his mother, as if reassuring her of his resurrection and final victory. The image depicts the love that binds Mary and Jesus to each other, but it also reminds us of the connection between Mary, as a representative of God's love, and ourselves. We too are God's beloved.

Our third icon is "Christ the Pantocrator." The Greek word *pantocrator* means "the Lord of Creation." Because first-century Christians took painstaking effort to pass on to succeeding generations their memory of Christ's words and image, we find an amazing continuity in the icons of Jesus, just as there are in the icons of Mary. Notice his dark, soulful eyes and ruddy, yet gentle, features. Even today, although the Bible says very little about bodily features, our Sunday school lessons continue to depict the apostle Peter with blazing red hair and Paul as bald.

"Christ the Pantocrator" tries to express Christ as truly God and truly human. Note the large halo containing crosslike lines that are only used in connection with Christ. Christ's right hand offers a blessing of grace and peace; his fingers form the Greek letters that abbreviate his name, IC XC, reminding us of God's mercy and compassion. His left hand holds a book, representing law and judgment, calling followers to accountability.

The Virgin of Vladimir

Christ the Pantocrator

Some Things to Think About

The icons pictured in this book are printed in black and white. However, color itself is an effective means of communication; the variety and richness of colors used
in icons adds another level of depth and meaning. Paying attention to the use of
colors in each icon enhances your understanding and experience of prayer. Blue signifies heaven and mystery, most notably in the cloak of Christ and the clothing of
Mary. Red is the color of blood and suggests vitality, life, and beauty. It can also be
associated with fire, connoting purification. Purple is linked to wealth and power,
and white to purity and innocence. Gold signifies sanctity, splendor, and the glory
of God. Green signifies fertility in a general sense and the earth's vegetation; it can
be seen in the clothing of the martyrs whose blood nurtures the Church. Brown is
linked to the earth and can be a sign of a life of poverty, as found in the icons of
Francis of Assisi.

Some Orthodox families commission an icon for each room of the house, so
they can move from room to room in prayer. To enrich your prayer with icons, I encourage you to buy a book of full-color icons, or purchase an icon for your home.
Most Orthodox churches, and many Roman Catholic churches, have icon prints for
sale; a few may even offer originals by a resident iconographer. You might decide to
commission a hand-painted icon, which, when completed, will be formally blessed
by a priest or religious official in your presence. Although courses in icon painting
are ever more available to individuals, the parish iconographer should really be a
person who has the necessary virtues and has been sanctioned to carry on the work.

Questions for Reflection

1. Have you noticed any icons in your place of worship, or in your home or
    community? Which one has most captured your attention? Why?

2. Have you ever visited a church that uses icons as a tool for prayer? How did you feel? What was your initial reaction? What did you discover about yourself and your spiritual life from this experience?

3. What icon might you commission to be written? What aspect of the Christian story would you wish to be reminded of? Why? What images, nuances, and colors would the icon hold? Where would you place it in your home? Why?

Other Resources to Continue Your Journey

Joan Chittister, *A Passion for Life, Fragments of the Face of God,* with icons by Robert Lentz (Maryknoll, N.Y.: Orbis Books, 1996). This is one of my favorite books of all time. The combination of the author's storytelling with the stunning contemporary icons is simply divine.

Jim Forest, *Praying with Icons* (Maryknoll, N.Y.: Orbis Books, 1997). Forest offers a simple introduction with special emphasis on the practical use of icons in the spiritual life.

Henri J. M. Nouwen, *Behold the Beauty of the Lord: Praying with Icons* (Notre Dame, Ind.: Ave Maria Press, 1987). With the help of these meditations, you'll be able to gaze at the icons with complete attention and pray with them.

Novenas

Too late I loved you, O Beauty so ancient yet ever new! Too late I loved you!
And, behold, you were within me, and I out of myself, and there I searched for you.

—AUGUSTINE, 354–430, NORTH AFRICA

Thoughts Before You Begin

Welcome to praying novenas, so named because they are based in some way on the number nine; the word itself comes from the Latin word *novem*, meaning "nine." Reciting a written prayer nine times in nine days is the usual pattern.

Where did this practice originate? Early Christians adopted and adapted this custom, called the "novendialia," from the Roman and Greek cultures, who observed a nine-day period of sorrow after the death of a loved one. There are also nine days between Jesus' first appearance to his followers after his death and Pentecost, the day when the Christian church was officially founded by the Holy Spirit. By the high Middle Ages, novenas became a frequently used folk religious practice to create nine days of prayerful preparation before important feast days such as Christmas or All Saints' Day or the Transfiguration. A special novena of nine days preceding Christmas Day was a folk custom adopted by seventeenth-century Christian Spain. Each day symbolized a month of Mary's pregnancy.

Praying a petition nine times helps us develop the habit of praying and ensures that our prayer is sincere and a product of intentional forethought. In fact, I have found that my own novena becomes more focused and clear-headed with each repetition. Some people who pray the novena pray a chosen prayer nine times in a row at one sitting for nine days in a row. This repeating action opens their hearts to God's will and grace. The more grace we invite into our hearts, the closer we draw to God's will.

Repetition of novenas is not associated with superstition. If you skip a day, or pray it eight times instead of nine, trouble will not befall you. Instead, novenas are used to develop a habit of prayer that gradually clears the mind of distraction and focuses on the true intention, allowing the heart to face real—and at times hard— questions.

The novena to the Holy Spirit, which you'll find here, is one of the oldest known novenas. It is addressed to the Third Person of the Trinity and is a plea for the virtues we need to live the Christian life. When Christ appeared to the disciples forty days after his crucifixion, he instructed them to go to Jerusalem to wait for the Holy Spirit and pray—which turned out to be for nine days. This particular novena to the Holy Spirit was written in the Middle Ages and is usually used during the nine days from the feast of the Ascension, a Thursday, until Pentecost Sunday, the fiftieth day after Easter.

Now Begin

The novena to the Holy Spirit, included here, is an abbreviated version of the original, so that you can experience its feeling and flow if this is your initial journey into novenas. This novena is divided into two parts: the act of consecration to the Holy Spirit and prayer for the gifts of the Holy Spirit. Pray this novena at least once a day for the next nine days. I suggest kneeling or sitting in a comfortable but attentive position as you begin.

DAY ONE: Before you recite the novena, enter into your session of prayer by making the sign of the cross as you pray: "In the name of the Father, and of the Son, and of the Holy Spirit. Amen."

The sign of the cross is an ancient prayerful bodily gesture expressing faith in the Holy Trinity. To make this sign, lightly place your fingers upon the center of your forehead, then move your fingers to your chest. Next, touch your left shoulder and then the right shoulder, and return your hand to the center of your chest.

Next, pray these three prayers: the Lord's Prayer, the Hail Mary, and the Glory Be. (Refer to the chapter "Prayer Beads" to find these prayers.) Make the sign of the cross before you begin and at the end of the three prayers—like parentheses.

After you have completed the three prayers listed in the preceding paragraph, pray the entire novena (part one and all of part two) and the concluding prayer.

DAY TWO: Pray the three prayers along with the sign of the cross as you did on day one, starting with "In the name of the Father, and of the Son, and of the Holy Spirit. Amen." Then continue with part one of the novena and add the petition from part two that corresponds to the second day. Always end with the concluding prayer: "Mark me, Holy Spirit, with the sign of your true disciples and inspire me in all things. Amen." Each of the remaining eight days has been given its own subject to contemplate. Make sure you pause each day to mention your "novena intention" before ending your session with the concluding prayer. An intention could include a petition for a sick friend, a newborn baby, or a son who is to be wed.

DAY THREE: Pray the three prayers along with the sign of the cross. Continue with part one of the novena, adding the petition from part two that corresponds to day three. Pause to contemplate the day's petition and your novena intention. End your session with the concluding prayer. Continue in this way with all eight petitions for a total of nine days.

(Part One)
Act of Consecration to the Holy Spirit

On my knees before the great multitude of heavenly witnesses I offer myself, soul and body, to you, Eternal Spirit of God. You are the strength and light of my soul. In you I live and move and am. I pray with all my heart to be kept from the smallest sin against you. Guard my every thought, and grant that I may always watch for your light and listen to your voice and follow your gracious inspirations. I give myself to you and ask you to watch over me in my weakness. Give me grace, O Holy Spirit. "Speak, Lord, for your servant is listening." Amen.

(Part Two)
Prayer for the Gifts of the Holy Spirit

DAY TWO: Holy Spirit, grant me the Spirit of Wisdom, that I may despise the perishable things of this world and aspire only after the things that are eternal

DAY THREE: Holy Spirit, grant me the Spirit of Understanding, to enlighten my mind with the light of your divine truth

DAY FOUR: Holy Spirit, grant me the Spirit of Counsel, that I may ever choose the sure way of pleasing God

DAY FIVE: Holy Spirit, grant me the Spirit of Fortitude, that I may overcome with courage all obstacles

DAY SIX: Holy Spirit, grant me the Spirit of Knowledge, that I may know God and know myself

DAY SEVEN:	Holy Spirit, grant me the Spirit of Holiness, that I may find the service of God sweet and amiable
DAY EIGHT:	Holy Spirit, grant me the Spirit of Reverence, that I may be filled with loving respect and awe
DAY NINE:	Holy Spirit, grant me the Spirit of Wisdom, that I may aspire only after the things that are eternal

CONCLUDING PRAYER

Mark me, Holy Spirit, with the sign of your true disciples and inspire me in all things. Amen.

Some Things to Think About

In times of urgent need some people pray a nine-hour novena instead of this nine-day version. There is also a "triduum" prayer: three days of intense prayer, continuous petition for seventy-two hours. The point in telling you this is that the novena is a form of intercessory prayer; whatever form you use, they all encourage the understanding that God is listening and will act when we ask for what we need.

People who pray using novenas have told me that repeating a novena opens them to the miraculous and the opportunity to receive God's grace. However and whenever you decide to use novenas, they require a discipline that ensures time spent in prayer.

Questions for Reflection

1. How did the experience of prayer change over the nine days that you used the novena? What did you learn as a result of this change?

2. As a prayer technique, is recitation a good or not-so-good practice for you? Is repetition helpful in your life of prayer? Why or why not?

3. It is the ordinary ground of everyday life where God acts in extraordinary ways. Has this been your experience? How have you seen God at work in your life?

4. Write your own novena. Do you have a nagging concern, like a strained relationship with a co-worker or family member, or a particular problem to solve? Are you seeking guidance and direction for an important decision? Write a prayer about it. Then pray your personal novena for the next nine days and look for new insights, greater peace, or the challenge of new direction for your life.

Other Resources to Continue Your Journey

Barbara Calamari and Sandra Di Pasqua, *Novena: The Power of Prayer* (New York: Penguin Putnam, 1999). This book helps you to pray novenas for a variety of circumstances, with the novenas being based on the lives of the saints. These novenas remember Christian men and women from ages past who experienced similar problems or concerns, and from whose memory we can draw inspiration.

Joan Chittister, *Life Ablaze: A Woman's Novena* (Maryknoll, N.Y.: Orbis Books, 2000). This contemporary prayer book draws on novenas for women to meditate and pray on such concerns as wisdom, understanding, and fortitude.

Prayers for the Dead

Dear Lord . . . there is the certainty that you are waiting for me and will welcome me home when I have persevered in my long journey to your house.

—HENRI J. M. NOUWEN, 1932–1996, HOLLAND

Thoughts Before You Begin

Death is one of the great realities of life that we all face—and to which the Church responds with the hope of God. Prayers for the dead celebrate the life and death of a person and help people of faith cope with bereavement.

Although the Jewish Pharisees prayed for their departed, the early Church—expecting the imminent return of Christ, understandably devoted little energy to such prayer. As more and more believers "fell asleep" (I Cor. 15:6, KJV) the Church began the slow process toward articulating a theology of the dead. From the walls of the catacombs, we know that early prayers were a confident celebration of the dead one's journey through the gates of death and into eternal life with Christ.

By A.D. 160–220, at the time of Tertullian, people prayed in order to remember the holy lives of departed souls on the anniversary of their death. From the fourth century we have the writings of Augustine, who prayed for his deceased mother, eagerly reminding God of her sinless life since her baptism. Prayers for the dead came to include petitions for their forgiveness, thus forming the seedbed of the belief in purgatory.

By the fourth century, it was common in worship for the congregation to pray set petitions for the "communion of saints" as part of their daily worship. Especially in the case of martyrs, lists of the dead were maintained in the churches for the purpose of prayer. The churches I served in the mountains of Pennsylvania kept an official "roll" of those who died, and whose funerals were held at the church, along with the registered names of the baptized and current members.

Today, remembering the saints who have gone before is a regular part of the prayers of the Church. Praying and commemorating "the departed" is a regular feature in the *Book of Common Prayer* of the Episcopal Church. The "prayers of the people" in the *United Methodist Hymnal* are a typical example of this petition, used in morning and evening prayer. It contains the prayers given here, during which any person present may offer a brief prayer of intercession or petition. After each prayer, the leader may conclude: "Lord in your mercy," and all may respond: "Hear our prayer."

Nine times out of ten, when "the communion of saints" is stated, I say aloud the name of my deceased ("sainted") husband, Richard: "So then you are no longer strangers and aliens, but you are citizens with the saints and also members of the household of God" (Eph. 2:19). I remember Richard and trust that he prays for me too, with the intercessions of the Holy Spirit, "because the Spirit intercedes for the saints according to the will of God" (Rom. 8:27).

Here is the prayer. Sometimes the leader pauses for a time of silent reflection, and other times the congregants are invited to interject their petitions after each request.

> Together, let us pray for
> the people of this congregation . . .
> those who suffer and those in trouble . . .
> the concerns of this local community . . .
> the world, its people, and its leaders . . .
> the Church universal—its leaders, its members, and its mission . . .
> *the communion of saints* . . . [you may add the names of those who "died to the Lord" (Rom. 14:7–8) here].

The Lord's Prayer is then prayed in unison (see the chapter "Lord's Prayer" or "Prayer Beads").

Now Begin

It can be important to mark the occasion on the anniversary of the death of a loved one. Through simple words and ritual, we can express our continuing loss and grief and show our love and respect for the one who died.

In her book *Remembering Well: Rituals for Celebrating Life and Mourning Death*, Sarah York writes, "The occasions when a grieving person feels most vulnerable provide opportunities for the healing power of ritual. During the first year after a death, each birthday, anniversary, and holiday is a painful reminder of absence and loss. These occasions are also opportunities to create rituals of remembrance and mark milestones of memory." Write down the name of the person you wish to commemorate or make a list of deceased persons for whom you wish to pray. Use the next prayer, from the *Book of Common Prayer*, inserting their names as directed. If you are praying for more than one person, you may insert all of their names, at one time, in the place provided. You may wish to light one candle for each person you name before beginning the prayer.

> O God, whose mercies cannot be numbered: Accept our prayers on behalf
> of your servant(s) [insert name], and grant [him or her or them] entrance
> unto the land of light and joy, the fellowship of your saints; through
> Jesus Christ your son our Lord, who lives and reigns with you and the
> Holy Spirit, one God, now and for ever. Amen.

Then sing or read this thoughtful song by H. F. Lyte:

> Abide with me; fast falls the eventide;
> The darkness deepens; Lord, with me abide!
> When other helpers fail, and comforts flee,
> Help of the helpless, O abide with me.

Swift to its close ebbs out life's little day;
Earth's joys grow dim; its glories pass away;
Change and decay in all around I see;
O thou who changest not, abide with me.

Hold thou thy cross before my closing eyes;
Shine through the gloom, and point me to the skies:
Heaven's morning breaks, and earth's vain shadows flee;
In life, in death, O Lord, abide with me!

Close the time of remembrance by reciting the Twenty-Third Psalm (see the chapter "Praying the Scriptures") or the Lord's Prayer (see the chapter "Lord's Prayer").

Some Things to Think About

Today the prayer for the dead continues to be rooted in the anguish of bereavement. Although the ritual given here is designed for individual use or a small group, prayer for the dead usually takes place in a service of divine worship, such as All Saints' Day, or at a funeral or memorial service. This service of prayer offers a celebration of resurrection; thanksgiving for the person that affirms, without false glorification, the life that has been lived; ministry to the surviving family, friends, and community in grief; and transition for the church to express farewell and adjust to a different life that is resumed without that person's presence.

Let me end here with more wise words from Sarah York: "The mending we do in our own grieving hearts will heal and bless us in our relationships. And it will do more than that: It will reconcile us with the holy order of the universe. It will heal and bless the world."

Questions for Reflection

1. Think back to a funeral or memorial service that you attended. Were there particular prayers that were helpful to you in your grief? Did repeating prayers in the days, weeks, and months after the service help to assuage the pain of your loss?

2. Many Christian funerals incorporate well-known prayers such as the Lord's Prayer and the Twenty-Third Psalm. In such circumstances as a death, what feelings arise in you as you pray them?

3. Have you ever privately prayed for a loved one who died? When? What were the circumstances? How did these prayers comfort you?

Other Resources to Continue Your Journey

Sarah York, *Remembering Well: Rituals for Celebrating Life and Mourning Death* (San Francisco: Jossey-Bass, 2000). Whether you are planning a memorial or funeral service, for yourself or a loved one, this comforting and affirming book gives you words and ways to express your loss and hope.

C. S. Lewis, *A Grief Observed* (Nashville, Tenn.: Thomas Nelson, 1998). Writing with love, humility, and faith, this celebrated author gives an intensely personal account of the meaning of his wife's death.

Adele Wilcox, *Mending Broken Hearts: Meditations for Finding Peace and Hope After Heartbreak* (New York: Berkley Books, 1999). With one hundred life-affirming meditations, this book addresses the issues and emotions that accompany the loss of a love.

Experiential Prayer

*O*pen your heart as you enter these experiential prayers that speak to your deep appreciation for the history and theology of particular practices. Because you are an individual who likes traditions, yet who wants to be grounded in the here and now, you will relish the opportunity to try some of these ways of praying and apply them in daily life as you work, play, eat, and even sleep.

Fasting
    Abstinence from Food
    Fasting as Prayerful Solitude
Breath Prayer
    The Jesus Prayer: Prayer of the Heart
Benediction and Blessing
Tallith: The Prayer Shawl
Centering Prayer
Meditation: Mental Prayer
Anointing for Healing

Fasting

So, if we pray, fast; if we fast, show mercy; if we want our petitions to be heard, hear the petitions of others.

—MEGAN MCKENNA, 1997, MARYKNOLL, NEW YORK

Abstinence from Food

Thoughts Before You Begin

Christian fasting seems rare these days. Among churchgoers, you hear more about church potluck suppers, dinner clubs, and ice cream socials than about fasting. Let's admit it, food and eating play a big role in many religious observances and functions, and food also holds a significant role in the pages of the Bible—and even in Jesus' ministry. So does fasting.

There are numerous examples of fasting from food in scripture. The Bible offers a variety of examples, from moderation in diet to partial abstinence of food, and even total food restriction. Queen Esther fasted along with her people for three days and nights in order to save her nation (Esther 4:16). Jesus, like Moses and Elijah before him, ate nothing for forty days in the wilderness and stood strong against Satan's temptations (Deut. 9:9, I Kings 19:8, Luke 4:2). Jesus knew that a prayer practice of fasting was an outward sign of inward spirit-induced restraint, one revealing, perhaps more than any other form of prayer does, the things that control us. In this humble secret attitude, Jesus fasted in preparation for his ministry (Matt. 4:2).

Jesus left no explicit command to fast. Instead, he said, very simply, "When you fast . . ." instructing us on a regular prayer practice of his day. The one condition

Jesus does place on fasting was that it be sincere (Matt. 6:16), and not just for show. The sincerity of our fasting is not judged by flaunting our restraint and sacrifice, but by keeping it to ourselves, and sharing our sincere intentions with God.

Other instances of fasting in the New Testament include the apostle Paul, whose penitential three-day fast immediately after encountering Christ for the first time (Acts 9:9) was a prayerful action signifying an inward change; and John, the baptizer, who invited people to join him in the desert, wear scratchy clothes, and eat insects—all forms of abstinence (Matt. 3:1–4). But these deprivations were not an end to themselves. Instead, they enabled inner change that prepared the way for God to enter their lives. It wasn't the grasshoppers or burlap that were of value but the changes in the mind and heart of God's people. What initially appeared to be an avenue of discomfort, in the case of John's community, became a life-changing source of light, inspiration, and healing.

Jesus said, "If any want to become my followers, let them deny themselves and take up their cross and follow me. For those who want to save their life would lose it, and those who lose their life for my sake will find it" (Matt. 16:24). Here, Jesus was speaking about the paradox of surrender. Surrendering one's life to God gives a person new life in return, dying to self in order to rise again. It is surrendering the demands and comforts of our physical existence that creates openness to growth into a new life centered on openness to others and to God.

I understand how anyone might resist the idea of surrender and powerlessness. No normal person (including myself) accepts this truth without a fight. We carry a sense of misguided security in our personal power and the control we think we have over our lives. We label this control self-discipline, though in reality it has significant limitations. Fasting prayer is a prayer of surrender; it is an admission of helplessness. The day we see ourselves as we truly are is the day we begin our journey toward surrender. We admit to ourselves and to our Creator that there are things outside the limits of our control, that life is bigger than our willpower. It is an acknowledgment of our inability to control even our own body.

Don't think you can fast by willpower alone. You can't. Willpower bases its existence on hype, excitement, or desperation (like those fad diets, where the dieter's enthusiasm lasts no longer than ten days). Willpower is not comparable to prayer. Willpower is momentary; it never sustains you in the long run. Prayer, however, gives you access to infinite power with no limit. When we pray as we fast, we connect to a source that is both within and around us. It sustains us, supports us, and fills us. The strength we receive through fasting prayer encourages us day and night and leads us to abundant life. Try substituting willpower for divine power; I'd rather rely on God's power any day rather than on my own. Wouldn't you?

Now Begin

John Wesley, founder of the Methodists, taught that "the man who never fasts is no more in the way to heaven than the man who never prays." Fasting is one prayer practice that you will want to add to your prayer life gradually, in progressive steps. Here are some basic guidelines to acquaint you with the how-to's of fasting.

1. Consider if you will fast alone, or in companionship with another, or if you should seek the guidance of someone like a spiritual director.

2. Start by eliminating any food or beverage that causes you withdrawal symptoms, such as caffeinated drinks. You'll want to do this in the days and weeks before undertaking a fast so that any withdrawal symptoms do not distract you from your prayer.

3. Begin with a partial fast, perhaps skipping one meal. Then the next time you try fasting, extend it to two meals, and three. Try this one day a week for three

weeks. In week four, increase your duration to twenty-four hours. Then determine if you feel called to fast for a longer period of time, and how often you feel called to fast—once a week, once a month, or some other interval. Writer Dallas Willard states that if fasting is to be a spiritual discipline, then "practice it well enough and often enough to become experienced in it."

4. Live your outward day regularly, not drawing attention to your fast, while inwardly being in prayer. This causes each duty to become a sacred act of devotion and praise. Devote the time you would normally eat to prayer practice, meditation, or spiritual reading.

5. Drink liquids to help you remain hydrated. Consume 100 percent fruit juices or protein supplement drinks and water when you first begin to fast. As you progress in your practice, you can move to water only. Break your fast with a light meal.

6. You'll feel some physical hunger. The slowing of your metabolism may make you feel cold, so keep warm. Although the bodily aspects of fasting are a concern, don't forget that the important work of the fast is in the spirit.

7. If fasting is difficult, I suggest you pray often. Ask God to open your heart to your body and to see hunger as a companion. Pray for compassion, which is an accurate view of yourself or the world. Until we see with the eyes of compassion, we do not see at all.

8. After you advance to a two-day or three-day fast, prayerfully discern if you are to fast for a longer period of time. Three days is a substantial time period, and it will have an impact on your life. You may encounter a heavy spiritual struggle, or joy and peace. The Russian mystic Seraphim of Sarov (1759–1833) gives us these wise words: "Prayer, fasting, watching may be good in themselves; yet it is not in these practices alone that the goal of our Christian life is found, though they are necessary means for its attainment. The true goal consists in our acquiring the Holy Spirit of God."

Another option is to fast as practiced in the Western rite churches. For forty days during Lent the fast consisted of giving up types of food rather than meals. Christians gave up fats, such as found in meat, oil, butter, and cream, as well as sugars. This form of fast may be more attuned to your lifestyle.

Some Things to Think About

Why fast today? Can fasting as an ascetic act of penance really have any meaning for contemporary life? Besides, hard things are not necessarily good things. How can conformity and self-repression be good in a culture that prizes freedom and self-expression? What is the value of self-subscribed discomfort? Some of us may have a real aversion to the idea of fasting. We have been taught that our three meals a day are a medical necessity. Or we think that there is something unnatural about fasting. But when we understand fasting in the context of the scriptures and tradition, we look into our past, our collective memory of an enormously rich tradition.

Here are some reasons to fast:

1. *Fasting teaches surrender.* Like the martyrs before us, we can experience the beginning of real strength through surrender. Surrender is a giant step forward on the spiritual journey and an opportunity to be freer and more alive than we ever imagined. Practice powerlessness, and remember that control is an illusion. Remember, too, that God is in charge; you need only surrender. You don't have to fear being powerless. Instead, celebrate it and watch God work in your body and in your life. Allow your struggle to be an agent of spiritual growth; let it move you into a deep and fearless experience of life itself. It is when we refuse to give in to what we *think* we want, and thereby find what we truly need, that we can become free. This freedom is so essential for those of us who wish to live life fully. Let our fast be the diet of this restoration to wholeness.

2. *Discover the mystery.* Fasting can expand your perception of life and break down one more wall that obstructs your view, introducing you to the greater mystery of God. As a form of prayer, fasting is a natural expression of our humanity, and it is designed to introduce us to the mystery of life and God. Fasting creates events, attitudes, and circumstances we do not expect. It makes you hungry, of course, but it also opens your heart and mind to a new vision of what it means to be a faithful disciple.

3. *Fasting reveals the things that control us.* This is a wonderful benefit for those who long to be transformed into the image of Christ. If we enter the desert and remove the distractions, we can face who we are. We can die to our self so that we may live for Christ; we are not the center of the universe. During our fast, we encounter the inadequacies of willpower and self-discipline. They work for a while, but then we succumb to our cravings. It is this unavoidable encounter with hopelessness that can become the vehicle for a breakthrough that can change us forever. We finally admit that we do not have control of our lives and that we need help in a way and at a level we may never have experienced before. Now we are ready to pray.

4. *Fasting helps us keep life in balance.* It strips away the nonessentials that take up unnecessary room in our lives. My friend Adele Wilcox, author of *Self and Soul,* calls greed the bottomless bucket. She says that it is out of our insecurities that we think we need more than we actually do. This desire can encompass food, sex, or material possessions. What you have to realize, she says, is that "you are pouring water into a bucket with a giant hole in it." Jesus taught his disciples, "Sell your possessions and give alms. Make purses for yourselves that do not wear out, an unfailing treasure in heaven, where no thief comes near and no moth destroys" (Luke 12:33). When our lives and hearts are empty, we collect things. Wilcox challenges us to ask ourselves, "When is enough enough?" Do we possess our belongings, or do they possess us?

5. *Dedicate your fast to God with your whole being.* Fasting is not to be confused with a hunger strike, which is used to gain attention to an issue or to acquire political power. Fasting also differs from dieting to lose weight for physical reasons. Remember that fasting prayer centers on God. As Richard Foster writes in *Celebration of Disciplines,* "It is God-initiated and God-ordained."

Questions for Reflection

1. What did you find to be the greatest benefit in fasting? the biggest difficulty?
2. What did fasting reveal to you about your life and what controls you?
3. What did your prayer fast teach you about yourself, your relationships, and God?

Fasting as Prayerful Solitude

Thoughts Before You Begin

Although we usually associate fasting with abstinence from food, in our fast-paced society there are other modes of fasting that are just as important. At its core, fasting is a way to create more time to be with God, to establish a closer communion with the Divine. This continuous communing in prayer while fasting can play an integral part in our spiritual growth. Fasting can regulate not only our food but anything that invites obsessive attention outside of God.

Fasting helps us keep balance in life. By abstaining from food or other "necessities," we can see what is nonessential and begin to simplify our lives. Fasting makes the statement that we are willing to leave the physical comforts of life so as to feast on God's Spirit, making inner room for God's will to be at work and brought to reality in us. Even as we fast, we are reminded that we are sustained, not by food but by God's word (Matt. 4:4). In this way, we humble ourselves before God, calling upon the resources of the Holy Spirit who lives in us and implores us to turn our attention to God.

Richard Foster, a Quaker who has written several books on prayer and other spiritual practices, says that at times we may choose to fast from speech. For five minutes, ten minutes, thirty minutes, or longer, we abstain from speaking.

If you are not used to solitude, these minutes may seem like a lifetime. Yet the spiritual work of prayerful solitude is as important as any task or project you have on your desk. Do not feel guilty about "wasting time." It is permissible to care for your own soul. Spending time with God on your spiritual journey is essential work.

Now Begin

Set the alarm on your watch, or use a timer so you will know when the time is up. If you are praying with a group, please respect the silence of others and signal with a bell or chime when the time of abstaining from speech is finished.

On your first attempt, begin with five minutes of silence. You may choose to take this time of solitude before beginning your workday or commencing a project. Start by taking ten slow, deep breaths in and out. Use this as an attitude adjustment time. This creates a space for you to center and quiet yourself. It also tends to help you focus and settle your thoughts. You begin to be aware of your own inner feelings, and you are more in tune with the needs of those around you.

On your next attempt, try a period of fifteen minutes. Observe your feelings and reactions. Become aware of what you are feeling in this time spent in solitude, time apart from the incessant noise and distraction of your daily life. Think about this: when you follow God's command to love your neighbor as yourself, you first take time to know and love yourself. Ask yourself, *What does this experience tell me about myself?* This is not a selfish love; it is genuine care for your own spiritual well-being, which enables you to give and be fully present to others.

As you become accustomed to more time in silence, try thirty minutes of solitude. Find a quiet space. Claim it as your own. You may want to move to a particular room or go outdoors. You will not grow in your prayer life if you do not set a regular time for reflective, meditative solitude. Teresa of Avila, who lived in the sixteenth century, says, "Settle yourself in solitude and you will come upon him [God] in yourself." *Silence* does not mean only the absence of speech but also a new openness to listening to God. Fasting and solitude remove the ways in which you have insulated yourself from God's approach at a deeper level, allowing you to be open to meet God intimately.

Some Things to Think About

To stop talking without listening to God is not true spiritual solitude. Constant talkers drain their inner energy without realizing it. In silence, we learn that we can turn off the chatter and still feel at ease. In the quiet, we also learn to listen to others. As you silence yourself, you learn to act with increasing sensitivity and gentleness toward others. Learning to listen and be still means being able to speak the word of compassion that is needed *when* it is needed. With practice, we may find that we like the discipline of silence as much as talking.

People who practice inner silence begin to learn the lessons of consistently maintaining a quiet place of mind and heart—a place designed for silence and solitude. This time of silence ripples out to the other parts of their lives. They begin to anticipate the snatches of quiet time here and there throughout their day—in the morning before the kids get up, or later in the day while sitting in the car at a red light. They stop for a moment of silence before they eat. Bit by bit, they learn to carry a portable sanctuary of the heart wherever they go.

Questions for Reflection

1. When do you abstain from speech? Make a list of times in your daily schedule when you can intentionally observe times of silence and reflection.
2. How does it feel to be in solitude? How does the experience change for you as you learn to remain silent for a longer period of time?

3. Can you spot any problems that might arise? Some individuals have difficulty locating a time and place to be uninterrupted. Others find that they have a short attention span or get restless after a brief silence.

Other Resources to Continue Your Journey

John Piper, *A Hunger for God: Desiring God Through Fasting and Prayer* (Wheaton, Ill.: Crossway Books, 1997). This is a comprehensive study of the topic. In addition, the appendix contains great historical quotes on fasting, from the early Church fathers to the present day. A drawback is that he doesn't refer to any women in his bibliography.

Richard Foster, *Celebration of Discipline: The Path to Spiritual Growth* (San Francisco: HarperSanFrancisco, 1983). Foster has a good chapter on fasting that gives crucial new insights into the simplicity of fasting. Topics include fasting in the Bible, the purpose of fasting, and the practice of fasting.

Anthony De Mello, S.J., *Awareness: The Perils and Opportunities of Reality* (New York: Image Books, Doubleday, 1992). De Mello's message is clear: you leave this go-go-go world of illusion and become aware of what you are doing and why you are doing it. This book challenges you to wake up in every aspect of your life.

Emilie Griffin, *Clinging: The Experience of Prayer* (New York: McCracken Press, 1983). Griffin talks about how "transparency" is a passage into the fullness that makes us want to fast. Her descriptions of prayer and fasting lead you into the actual experience of praying.

Cheri Huber, *That Which You Are Seeking Is Causing You to Seek* (Mountain View, Calif.: Center for the Practice of Zen Buddhist Meditation, 1990). We need only to stop, sit down, be still, and pay attention in order to draw closer to God. This simple little book assists you in doing just that.

Breath Prayer

Prayer unites the soul to God.

—JULIAN OF NORWICH, 1342–1416, ENGLAND

Thoughts Before You Begin

The breath prayer is a short prayer of petition or praise that helps us become aware of the presence of God. This practice was given its name because prayer is to be as natural as breathing. Physical breath is a scriptural symbol of God's Spirit. Remembering that the Hebrew word *ruach* means *wind* or *breath* but also *spirit* helps us understand how the breath allows us, in a very real sense, to be praying always *within.* Just as breath is an innate function of our bodies, prayer can be rooted naturally within our being. It is a way to have on our lips what is always in our heart. The goal of this form of prayer is to integrate our interior thoughts and exterior actions.

The original breath prayers grew out of the psalms. Short phrases or verses were uttered, reminding the individual of the whole psalm. A breath prayer is a brief petition that arises from our deepest needs, clarifying who we are and helping us understand our relationship with God. It can be drawn from scripture or from our imagination; two simple examples are "Physician, lead me to wholeness" or "Shepherd, guide me to do your will." I have found it helpful to break down the petition into parts so that with each breath, or a number of breaths, the petition grows smaller, simpler, and more specific:

Jesus, help me.
Jesus, help.
Jesus.

Guidelines for breath prayer:

- Be honest and humble in your petition.
- Choose a short phrase. Pray a natural rhythm of six to eight syllables.
- Allow yourself to search for one or two days to find the most comfortable and personal words, and then pray them unchanged for at least a month.

♦   After a month, change your prayer as new insights come and your life situation changes.

In this slowed-down experience of serenity and calm, you intentionally choose to
rest in the presence of God, putting aside external and internal distractions and focusing on the present space and time of prayer. Metropolitan Anthony, a Russian
Orthodox bishop of London, gives us wise council: "you must decide that within
these two minutes, five minutes, which you have assigned to learning that the present exists, you will not be pulled out of it by the telephone, by a knock on the door,
or by a sudden upsurge of energy that prompts you to do at once what you have left
undone for the past ten years."

Now Begin

STEP ONE: Sit for a moment in silence and remember that God holds
you in a loving presence. Determine the amount of time you
desire to designate to your breath prayer, then say, "God,
here I am."

STEP TWO: As you settle yourself into a comfortable position, breathe
comfortably, with regular breaths. Our desire in prayer is to
breathe slowly and deeply into our abdomen. Breathing in
prayer should be a slow, natural, rhythmic action involving
the entire torso. Too many people coming to prayer breathe
poorly, never fully using their lungs; they take shallow
breaths, making little use of the diaphragm. These rapid
shallow breaths can cause tension. Breathing for maximum
awareness means breathing through your nose as you inhale
and exhale the lungs fully. The more used air we breathe out,

the more new air we can take in. Take three or four slow, deep breaths.

STEP THREE: Next, you may want to close your eyes as you silently recall the words "Be still, and know that I am God," from Psalm 46:11. Pause after each phrase to take three or four deep breaths before moving to the next phrase:

Be still, and know that I am God.
Be still, and know that I am.
Be still, and know.
Be still.
Be.

STEP FOUR: For the next five to ten minutes, just breathe. Become aware of the natural pauses in the ebb and flow of your breath. These are called *stillpoints.* Watch each moment of breath, the inhalations and exhalations and stillpoints, with calm awareness. In Christian spirituality the stillpoint is identified as God's fullness. It is a point of rest. When we rest in God, there is nothing more to do, nothing to be, nowhere to go. Augustine prayed about this stillpoint: "You move us to delight in praising you; for you have made us for yourself, and our hearts are restless till they find rest in you." Continue to observe each moment of breath with calm awareness.

STEP FIVE: When thoughts arise, simply acknowledge them and let them pass. Do not make judgments about them. Try not to take a ride with them or become involved. Thoughts will come and go; they don't have to be given any energy, named, or held onto. The point is not to suppress thought but to surpass it. Simply return to your breath. Keep your awareness on the breath.

STEP SIX: Return to the phrase from Psalm 46. As before, take three or four deep breaths between phrases. Rest with God in the inhalation, the exhalation, and the stillpoint of each breath:

Be still, and know that I am God.
Be still, and know that I am.
Be still, and know.
Be still.
Be.

STEP SEVEN: Gently, slowly open your eyes. How are you feeling? As the Spirit releases you from this time of breath prayer, carry its calm awareness with you as you move on with your day.

Some Things to Think About

It is important to calm ourselves and take the time to be open to God's Spirit, simply to observe and not control what happens within us. Check on your body tension, and slow your breathing so you can relax. As you relax in this mindful presence before God, you become more spiritually aware. You are alert and perceptive in the present moment.

Episcopal pastor Ron DelBene says that the feeling in breath prayer is like the yearning that lovers have for each other. It is a yearning not of the mind or heart alone but of our *whole being.* Our bodies, our intentions, our lives, and our very selves become prayer. Dame Gertrude More captures the essence of this intention:

O my God, let me walk in the way of love which knoweth
not how to seek self in anything whatsoever.
But what love must it be?
It must be an ardent love,
a pure love,
a courageous love,
a love of charity,
a humble love,
and a constant love.
O Lord, give this love into my soul,
that I may never more live nor breathe but out of a pure love of Thee,
my All and only Good.

Questions for Reflection

1. Some users of breath prayer find that it is helpful in restoring calm so
   that they can then enter into other forms of prayer. When might you use
   breath prayer?
2. How often are you challenged to *become* prayer? How often are you challenged to believe that the very person you are can be a prayer to God and
   a prayer for others?

The Jesus Prayer: Prayer of the Heart

Thoughts Before You Begin

The prayer of the heart is a simple form of breath prayer in which a mantra or short phrase is repeated to keep one's attention focused, to attend to the presence of God in the moment. Short prayers can be used in time of need, stress, or joy ("Jesus, help me"; "O Lord, hear my prayer," "Praise be to thee, O God!" and so on).

From the Christian tradition of the East comes a prayer of the heart called the Jesus Prayer. It is a unique form of prayer of the heart because it strictly employs one mantra: "Lord Jesus Christ, Son of God, have mercy on me, a sinner"—or the even further condensed "Lord Jesus Christ, have mercy on me," which we employ to introduce this prayer practice.

Now Begin

Discern how much time you plan to pray: two minutes, five, ten, or more. Sit alone and in silence; bow your head and close your eyes; relax your breathing, and with your imagination direct your mind from the head into the heart. Regulate your breathing; rhythmic breathing disperses distracting thoughts. While inhaling, say "Lord Jesus Christ." As you exhale continue with "have mercy on me," either softly with your lips or silently in your mind. Continue until you can relax. Allow God's peace to settle over you and rest your mind. Isaac of Syria, a sixth-century Eastern Church pastor, wrote, "Endeavor to enter into your inner treasure house and you will see a heavenly treasure. The ladder leading into the kingdom of heaven is hidden within you, in your heart." Find that "place of your heart" and abide there.

When distracting thoughts enter your mind, set them aside. Be patient and peaceful and repeat the process frequently. As a beginner you may experience discomfort in the form of troubling thoughts or a wandering mind. You may even wonder why you are "wasting time." But, if you persist you will attain increasing joy.

Some Things to Think About

The ceaseless Jesus Prayer is an uninterrupted call on the holy name of Jesus Christ with the lips, mind, and heart. John Main, with his Irish wit, once instructed, "The only important thing about breathing is to continue to do so for the full time of your meditation." This is not to say that Main was not well aware of the breath's importance. He was. He simply believed, and I also have found it true, that with time and practice one's mantra and breath gradually and naturally regulate themselves into a comfortable rhythm.

Simeon the New Theologian, an Eastern Christian of the eleventh century, gives these additional instructions:

> First you must observe the following three conditions: You must be free
> from all cares, not only from vain and unholy cares but even from good
> things. In other words, you should be dead to everything; your conscience

should be pure and it should not denounce you in anything. You should be completely free from passionate attachments; your thoughts should not be inclined toward anything worldly.

Then sit alone in a quiet place, close the door, take your mind from every temporal and vain thing. Bow your head toward your chest and stay attentively inside of yourself, not in the head but in the heart, and holding the mind there with your inner eye watch your breathing. With your mind find the place of the heart and let it abide there.

Questions for Reflection

1. Which mantra or short phrase did you choose to use? Why?
2. Are Saint Simeon's instructions different from how you have prayed before? Which concepts are different? Which are familiar?

Other Resources to Continue Your Journey

James Finley, *The Contemplative Heart* (Notre Dame, Ind.: Sorin Books, 2000). The author's meditation instructions, precise and poetic, help you in whatever stage you are at in the contemplative experience.

E. Kadloubovsky, *Writings from the Philokalia on Prayer of the Heart*, G.E.H. Palmer, trans. (London: Faber and Faber, 1975). Hear the wisdom of seventh-century spiritual men and women. This translation of their spiritual writings holds gems that you won't want to miss.

Helen Bacovcin (trans.), *The Way of the Pilgrim and the Pilgrim Continues His Way* (New York: Doubleday, 1978). Come with this anonymous nineteenth-century Russian pilgrim in search of the answer to his question, How does one pray without ceasing? With him you'll discover the Jesus Prayer.

Ron DelBene, *The Breath of Life: A Simple Way to Pray* (Minneapolis: Winston Press, 1981). The breath prayer is a short, simple, ancient prayer that helps us experience the presence of God. DelBene walks you through the process step by step.

Robert Faricy, S.J., and Lucy Rooney, S.N.D, *The Contemplative Way of Prayer: Deepening Your Life with God* (Santa Barbara, Calif.: Queenship, 1986). "Contemplating Jesus" simply means looking at Jesus with love. This book helps you sit at Jesus' feet, listen, and receive God's love.

Benediction and Blessing

May the road rise to meet you,
May the wind be always at your back,
May the sun shine warm upon your face,
May the rain fall softly on your fields,
May God hold you in the hollow of his hand.

—TRADITIONAL GAELIC PRAYER

Thoughts Before You Begin

The formal worship service is drawing to a close, and the pastor dismisses the congregation with a blessing in the name of God. You've likely heard this many times in your life. A benediction is a blessing that pronounces God's favor and usually ends with the trinitarian formula "In the name of the Father, the Son, and the Holy Spirit."

Benedictions are found throughout the Old Testament. Sarah and Abraham are blessed by God: "I will bless her, and moreover I will give you a son by her. I will bless her, and she shall give rise to nations; kings of peoples shall come from her" (Genesis 17:16).

A blessing that is still commonly used today comes from Moses' blessing of the Israelites: "The Lord bless you and keep you; the Lord make his face to shine upon you, and be gracious to you; the Lord lift up his countenance upon you, and give you peace" (Numbers 6:24–26).

Two other benedictions are commonly used simultaneously with the sign of the cross. The pastor motions with an outstretched hand from head to chest, and then left to right: "The grace of the Lord Jesus Christ, and the love of God, and the communion of the Holy Spirit be with you all," or "Almighty God, Father, Son, and Holy Spirit, bless you now and forever. Amen."

You can also use benedictions. Just as a pastor offers God's blessings to the congregation, you can extend a benediction reminding one another of God's goodness and grace. I use the simple benediction "Blessings" or "Blessed be" as a salutation at the end of a letter or e-mail. I also hug close friends as we part and in the hug whisper in her ear, "The Lord bless, keep you and give you peace" (a short version of the passage in Numbers 6). There is no greater wish that we can bestow upon another.

Now Begin

These instructions are written for prayer with a partner.

Face your partner. You will recite this exchange two times, reversing roles the second time, so that you each act as giver and receiver.

With your thumb, trace the cross upon each part of the body of your partner as it is mentioned. Your partner may respond by simply saying "Amen," or by using the response in the script:

PARTNER ONE: Receive the cross on your ears, that you may hear the gospel of Christ, the Word of life.

PARTNER TWO: Glory and praise to you, Almighty God.

PARTNER ONE: Receive the cross on your eyes, that you may see the light of Christ, illumination for your way.

PARTNER TWO: Glory and praise to you, Almighty God.

PARTNER ONE: Receive the cross on your lips, that you may sing the praise of Christ, the joy of the church.

PARTNER TWO: Glory and praise to you, Almighty God.

PARTNER ONE: Receive the cross on your heart, that God may dwell there by faith.

PARTNER TWO: Glory and praise to you, Almighty God.

PARTNER ONE: Receive the cross on your shoulders, that you may bear the gentle yoke of Christ.

PARTNER TWO: Glory and praise to you, Almighty God.

PARTNER ONE: Receive the cross on your hands, that God's mercy may be known in your works.

PARTNER TWO: Glory and praise to you, Almighty God.

PARTNER ONE: Receive the cross on your feet, that you may walk in the way of Christ.

PARTNER TWO: Glory and praise to you, Almighty God.

After you have blessed each other, you might wish to extend the peace of Christ to one another with the ancient words, "The peace of the Lord be with you." The response is, "And also with you."

Some Things to Think About

Perhaps you recognized the blessing. Although an ancient rite, it is still used today in the Christian church to welcome "hearers" into the assembly. The sign of the cross—a symbol that was used by the earliest Christians to mark the blessing of the divine upon their lives—is used today in the rite of initiation. This prayer was used to mark a seeker's first step into formal catechesis. In the past, you may have thought of catechesis as rote memorization of answers to questions. Instead, true catechesis is grounded in relationships between reliable spiritual guides and people who are seeking to know the way of dying and rising with Christ in their daily life.

Questions for Reflection

1. How did you feel as the receiver of the blessing? As the giver?
2. Write or adapt a benediction to close this time of communal prayer. Say the benediction aloud to your partner.

Other Resources to Continue Your Journey

Philip Dunn, *Prayer, Language of the Soul* (New York: Bantam Doubleday Dell, 1997). More than three hundred prayers from around the world offer the right words for private devotion and meditation.

Marcia Falk, *The Book of Blessings: New Jewish Prayers for Daily Life, The Sabbath, and the New Moon Festival* (Boston: Beacon Press, 1996). This is a book that brings the ancient prayers alive for Jews and non-Jews alike.

Susan Langhauser, *Blessings and Rituals for the Journey of Life* (Nashville, Tenn.: Abingdon Press, 2000). The author offers forty-one ready-to-use, easily adaptable blessing rituals for a variety of community occasions.

Tallith

THE PRAYER SHAWL

I ran inside, grabbed a prayer book, scurried back outside, wrapped myself in a sheet, said the blessing for putting on the prayer shawl, and felt the Presence gently embracing me with arms of sunlight. . . . I could feel the Presence bathe me in Her loving laughter.

—JUDY PETSONK, 1991, OHIO

Thoughts Before You Begin

To learn how to pray as Jesus did, you'll want to experience using the tallith, a Jewish prayer shawl. It will remind you of the fabric prayer stole worn by your Christian pastor or priest on Sunday mornings. The Jewish *tallith* (pronounced *tä-lət* or *tent-it* as in the word *little;* the *th* is pronounced as a *t* and not as a *th*) is worn over the shoulders or head. A practicing Jew typically wears the tallith during morning prayer and other daytime prayer, on the Sabbath, and on religious holidays. The owner is also lovingly wrapped in it and buried with it at his or her death.

This rectangular four-cornered garment has four fringes or tassels, called *tzitzit* (pronounced *tsēt'-sēt),* which are always white, representative of purity.

The typical size of the shawl is five feet by two feet; larger ones measure up to six feet by four feet. Your imagination, creativity, sensitivities, and taste determine

Tallith Prayer Shawl

the size and fabric of the tallith you choose, as well as when you use it. I own a silk prayer shawl that measures three and a half feet by six and a half feet. I like the larger size because it reminds me that I am wearing not a scarf but a prayer garment. I can easily enwrap myself in this prayer shawl and, hiding in its tent, immerse myself in prayer. But my rabbi friend reminds me that it is not just about the shawl enfolding us. The shawl is simply the vehicle that enables us to pray. Wearing the tzitzit reminds us of God's commands.

Now Begin

I have taken some liberty in combining a number of Jewish prayers and rituals that are used with the prayer shawl so that you can get a taste of the tallith's helpfulness while praying. To pray the prayers in full and enact the rituals in their entirety as they are used in worship today, refer to the recommended texts at the end of this instruction.

The prayer begins with a step-by-step ritual process for putting on the prayer shawl. The sequence moves in an outward progression, from your personal space enveloped within the prayer shawl, to the shared space of the community, to the whole of the natural world.

STEP ONE: Standing is the usual position for Jewish prayer. Spread the folded shawl across your outstretched arms and hands. (The shawl is often folded in a way that allows it to fit into its specially made cloth storage bag; there is no one proper way to fold the shawl.) This ancient ritual inspects the shawl to ensure that it is made with the correct cloth and its tzitzit are intact. Read this passage as you make your examination. The first paragraph of the prayer is lifted directly from Psalm

104. The second paragraph of the prayer is a meditation from the traditional Hebrew prayer book called the *Siddur* (pronounced si-dər):

Bless the Lord, O my soul; O Lord, my God, you are very great; you are clothed in glory and majesty, wrapped in a robe of light; you spread the heavens like a tent cloth.

For the purpose of unifying with the Holy One I wrap myself in this tallith. My soul is wrapped in the light of the tzitzit. And just as I am covered by a tallith in this world so should I be worthy of a dignified cloak and beautiful tallith in the world to come—in the Garden of Eden. And as I fulfill God's command may my soul, spirit, holy spark, and prayer rise to you. May the tallith spread its wings over us and save us, "as an eagle that stirs its nestings, fluttering over its chicks." Amen.

STEP TWO: Gather all the strands of the four corners of the tzitzit together and hold them in your left hand to symbolize the gathering of the four corners of the earth into unity with God. Wrap the strands of the fringe around your index finger and pray:

Hurry, and quickly bring upon us blessing and peace from the four corners of the earth. You have brought us close to your great name, with love and truth, so that we can praise you and live in love.

To experience the full effect, open to the Numbers passage in your own Bible, instead of relying on the reprinting here. Touch the Bible with the fringes of your tallith and then kiss the fringes to show respect for God's commandments. Now continue with the reading. Kiss the tzitzit fringes three times, once for each time the word *fringe* is used as you pray this third section of morning prayer, called the *Shema*. This prayer of affection for God and God's commandments comes from the Hebrew scriptures, Numbers 15:37–40:

The Lord said to Moses as follows: Speak to the Israelite people and instruct them to make for themselves fringes (first kiss) on the corners of their garments throughout the ages; let them attach a cord of blue to the fringe (second kiss) of each corner. That shall be your fringe (third kiss); look at it and recall all the commandments of the Lord and observe them, so that you do not follow your heart and eyes in your lustful urge. Thus you shall be reminded to observe all my commandments and to be holy to your God.

STEP THREE: Now, fully open the tallith, spreading it on a table or draping it in front of you. As you open it, use this prayer of praise:

Blessed are you, Lord our God, Ruler of the Universe, who has sanctified us with God's commandments, and directs us to enwrap ourselves in a tallith with tzitzit.

Now kiss each end of the "crown" of the shawl as an act of love and endearment for God and the commandments. The crown, also called the *attarah,* is the area often designated with a band that lies on the outside of the garment, over your neck. It might be decorated with a biblical saying or special decorative fabric.

STEP FOUR: Stretch your arms behind you, and holding the tallith like a cape, rest it upon your shoulders. Next, bring the shawl up from your shoulders and cover your head. Now begin to sway with a back and forth motion as if you were in a rocking chair. Swaying symbolizes Psalm 35:10, "All my bones shall say, 'O Lord, who is like you?'" and is the most recognizable movement associated with Jewish prayer. Some people make this movement exaggerated and rapid, while others rock slightly and slow. I tried swaying to and fro and it made me feel as though my entire body were caught up in prayer. It kept my attention fully focused in the moment. Until I got the hang of it, it was awkward to keep my balance standing and swaying. So I sat down. Try both standing and sitting and decide which is best for you—swaying or being still, whichever helps you to concentrate on your prayers. Now, in position, pray:

How precious is your kindness, God. We take refuge in the shadow of your wings. Recalling the generations, I wrap myself in the tallith. May my mind be clear, my spirit open, as I envelop myself in prayer.

This is where you simply spend time with God in prayer—for five minutes or an hour, or longer. At the conclusion of your prayers, say "Amen" aloud and return the tallith from your head onto your shoulders. Remove the prayer shawl gently, reluctantly, folding it neatly and returning it carefully to its holder, which can be a specially made cloth bag or a simple plastic covering.

Some Things to Think About

You can make a simple homemade tallith prayer shawl along with its tzitzit fringe to use in public worship, at home, or on the road. Similar to using prayer beads that count prayers, the tallith is used to keep count of the prayers of the traditional Jewish blessing path, in which an individual prays one hundred blessings a day. Therefore a more elaborate (and complete) tallith has the four tassels, eight strings, and five knots, as on the one you'll be making; it also contains six hundred fringes. These details all have meaning. The numerical equivalent of the Hebrew word for *fringe* is 600; after adding the numbers 8 and 5 (eight strings and five knots in each corner), the sum is 613, representing the number of commandments *(mitzvot)* in the Jewish tradition.

You can use a shawl that you already own or purchase any woven piece of cloth at a fabric store. A tallith can be made of any type of fabric, but there is a caveat not to mix linen and wool in the same garment. When selecting material, pay attention to the weight and lay of the cloth. You want it to be flexible and not too heavy. The rectangle can measure four feet by six feet. To make a finished edge, turn and fold the ends of each of the four sides one-half inch. Crease the folds with an iron. Again, turn and fold each edge one-half inch a second time and crease with an iron. Secure the edges with a hem stitch (by hand with a needle and thread, or with a sewing machine) or by using a special iron-on tape that you can buy at the craft store.

Make slits for button holes one-quarter inch long at the four corners. These can also be done by machine or by hand. I couldn't remember how to make these holes from my high school home ec course, so my local tailor put them in for me.

To make the white tassels that go on the four corners of your shawl, I suggest you first practice using twine before attempting the fringes in more expensive thread of wool, silk, or linen. I used a substantial twine, one-half inch in diameter.

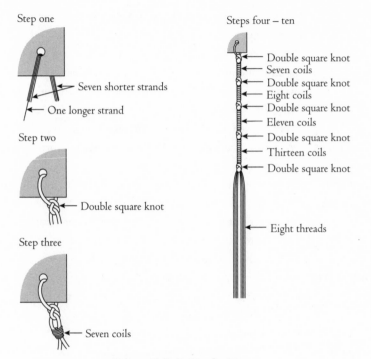

Step one

Seven shorter strands

One longer strand

Step two

Double square knot

Step three

Seven coils

Steps four – ten

Double square knot
Seven coils
Double square knot
Eight coils
Double square knot
Eleven coils
Double square knot
Thirteen coils
Double square knot

Eight threads

Tying a Tzitzit, Step by Step

Here is how to make one tassel in ten steps:

STEP ONE: Cut one strand of twine nine feet long and three strands five feet long, for a total of four stands.

STEP TWO: Even up the four strands at one end and fold them in half at two and a half feet. Allow the one longer strand to hang to one side. Secure them around a tying post such as a doorknob or onto the post on the back of a chair so that you now have eight strands (I used the post of a kitchen chair). Holding four strands in each hand, tie a double square knot snug against the tying post. To make a double square knot, wrap and tie the rope right over left and under and through, then left over right, and under and through. This keeps both sides an even length. The rest are short easy steps.

STEP THREE: Wind the one long strand around the seven shorter strands seven times to make seven coils.

STEP FOUR: Make a second double square knot, as you did in step two.

STEP FIVE: Wind the long strand around the shorter strands eight times to make eight coils ($7 + 8 = 15$ is a numerological formula that represents the first two Hebrew letters of God's name).

STEP SIX: Make a third double square knot.

STEP SEVEN: Wind the long strand around the shorter strands eleven times to make eleven coils (eleven represents the last two letters in God's name in Hebrew).

STEP EIGHT: Make a fourth double square knot.

STEP NINE: Wind the long strand around the shorter strands thirteen times to make thirteen coils. (Thirteen is equivalent to the Hebrew word "one" and emphasizes that "God is one.")

STEP TEN: Secure the end of the long thread by tucking it up into the last set of coils.

Once you have learned this process, you are ready to place the tassels on your prayer shawl. This time you push the clusters of threads through the buttonholes that you made in the corners of your shawl.

Questions for Reflection

1. How did you design your personal tallith? Did you use your imagination, creativity, sensitivities, and taste? What fabric did you use? What size is your prayer shawl?
2. Your shawl is a vessel that will enable you to pray. What did you pray about when you enwrapped yourself and hid in its tent? Were you able to shut out any intrusions and immerse yourself in prayer?
3. Swaying is the most recognizable movement associated with Jewish prayer. How best did you perform and experience this rocking motion? Exaggerated and rapid? Slight and slow? Did you sit, kneel, or stand?

Other Resources to Continue Your Journey

Michael Strassfeld, *The First Jewish Catalog: A Do-It-Yourself Kit*, Richard Siegel, Michael Strassfeld, Sharon Strassfeld, eds. (Philadelphia: Jewish Publication Society, December 1989).

Hayim Halevy Donin, *To Pray as a Jew: A Guide to the Prayer Book and the Synagogue Service* (Cambridge, Mass.: Basic Books, 1980). This book is Jewish liturgy 101 for beginners. You'll be guided through Jewish prayer passage by passage and ritual by ritual.

Marcia Falk, *The Book of Blessings: New Jewish Prayers for Daily Life, the Sabbath, and the New Moon Festival* (Boston: Beacon Press, 1996). If you are looking for the heart, soul, and bones of Hebrew prayer, you will find them all in the *b'rakhah*, or blessing. Falk serves as both poet and translator to give us this gender-inclusive prayer book written in Hebrew as well as English.

Centering Prayer

One whom God possesses
lacks nothing,
for God alone suffices.

—TERESA OF AVILA, 1515–1582, SPAIN

Thoughts Before You Begin

During the initial sixteen centuries of Church history, contemplative prayer was the understood goal of Christian spirituality. After the Reformation, this heritage, at least as a living tradition, was virtually lost. However, throughout the 1970s, a group of Trappist monks at St. Joseph's Abbey in Spencer, Massachusetts, taught a form of centering contemplative prayer to the world in an effort to renew the teaching of this Christian tradition in an up-to-date form and to put a certain order and method into it. Two leaders in this movement, William Menninger and Basil Pennington, developed the practice of centering prayer based on the fourteenth-century classic *The Cloud of Unknowing*. Adapting the contemplative practice of the early desert fathers and mothers, sixteenth-century mystics John of the Cross and Teresa of Avila taught centering prayer as a process of interior transformation, a conversation initiated by God that leads, if we consent, to divine union.

Centering prayer is not contemplative prayer itself but a method of reducing obstacles to contemplation. It seeks to help us become aware of the presence of God by withdrawing our attention from our ordinary flow of thoughts. The cultivated interior silence of centering prayer enables us to move into a spiritual realm and a gradual development of intimacy with God—to an interior experience of God's presence. This intimacy is expressed in the mutual sharing of thoughts, feelings, problems, and spiritual aspirations that gradually develop into spiritual friendship with God.

To listen for God, we become quiet and still. Centering prayer brings the distracted mind to stillness, silence, and concentration. In this quiet, selfless concentration, we follow the words of the psalmist: "Be still, and know that I am God," seeking to be with God and to experience the presence of Jesus. The aim is to allow God's mysterious and silent presence within us to become our reality, giving our lives meaning, shape, and purpose.

Through centering prayer your way of seeing reality changes. The restructuring of consciousness that takes place empowers you to perceive, relate, and respond with increasing sensitivity to God's presence in, through, and beyond everything that exists. Centering prayer awakens us to the presence and action of the Spirit in us. The Spirit prays in us and we consent. It is the opening of mind and heart—our whole being—to God, the Ultimate Mystery, beyond thoughts, words, and emotions.

Now Begin

STEP ONE: Choose a short "sacred word" of one or two syllables, such as "love," "joy," "peace," "Lord," "Jesus," or another. This word, sometimes called a mantra, is a symbol of your intention to consent to God's presence and action within.

STEP TWO: Sit in a comfortable position with your eyes closed. Breathe calmly and regularly for at least two minutes. Sometimes when you close your eyes and breathe, you sink into interior silence as soon as you sit down. You are receptive to God's presence, which is already there. Other times, when you first begin, you confront the chaotic din and distractions of your mind, but by persevering with the mantra you move to a deeper level of consciousness.

STEP THREE: Silently repeat the sacred word as a means of centering your thoughts on your yearning for God. Remember that this word, as a vehicle of centering prayer, is more about your intention than your attention. It is not simply a focal point to return to when you notice you are wandering away; the word is like a sign or an arrow pointing in the direction you intend to take. The word points us to the Source who dwells in our inmost being.

STEP FOUR: Whenever an emotion, image, memory—even a helpful thought or a thought about God—enters your mind, put it aside. Set any self-generated thoughts out of your mind, letting go of not just ordinary thoughts but also devout reflections and aspirations. Augustine said, "Our hearts are made for you, O Lord, and they will not rest until they rest in you." Our restless hearts find that place of rest they seek, not by finding out *about* God but by finding God, experiencing God, and coming to know God.

STEP FIVE: Repeat the word or verse you have chosen in the silence of your mind in a calm, steady rhythm. After a while, and as long as distracting thoughts are leaving your mind of their own accord, you don't have to think of the sacred word. It can be hard to turn off the ordinary thoughts and your habitual way of thinking. If your mind wanders, gently return to the word as easily as possible.

The object is not simply to let go of all thoughts but to deepen your contact with God. It is not just sustained attention to a word but the surrender of one's whole being to God. As your attentiveness and receptivity grow, you move into your own silence, surrender your life to God, and realize your absolute dependence on God.

STEP SIX: After twenty minutes have elapsed, return to ordinary thought by reciting the Lord's Prayer. To know when twenty minutes have gone by, use a countdown timer or musical recording that is twenty minutes in length. (Peeking occasionally at a watch or clock works, but it interrupts your cultivation of inner stillness.) The next thing you know, you'll catch yourself thinking, "Where was I?" The time will have passed in a twinkling of an eye, and you will return to daily life carrying a joyful awareness of your life in God.

Some Things to Think About

There are times when we may choose not to answer the door or telephone, to rest in silence from everything. The world can wait five minutes. No matter how busy we are, no matter how well organized, no matter how little rest we allow ourselves, we will never do *everything* that needs to be done. But to do well at the essential tasks in our lives, it is necessary to nurture a capacity for inner stillness. Such quiet, deep-down listening is itself prayer.

In our most blessed moments, what moves us to pray is not a sense of duty but the yearning of love. A lover can hardly stop thinking about how wonderful the beloved is. We pray out of sheer joy. But if we wait until we are in such a mood to pray, we may find we haven't much of a prayer life. Prayer is not just for moments when we are spontaneously and deeply moved; prayer is also a discipline that helps shape each and every day.

In this prayer practice, I have attempted to bring together the methods of a number of teachers of contemplation into a coherent whole to describe a practice of contemplative prayer. I have drawn primarily from the work of John Main and Thomas Keating, both of whose contemplative methods move the individual beyond thought to the presence of God.

Keating's contemplative teachings have a strong Buddhist influence as well as reflect the practices of Zen *sesshin*, with significant time spent in silent meditation—long periods of nonprogrammed prayer. Keating said that centering prayer, cultivating interior silence, was designed to reduce the obstacles to contemplative prayer and "to facilitate the process of inner transformation and intimacy with God."

Main centers his contemplative prayer on what he calls Christian meditation. He writes, "Prayer is the life of the Spirit of Jesus within our human heart." Centering-contemplative prayer is inspiration, "our awakening to the presence and action of the Spirit" in us: "The Spirit prays in us and we consent. Our task in meditation is to allow our unity to be restored and for our scattered parts to move back into their proper harmonious alignment to the center of our being."

A primary difference between the two is that Main's mantra is maintained throughout the method, while Keating instructions (as do my own) advise us to let go of the mantra as God's self takes its place.

Questions for Reflection

1. What sacred word did you choose? Why?
2. What emotions, images, memories, or thoughts appeared to you during your prayer time? Were you able to turn from them and return to your word?
3. Do you pray when you are in the mood, or do you encourage yourself to pray even when you are not in the mood? Why or why not? What steps can you take to reduce obstacles to prayer?

Other Resources to Continue Your Journey

Thomas Keating, *Intimacy with God: An Introduction to Centering Prayer* (New York: Crossroads, 1994). Filled with practical advice, this book offers the history of centering prayer along with sound wisdom on how centering prayer can deepen your relationship with God.

William Johnston (ed.), *The Cloud of Unknowing and the Book of Privy Counseling* (New York: Doubleday, 1973). The anonymous fourteenth-century author of this classic explains how all thoughts and concepts are buried beneath a "cloud of forgetting," while our love rises toward God, who is hidden in the "cloud of unknowing." Johnston also offers a good introduction to the history of this text and its relevance through the ages.

M. Basil Pennington, *An Invitation to Centering Prayer* (Liguori, Mo.: Liguori, 2001). In this short and simple book, Pennington, a Trappist monk, explains how to use centering prayer to reach an inner communication with God and experience this traditional Christian way to pray.

Meditation

MENTAL PRAYER

God showed me too the pleasure it gives him when a simple soul comes to him, openly, sincerely, and genuinely.

—JULIAN OF NORWICH, 1342–1416, ENGLAND

Thoughts Before You Begin

The practice of meditation is found in all religions, though each tradition employs its own techniques and explains it in different terms. In the Christian tradition, meditation is a method of prayer in which we spontaneously respond to God by pondering God's activity and presence in human history and in our lives. It is a conversation with God that can be prayer no matter what the circumstances of your daily life. Mental prayer has no set formula. It is a spontaneous conversation with God, where we use our conscious thoughts in the form of a dialogue with God to expose our deepest concerns, questions, longings, and joys.

Melete, the Greek word for meditation, means "study," "care," and "exercise." The Latin root *med* denotes care and cure; the word itself conveys "practice and preparation." The root Hebrew word *haga* is translated as "meditation" in Psalm 19:14: "Let the words of my mouth and the meditation of my heart be acceptable to you, O Lord, my rock and my redeemer." It is the "heart," not the mind that meditates.

Meditation, then, can be understood as a disciplined spiritual exercise that prepares us to enter into a profound listening and intimate relationship with God. To enter into this place of intimacy, you need to begin with a foundation of interior silence, simplicity, and an awakening to the silent presence of God within. In this way you can cultivate your receptivity to God's voice, deepening your union with God. Once all the distractions are faded, you enter a still place where you can focus your whole attention. There God speaks directly to your heart.

There are numerous ways to meditate. I confess that I tend to meld meditation (strictly regarded as mental consideration of something) and contemplative prayer (placing oneself in a disposition of resting in God's presence), for my essential goal is to still the constant movement of the mind and open myself to deeper union with Christ's indwelling and guiding presence. Through practice, you learn what works for you.

Now Begin

STEP ONE: Choose a time of day that is usually quiet and uninterrupted so that you can develop a daily practice of meditation.
Many people prefer the early morning for this reason.

STEP TWO: Decide how much time is best for you. Thirty minutes is usually considered optimal. Anything less does not give you the
necessary time to let go of your usual ways of thinking, to
give your full attention to your prayer. You will also require
a leisurely pace afterward to return from your prayer to your
day's work.

STEP THREE: Find a comfortable sitting position with your body balanced,
your hands resting, and your back straight. Using one position consistently soon triggers the response of quieting yourself. Your body lets your mind and heart know that it is time
for prayer.

STEP FOUR: Focus. There are four common ways to focus. Choose one
that works best for you, or a combination of two or more:

1. *Follow the breath.* Slow your breathing, and notice how you inhale and exhale
rhythmically.

2. *Use a mantra,* a sacred word or phrase (such as the ancient Aramaic prayer
"maranatha," which means "Come, Lord Jesus"), or the word "love." A mantra may
employ a word that has universal meaning, such as "peace" or "joy," repeated in a
calm, steady rhythm. John Cassian, a monk and a contemporary of Augustine's,
taught that constant recitation of a name for God, such as Spirit, Father, or Jesus,
or an adopted word or phrase that speaks to your heart, such as "Be still and know"

or "Lord God, have mercy on me," can lead you to the state of continuous prayer that is enjoined by Christ, who told us to "pray always and not to lose heart" (Luke 18:1).

3. *Choose an image.* Turn your focus on an object such as a cross, candle, or flower. Contemplating this image is a way to quiet the rumblings of your heart, making the transition from current thoughts to inner stillness and calm.

4. *Employ a sacred text.* Benedictine monk John Main states that this does not mean analyzing or evaluating the scripture, but rather just entering it into your subconscious and keeping your mind free during the process. This passage can help direct and inspire you. You may want to learn how to pray the scriptures as you enter into meditation. Lectio divina prayer practice (found in the chapter "Praying the Scriptures") instructs you in another way.

STEP FIVE: Sit in silence, using whichever of the four methods you decide upon. Be receptive; do you hear the still, small voice of God? What is God saying to you out of the silence? Eventually these tools of meditation (breath, mantra, image, or sacred text) may lead to inner silence and completely still the thoughts. In that moment, you are in the fullness of God. You are now ready to hear God's message of love and peace.

STEP SIX: As you end your meditative time, sit quietly and take time to refocus on your surroundings. When you are ready, close your prayer time with a short memorized prayer or benediction, or the Lord's Prayer.

Some Things to Think About

Meditation as a foundation for spiritual life leads not to escape from reality but to a deeper knowledge of God, who is present with us and in all creation. God bids us to "be still and know that I am God. I am exalted among the nations. I am exalted in the earth" (Ps. 46:10). Meditative prayer is an interior sacrifice that, through commitment and perseverance, allows us to turn away from selfishness and to co-operate with the transforming grace of the Holy Spirit to discover our true self in Christ. Like those who prayed in the city of Galatia, we know that "it is no longer I who live, but it is Christ who lives in me" (Gal. 2:20). Sustained meditation leads beyond our distracting, self-conscious, and inwardly focused thoughts to a state where we are receptive to the voice of God. In meditation, the true self is inseparable from God in Christ.

Questions for Reflection

1. Do you have a place to sit quietly and meditate? What is your focal point?
2. What mantra or image would you select to still your thoughts?
3. Is there a special biblical passage or sacred writing that you might use to begin your meditation time?

Other Resources to Continue Your Journey

Paul Harris, *Christian Meditation: Contemplative Prayer for a New Generation* (Toronto, Ont.: Novalis, 1996). Harris answers basic questions: "How do I sit?" "How can I still my mind?" "What if I fall asleep?" The novice will definitely find it helpful.

John Killinger, *Beginning Prayer* (Nashville, Tenn.: Upper Room Books, 1993). This introductory primer assists you in thinking about your attitude in prayer, time of day for prayer, place for prayer, and more.

John Main, *Moment of Christ: The Path of Meditation* (New York: Continuum, 1998). Main says that the process of mediation is absolute simplicity. He also knows that the way of silence and stillness is a demanding discipline. He gives special emphasis on the how-to of the mantra and setting aside distractions.

Anointing for Healing

The practice of healing prayer will always be something experienced before it is understood, known by the heart before it is grasped by the mind.

—TILDA NORBERG AND ROBERT D. WEBBER, 1998, NEW YORK

Thoughts Before You Begin

Good people in times of grave illness sometimes say, "We've done everything we can. Now, all we can do is pray"—even when they know in the deep of their heart that prayer is a *primary* response and not a last resort. If you ask them, most will tell you—that whatever the calamity they have been praying all along.

The first-century A.D. community of James records for us its understanding of the prayer practice of anointing for healing:

> Are any among you sick? They should call for the elders of the church and have them pray over them, anointing them with oil in the name of the Lord. The prayer of faith will save the sick, and the Lord will raise them up; and anyone who has committed sins will be forgiven. Therefore confess your sins to one another, and pray for one another, so that you may be healed. The prayer of the righteous is powerful and effective [James 5:14–16a].

The root of the word healing is *sōzō* (Greek). Sōzō also means salvation and wholeness. When we prayerfully anoint someone for healing or are anointed ourselves, we intentionally cooperate with the medical community and with God. We open ourselves to God's will as the Holy Spirit brings fresh options to a seemingly impossible situation. Think of anointing and healing prayer not as your effort to change God's mind but as a way to make you more receptive to receiving God's gracious actions. God yearns for *sōzō* in our lives and waits patiently for our response to the prompting of the Holy Spirit and cooperation with God's trustworthy will. Our prayer of healing is, "O God, help and heal us, according to your yearning, and your loving desire."

How you anoint and pray for a person depends on your church tradition and the need of the moment. In some churches, when viewed as a sacrament, anointing is "performed" by a pastor or priest. Here, in this instance, we are not talking about anointing in a sacramental context, like communion, but as the loving response of prayer from people who act as a channel of God's love. To touch gently and lovingly is a natural response to those in need. It is an expression, through us, of God's intentional will for our spirit, all of who we are, to have health and wholeness in body, mind, and relationships. Jesus touched others as he offered healing—blessing children, washing feet, healing injuries and disease, and even raising people from the dead. When we touch, with or without oil, our action points beyond ourselves to the actions of the Holy Spirit.

Anointing is a *sign act*, a term used by theologians to indicate a tangible, earthy expression from God through us, a material sign of God's covenant with us. Because such signs as communion, anointing, and baptism are mediated through the created world using real wine and bread, water, and oil, they assure us that God is intricately involved and acting through the physical world. Sign acts have a hidden quality: their meaning is not at first evident to the casual observer, and they elicit and reinforce faith both within the person giving and the one receiving the oil.

If feelings fail, we can look to these visible signs of God's presence and find strength. In times of great loss and grief we forget God's promises, as well as what God has already done for us. When we are sick unto death, we easily can forget that we belong to God. That is when and why it is important to remember God's presence through anointing. When life gets us down, we are reminded of both who we are and whose we are, and we demonstrate God's faithfulness in the face of our brokenness.

Anointing with oil is a powerful biblical symbol for healing. Why and under what circumstances might you anoint someone with oil and pray with them? Let me share a few of my experiences. I anoint with prayer at healing services and at the altar rail following communion. On those occasions I like *lots* of oil and use it generously. I've anointed many who were sick in the hospital; once at a meeting, I anointed a woman with a terrible headache. I've anointed individuals who came up and shared following a speaking engagement. In their homes, I've prayed and anointed a woman who was going through divorce as well as a grieving widower. Location is not important: I've discreetly anointed people (always with their permission and full participation) at the mall, on the street, in my home, and even in the fruit section of the grocery store.

In most instances, there is already an atmosphere of intimacy and trust in our relationship before the anointing. The anointee and I have made a deeper connection, for a moment or an hour. After asking the person if I can pray with her, I lean into her ear and pray a simple sentence prayer that only the two of us can hear. With the oil stock at the ready, I dip in to retrieve some oil on my thumb and discreetly take her hand in mine and rub the oil into the palm of the hand.

If it is in a less public place, I put oil, using the sign of the cross, on the forehead and quietly say, "I anoint you in the name of the Father and the Son and the Holy Spirit, Amen." The sign of the cross and touching with hands, called the laying on of hands, are reminders of the centrality of Christ in healing. Naming the Holy Trinity or the name of Jesus while anointing invokes the Holy Spirit. Other times I pray silently and then anoint. In either case, as a personal gesture, a hug usually follows.

Almost all of these occurrences were private and personal. I never worried about what to say, but only listened intently. I get out of the way and let God do the work. God is the healer. My role is to love the individual.

My prayer, usually slow, quiet, and brief, goes something like this: "Love Divine, I know that you have heard everything that [the individual's name] and I have talked about. [Here I might be specific, and name the son who is struggling with drugs, or the pain or illness that the person is experiencing.] I ask you now to continue to surround [him or her] with your comfort and love. Amen."

Now Begin

Olive oil and sweet oil (olive oil with preservatives) are traditionally used. I use body oil from the pharmacy that is hypoallergenic and has a very light fragrance. I like it because it is nongreasy and easily soaks into the skin. It also comes in a plastic bottle with a squeeze top for transporting. (I admit, in this instance, I'm more practical than romantic.)

The oil can be placed on the communion table, "blessed," and offered for God's use along with the bread and wine during the prayer of Great Thanksgiving of Holy Communion. The presider might adapt the prayer this way: "Pour out your Spirit on us gathered here, and on these gifts of bread, wine *and oil.*" Another option is for you to bless the oil with this prayer:

> O God, the giver of health and salvation,
> we give thanks for the gift of oil.
> As your holy apostles anointed many who were sick and healed them,
> so pour out your Holy Spirit on us and on this gift,
> that those who in faith and repentance receive this anointing
> may be made whole. Amen.

Always ask permission to pray and anoint someone. Individuals are usually eager to receive prayer, but occasionally someone will say no. In such an instance, I respect the decision, saying something like, "I just want you to know how much you are cared for," and then move on in our conversation.

When you anoint another with oil, it is usually placed upon the forehead using the sign of the cross. Make the cross signature using the pad of your thumb. Other parts of the body can also be anointed as seems appropriate and if you feel at ease doing so. For example, if someone has a hurt leg, you might want to anoint the leg.

In your prayers of anointing, use the name for the Divine Presence that is acceptable to the person being anointed as well as natural and comfortable to you. When anointing, you may simultaneously use these or similar words:

[Name], I anoint you with oil in the name of the Father, Son, and Holy Spirit. Amen.

or

[Name], I anoint you in the name of Jesus, the Christ, your savior and healer. Amen.

If oil is not available, or laying on of hands feels more appropriate, you can use these or similar words:

[Name], I touch you now
In the name of the Father, Son, and Holy Spirit.
May the power of God bring your spirit to
wholeness of body, mind, and relationships. Amen.

or

[Name], may the blessed hands of God,
your Creator, Redeemer, and Sustainer,
cover you with healing and give you peace.

A final note: be brief in your prayer. Keep it private and personal. Confidentiality is important. Use the person's name and mention the concern. You don't need to detail the problem to God; God already knows. The prayer and anointing do not do the healing; God does. Praying with individuals for healing and wholeness, lifting them up into the healing light and love of God, is a holy privilege.

Some Things to Think About

For these on-the-spot anointings, I carry an oil stock in my purse or pocket. About the diameter of a quarter, an oil stock screws closed tightly and is attached to a ring that slips easily over your finger to keep hands free. Oil stocks can be purchased at a religious supply store, where you may also find small vials of oil that can be conveniently carried and used.

If possible, you'll want to have your oil blessed before using it. The traditional day to have a year's supply blessed is at the communion service on Maundy Thursday, during the Holy Week before Easter.

The gift of anointing another is yours; we too are blessed abundantly. By participating in God's gift of anointing, you return to your daily life better able to sustain others and more intent on extending God's healing presence. You walk away more mindful of God's care so that you can live faithfully each day, touching your life to the lives of others and growing stronger in depth and integrity.

Questions for Reflection

1. What area of your life still needs healing and wholeness? Might you wish to be prayerfully anointed?
2. Write a prayer for someone you know—perhaps a friend who is sick, or a relative experiencing a broken relationship, or a colleague who is filled with anxiety. Pray it on the person's behalf.

James K. Wagner, *An Adventure in Healing and Wholeness: The Healing Ministry of Christ in the Church Today* (Nashville, Tenn.: Upper Room Books, 1993). As a facilitator of healing ministry training sessions for congregations, I recommend you contact the Upper Room to attend one of their weekends.

Tilda Norberg and Robert D. Webber, *Stretch Out Your Hand: Exploring Healing Prayer* (Nashville, Tenn.: Upper Room Books, 1998). The authors believe that whenever you open yourself to the activity of the Spirit, healing happens—sometimes physical, other times emotional or relational.

The Order of St. Luke is a ministry of Christian healing. They can be contacted at Box 13701, San Antonio, TX 78213, tel. 210/492–5222; this is another excellent resource.

Relational Prayer

*A*s someone who pays attention to emotions and who is in touch with the longings of the heart, you will feel at home with these relational ways of praying. Get ready to be inspired, and then extend yourself to awaken others, as you hear the faith stories of others who walk with God.

Adoration Prayer
Affirmation Prayer
Prayers of Confession
Prayer of Examen
The Daily Office
Tongsung Kido
Prayer Walks
   An Emmaus Walk
   Stations of the Cross

Adoration
Prayer

Jesus, strengthen my desire to work and speak and think for you.

—JOHN WESLEY, 1703–1791, ENGLAND

Thoughts Before You Begin

"The adoration of God is a mixture of gratitude and reverence and awe," wrote Quaker philosopher Douglas Steele. Adoration as a prayer of thanksgiving and veneration has been, and continues to be, a mainstay of Christian prayer, expressing gratitude for God's gifts and for God's self, constancy, and goodness. Steele goes on to describe adoration as "a firsthand feeling of being moved to the core, of being made to feel abased and yet drawn up to the pinnacle of one's being simply by the face of his [God's] Presence."

A prayer of adoration addresses God in joyful unending love. Adoration accepts, deepens, and intensifies our relationship with God. We adore Christ for what he has done and continues to do in his personal concern for us individually and collectively. With prayer, we praise and thank God by accepting that activity and its purpose in our lives and in the world, and we give ourselves to God in return.

During the seventeenth century the French School, a reform movement led by teacher and priest Pierre, Cardinal of Berulle, and his successor Jean-Jacques Olier, developed a spirituality of adoration that connected times of prayer with works of ministry. They believed that an attitude of gratitude—which gives God the credit—undergirded all of one's life of prayer and personal ministry. Their adoration prayer practices centered on a threefold spiritual synthesis:

1. To look at Jesus, meaning to hold the presence of Jesus in constant awareness that leads to acts of holiness
2. To unite in Jesus, meaning to surrender to him in all matters; it is the movement of the heart to the beloved that leads to union with God
3. To act in Jesus, or as my sixteen-year-old's WWJD bracelet reminds him, "What would Jesus do?"

This action leads to the ability to live more richly in the power of a Christ who prays in us, with us, and for us. A sacred text from Philippians 2:5–9a explains this concept clearly: "Let the same mind be in you that was in Christ Jesus, who, though he was in the form of God, did not regard equality with God as something to be exploited, but emptied himself, taking the form of a slave, being born in human likeness. And being found in human form, he humbled himself and became obedient to the point of death—even death on a cross. Therefore God also highly exalted him. . . ."

When we give our lives over to Jesus, we accept the Spirit's power to live all of life's possibilities to their fullest, and not just muddle through our existence. Jesus invited us to relinquish our plans in order to live and be open to God's new possibilities: to die to the doubts, frustrations, and anxieties that diminish us so we can live boldly and claim God's power.

A pastor friend of mine went to his doctor complaining of nervous tension, which revealed itself in headaches and compulsive shaking. After a physical, the doctor said to the pastor: "You're anxious and tense. Either I can give you some pills, or you can begin to practice what you preach."

Individuals who prayerfully adore God have learned the meaning of gratitude. They give up the frantic interior anxiety about themselves and their life, and they begin to live their daily lives in a new way. Trusting God, they live differently, manage money differently, speak differently.

Karl Rahner, a great spiritual thinker and teacher of prayer, in his eightieth year wrote that prayer is the last moment of speech before the silence, the act of self-surrender just before letting oneself fall into the infinite fullness and silence that we can never entirely grasp. I hope that as you kneel with your heart before holy mystery, you will (as I have) experience the silent presence of God's love for you.

Now Begin

The prayer of adoration included here captures the spirit of the Berulle French School practice.

Move into a kneeling position with your arms out and palms facing up, or choose any body position that demonstrates adoration. Closing your eyes may help you focus. Pray the prayer that follows in "awakened contemplation." This means that you are alert and fully conscious of your prayer, not dull or in a relaxed stupor.

STEP ONE: Say aloud the word "Look." Then pause for two or three minutes and be silent in the presence of Jesus. Contemplate the face of Jesus as you imagine it, and as he appears in others (such as your children or parents or friends).

STEP TWO: Say aloud the word "Unite." Again, pause for two or three minutes and be silent as you unite your desires and needs with the will of Jesus. This is the movement of the heart to the beloved, an immense longing. It is the mysterious pouring out of one's own being into the beloved *thou*. Feel the presence of Jesus as your companion. Consciously feel the companionship of others in your life, whom you also love.

STEP THREE: Say aloud the word "Power." Pause for two or three minutes of silence one last time as you open yourself to accepting Jesus' power to live enriched and whole, joyous and free. Accept the holy, silent mystery that fills any emptiness in your life. Remember that you are loved, and that the Spirit frees you to live out your life in a God-conscious way. The strong arms of God's divine strength lift you to a higher place.

Use this reflective prayer (from Mechtild of Magdeburg) to end your prayer time:

Lord, you are my lover,
My longing,
My flowing stream,
My sun,
And I am your reflection

Some Things to Think About

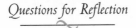

The other side of adoration is our total self-surrender before the absoluteness of God. We accept our full dependence on God. Because there can be no language to completely express our adoration, the prayer of adoration may be silent. But it is a silence that expresses a fullness that words cannot capture. It is our surrender to the silent mystery that embraces all life. Adoration therefore often finds expression in gestures—bowing, kneeling, prostrating, and genuflecting.

Questions for Reflection

1. How do you relinquish control of your life and surrender to God's guidance and will?
2. Do you really believe that God loves you, warts and all, in your imperfection and incompleteness? Are you willing to surrender to God's greater love? If not, what is holding you back?

Other Resources to Continue Your Journey

Keith Beasley-Topliffe, *Surrendering to God: Living the Covenant Prayer* (Orleans, Mass.: Paraclete Press, 2000). If you liked *The Prayer of Jabez*, you'll love this book. I pray the covenant prayer often, and it never fails to inspire and move me into a more satisfying relationship with God. You can also pray it using prayer beads (see the later chapter by that name).

George McClain, *Claiming All Things for God: Prayer, Discernment, and Ritual for Social Change* (Nashville, Tenn.: Abingdon Press, 1998). This book helps you integrate your daily active life and your spiritual life. The author accomplishes this by offering a four-step "prayer-action cycle" model that moves you from awareness to analysis, to reflection, and finally to action, through discerning the promptings of the Spirit. The book also offers expressive rituals for group use.

Karl Rahner, *The Need and the Blessing of Prayer* (Collegeville, Minn.: Liturgical Press, 1997). This is one of the most recent significant books on prayer. Rahner's writing opens up a creative understanding of prayer by challenging the reader to "pray in the everyday" to the God who can be found in all things. His eight thoughtful chapters challenge you to look more closely at what is actually going on in the depths of your daily life.

Affirmation
Prayer

Such is the nature of love: the nearer we draw to God in love,

the more we are united together by love for our neighbor;

and the greater our union with our neighbor,

the greater is our union with God.

—DOROTHEUS OF GAZA, SIXTH CENTURY

Thoughts Before You Begin

Affirmation prayers are a declaration of our readiness to God's movement in our lives. They are powerful, positive statements that declare how we want to live. If we allow ourselves to say yes to the workings of the Spirit, we are able to change and move on. Whatever our circumstances, we are all in need of God's grace. God's grace, and our efforts to acknowledge and embrace that grace, are what affirmation prayers are all about.

As we read or write prayer affirmations, we establish a dialogue with our self, with God, and with others. We ask, "What feelings, aspirations, or desires are emerging within me?" As we write and use affirmations, we are encouraged and empowered to follow our intuition and lifelong dreams. Our deepest desires come to the surface. We are inspired to write down what we really think and believe, and from that we go to God with a new attitude in our prayer. We are ready to listen, speak, and act. We are open in a new way for the Spirit to do God's purposeful work in our lives.

Now Begin

Choose one of the three affirmations given here, and read it aloud to yourself. (Feel free to choose more than one, if you'd like.) Then make copies and place the written affirmation where you will see it for the rest of this week, perhaps on the refrigerator, the dashboard, or the bathroom mirror. Read it aloud to yourself each day. If none of these prayer affirmations fits, skip this step and follow the guidelines below to create one that suits your particular circumstances.

FIRST AFFIRMATION PRAYER:
FOR HEALTHY RELATIONSHIPS

> Dear God, today I am better equipped to live in intimacy with another person. I have a deepened self-awareness, which leads me to a relationship that is healthy and whole.
>
> I no longer deceive myself by entering into harmful relationships that cannot fulfill my real needs. I have a greater sense of my own needs and an understanding of my past. I am ready to accept the challenges of true intimacy. Amen.

SECOND AFFIRMATION PRAYER:
FOR A HEALTHY BODY

A woman who adopted the name Peace Pilgrim walked more than twenty-five thousand miles, carrying in her blue tunic her only possessions. She crossed the United States for nearly three decades bearing the simplest of messages: "This is the way of peace—overcome evil with good, and falsehood with truth, and hatred with love." This affirmation comes from her writings:

> I know enough about food to nourish my body properly and I have excellent health. I enjoy my food, but I eat to live. I do not live to eat, as some people do, and I know when to stop eating. I am not enslaved to food.
>
> People can still be hungry after eating large quantities of wrong foods. In fact, you can suffer from malnutrition even though you consistently over-eat wrong foods. You can begin a healthy diet by having good, wholesome foods available. Eat slowly and chew your food well. . . . Then

make food a very incidental part of your life by filling your life so full of meaningful things that you'll hardly have time to think about food.

God, today I eat in healthy ways so that my body can return to its most healthy and balanced state. Amen.

THIRD AFFIRMATION PRAYER: FOR HOLINESS

Loving Jesus, today I take time to be in the presence of God and nurture my soul. I am a person who lives in holiness. Amen.

WRITING YOUR OWN AFFIRMATION

Write an affirmation about a challenge that you are working to meet, or a struggle that you need strength to face. To write your own prayer affirmation, here are a few guidelines:

♦ Write in the first person singular and in the present tense (not "*I will* become patient" but "*I am* patient"). This "I am" format affirms that I am created in the image of God, and it echoes the name of God ("I Am that I Am").

♦ After you write your affirmation, pray it aloud. As you think, write, read, and say the words aloud, the affirmation is reinforced and placed firmly in your heart.

♦ Beware of negative thoughts that try to take over, or statements that negate your worth as a person of God. Don't write, "I *will not* forget to pray." Instead write, "Everyday I pray."

♦ Let the scriptures inspire your affirmation prayers. You can use the fruits of the Spirit found in Galatians 5:22 to pray: "Spirit of God, I thank you for the fruits that are in my heart and continue to grow: love, joy, peace, patience, kindness, generosity, faithfulness, gentleness, and self-control. Amen." Or recall the story told in the book of Luke 13:10–17, of the woman who was once bent over but now healed by Jesus: "Jesus, you have healed me and set me free. I am no longer stooped, but stand straight and praise you with a life well lived."

Some Things to Think About

Affirmations are not a new concept. The letters to the Philippians written by Paul, the first-century apostle, contain words of affirmation. In fact, more than half of his letters to the church at Philippi consist of praise and thanksgiving to God and affirmation about his faithful friends. He knew there would be hard days ahead. His letters, read aloud at assemblies, gave these first Christians a heart full of courage.

If you want to replace your critical inner dialogue and prayer with positive, life-giving language, then affirmation prayers are for you. The conversations we repeat to ourselves and to God are crucial in determining our attitude, outlook, behavior, and path.

Questions for Reflection

1. If prayer is not a quick fix to make everything all right, then what is it?
2. Which affirmation(s) did you try? How did you feel about using it (them)?
3. If you wrote your own positive prayer affirmations, what subject or life situation did you choose? Write one today and use it in the coming week.

Other Resources to Continue Your Journey

Patricia D. Brown, *365 Affirmations for Hopeful Living* (Nashville, Tenn.: Abingdon, 1992). This work includes daily affirmations on topics such as relationships, courage, trust, self-acceptance, and more. Each begins with a scripture and ends with a sentence prayer.

Anne Wilson Schaef, *Meditations for Women Who Do Too Much* (San Francisco: Harper-SanFrancisco, 1993). This one made the best-seller list when it was first published, but if you missed it the first time around you can still pick it up.

Peace Pilgrim: Her Life and Work in Her Own Words (Santa Fe, N.Mex.: Ocean Tree Books, 1994). Reading about the life and teachings of Peace Pilgrim is an inspiration. You can find this book at your local bookstore, or for a free copy write to Friends of Peace Pilgrim, 43480 Cedar Ave., Hemet, CA 92544.

Prayers of Confession

The work of purging the soul neither can nor should end except with our life itself. We must not be disturbed at our imperfections, since for us perfection consists in fighting against them. How can we fight against them unless we see them, or overcome them unless we face them?

—FRANCIS DE SALES, 1567–1622, SWITZERLAND

Thoughts Before You Begin

Confession as a dimension of conversion is an ever-present dynamic of the Christian life. Prayers of confession are said as a community during public worship as well as by individuals, who usually do so in private to acknowledge their personal sin or short-comings before God. When we confess, we acknowledge our individual and community responsibility for our actions. Confession forces us to examine our own lives and compare how we *are* living with how we know we *ought to* live. In this way, confession spurs our growth in likeness to Christ under the guidance of the Holy Spirit.

When I speak of confession, I am not referring to the "confessions" that are statements of doctrine and belief used by the Protestant Reformed traditions. Nor am I referring to the *Confessions* of Saint Augustine, important foundational writings of the Christian faith. In the context of this particular style of prayer, confession is our own personal acknowledgment of our failure or wrongdoing. The early church understood confession as an individual's hatred of his own sin and his desire to change. In Luke 5:8–11, Peter confesses that he is a sinner even as he follows the call to follow Jesus. Jesus understands that Peter's true desire is to change, to stop being afraid, and to follow Jesus' call to lay down his fishing net and, from then on, be "catching people." Acts 19 tells the story of some of the first converts to the Christian faith. Here, confession was part of what it meant to be converted, to give one's whole life to Christ: "Also many of those who became believers confessed and disclosed their practices" (Acts 19:18). The parable of the prodigal son in Luke 15:11–32 shows us how the son's confession builds from *repentance* for what he has done, to *reconciliation* with his father, and finally to the *celebration* of his homecoming. Confession is not a static action but one that moves a person back into healing relationship with others. Perhaps this is why James 5:16 urges Christians to "confess your sins to one another, and pray for one another, so that you may be healed."

By the second and third centuries, individuals who had fallen away from Christian practice went through a long and arduous act of public confession and repentance. Called *penitents*, those enrolled in this process were segregated from the congregation and kept from receiving Holy Communion for a period of time. Instead, each Sunday they received a special laying on of hands by the pastor along with prayers. They were finally reinstated into the full assembly on Maundy Thursday (the Thursday before Easter). More important, this process could be undergone only once in a lifetime, so Christians took the idea of confession and repentance very seriously.

By the fifth century, this more serious approach was replaced by private confession and could be undertaken multiple times as needed. By the time of the Fourth Lateran Council of the Church in 1215, every Christian confessed his or her sin once a year by self-examination and performed acts of penance to atone for sin. Penance could consist of a dangerous pilgrimage, sustained fasting, and other similar discomfort.

Today the act of confession is making a healthy comeback. The standard confession prayed aloud in weekly worship is an attempt to identify and name what we have done that broke communion with God and our neighbor. It is based on the version developed by the Council of Trent in 1552, and revised and adopted in 1549 by the Church of England's *Book of Common Prayer* in an attempt to find a middle route between the Roman Church and the Protestant movement. It contains these (or similar) words:

> Most merciful God, we confess that we are in bondage to sin and cannot free ourselves. We have sinned against you in thought, word, and deed by what we have done and by what we have left undone. We have not loved you with our whole heart; we have not loved our neighbor as ourselves. For the sake of your Son, Jesus Christ, have mercy on us. Forgive us,

renew us, and lead us, so that we may delight in your will and walk in your ways, to the glory of your holy name, Amen.

Of course, God does not leave us standing naked in our sin. Along with confession comes forgiveness. The typical words of forgiveness, spoken by the pastor or the congregants to the pastor and to each other, are these: "Hear the good news. In the name of Jesus Christ you are forgiven. Glory to God! Amen."

We have other tools that can assist us in our self-examination. Among these are the Ten Commandments, which tell us not to lie or to covet another's property; and the eight Beatitudes, which admonish us, among other things, to be meek, merciful, and pure in heart. Adherents to the Wesleyan tradition of the 1700s inquired of their members' souls by asking such hard questions as "Do you desire to be told of your faults?" and "Do you desire that every one of us should tell you, from time to time, whatsoever is in his heart concerning you?" and finally, "Do you desire that, in doing this, we should come close, as close as possible, that we should cut to the quick, and search your heart to the bottom?"

The truth is that most of us grow queasy just thinking of opening ourselves up to another person in such an intimate manner. It feels like placing our neck into a vice. Yet we are to correct each other and confess to one another. This kind of confession is a deeper truth telling than going to our therapist or pouring out our heart to a sympathetic friend. Thinking in this way helps us understand why earlier Christians went to their pastor or personal spiritual director—someone who had taken a pledge of silence to the community—to confess their deepest sins and to seek advice.

I have had a number of confessors over the years. They were individuals who listened in a way that helped me confess. They had a capacity that inspired me to *want* to be seen and to reveal things about myself that needed to be confessed. I was well aware that this person—this confessor—was not perfect, but someone who also has her own confessor and may even have more to confess than I do. I confess not to her but to Christ in her presence; she is the witness of my confession. Then when I grow quiet and my list of sins is exhausted, I listen. As she helps me reflect on my sins, usually there is something helpful if I am willing to hear from both her and God— a suggestion or an insight that the old-fashioned word *penance* fits, for usually we come to the conclusion that I need to pray more, or fast, or mend some relationship.

When you ask a trusted person such as your pastor to be your confessor, don't imagine that he thinks less of you for what you reveal to Christ in his presence. Neither is he carefully remembering all your sins. As a pastor to seven congregations, I can assure you that confessions of those who came to my office blur together, and the only sins I remember are my own. I serve as a fellow sinner trying to stay on the path.

Now Begin

Here are two prayers of confession, one for you to do alone and a second to be used with a partner.

ON YOUR OWN

This short prayer, written in the fourth century by Ephraim the Syrian, can help you examine your life. It is recited in Orthodox churches every Sunday of Lent (the Sundays preceding Easter). Reflect on the prayer phrase by phrase, and let it probe the hidden places in your heart:

> O Lord and Master of my life, take from me the spirit of sloth, despair, lust of power, and idle talk. But give to me, your servant, the spirit of

chastity, humility, patience, and love. O Lord and King, grant to me to see my own faults and not to condemn my brother and sister. For you are blessed unto the ages of ages. Amen.

WITH A PARTNER

You will need a partner for this prayer. This is called the "I–2–2–I prayer"—that is, one minute of silence, two minutes of confession, two minutes of confession, and one minute of silence.

In this prayer of confession, share as you are comfortable. The time constraints necessarily keep it short and to the point. There is no need to elaborate; God already knows the details. Of course, be truthful in your own heart about what you have done, or what you have failed to do, and then speak it in a way that is comfortable for you.

When your partner shares with you, ponder it in your heart. Hear it as the sacred confession that it is, and allow it to flow through you to God.

Sit facing another person. The purpose is to listen attentively to what your partner tells you. Receive his or her story as a gift without much comment or questioning. Begin with one minute of silence between you as you contemplate and pray on this question: "What is some way you have felt you let God down on your journey since we last met?" The answer may be something very simple, such as losing your temper or not responding to a need.

After the minute of silence, give two minutes or so for each person to share his or her confession. One of you should serve as the timekeeper, or set a timer to keep track.

After both of you have shared, spend at least one minute in silent prayer. Closing your eyes, picture the face of your partner, silently praying for that person and lifting up her concern to God. Or you may prefer to offer a "sentence prayer" for each other (oh, the discipline of a single sentence!). Keeping your prayer to one sentence saves you from the temptation of projecting your own interpretation on the matter. The sentence prayer should simply restate what the person has shared with you and include her desire to seek God's forgiveness. The prayer could be something like this: "Dear God, I know you heard what my partner shared about losing her temper with her daughter, and she asks your forgiveness. Amen."

Whether you pray aloud or silently for each other, close by praying this prayer aloud in unison: "Go, and sin no more. In the name of Jesus Christ, we are forgiven. Glory to God. Amen."

When you are ready, give your friend some sign of Christ's peace, such as a handshake, or the benediction "the peace of the Lord be with you," or a hug.

Some Things to Think About

A young monk said to the great ascetic Abba Sisoes, "Abba, what should I do? I fell." The elder answered, "Get up!" The monk said, "I got up and fell again!" The elder replied, "Get up again!" But the young monk asked, "For how long should I get up when I fall?" "Until your death," answered Abba Sisoes.

This saying of the desert fathers illustrates the nature of our lives, as we sin, confess, and repent. Because we all need to get up when we fall, I am glad that today's church has again started to emphasize our ongoing renewal and transformation through the use of confession, both in public worship and in one-on-one designated time with a pastor or spiritual guide.

Questions for Reflection

1. What do you think about the need for confession in your own life?
2. How did you feel as you confessed your concern with a partner? What did that person's prayerful response mean to you?
3. Have you ever prayed the more formal 1552 prayer of confession in community worship? After the group has said the prayer, how important are the leader's closing words of forgiveness ("In the name of Jesus Christ, you are forgiven")?

Other Resources to Continue Your Journey

Jim Forest, *Confession: Doorway to Forgiveness* (Maryknoll, N.Y.: Orbis Books, 2002). Once a defining part of the Christian life, confession was sidelined with the advent of the Reformation. Forest's book demonstrates how repentance, confession, and forgiveness can be core elements of our Christian faith.

Eddie Ensley, *Prayer That Heals Our Emotions* (Columbus, Ga.: Contemplative Books, 1986). Guided prayer experiences are designed to bring clarity and calm your soul.

Michel Quoist, *Prayers* (Kansas City, Mo.: Sheed and Ward, 1963). A trusted friend gave me this book, and now I share it with you. Using the stinging simplicity of everyday speech, this book helps you pray as relevantly—honoring all creation with high regard and utmost respect—as you try to live.

Prayer of
Examen

When we speak with God, our power of addressing him, of holding communion with him, and listening to his still small voice, depends on our will being one and the same with him.

—FLORENCE NIGHTINGALE, 1820–1910, ENGLAND

Thoughts Before You Begin

The word *examen* sounds rather like the English word *examination*, and in a way the prayer of examen is an examination of our lives, a way of assessing our lives before God regularly. This type of prayer is popularly attributed to Ignatius, the founder of the Society of Jesus; it focuses our recollection on a narrow time span, perhaps the previous day or week. By regularly taking time to reflect on our completed day or week, we prevent ourselves from living an unexamined life, and we are more conscious of how we can increase our attentiveness to the Spirit of God. This examination is not intended to be a tallying of failures and successes but an interior and exterior evaluation of the spiritual state of our union with God. The prayer of examen always ends with a word of grace. Examen may be practiced in solitude, but it is ultimately about community; one's relationship to one's self, God, and others.

Because it is a time of reflection on (usually) the day just completed, the examen prayer is best practiced in the quiet of the evening. It takes about fifteen minutes. There are five basic movements in the examen prayer, or examination of conscience: (1) celebrate and give thanks; (2) pray for God's illumination; (3) examine the events and encounters of the day; (4) sift through the joys and sorrows, struggles, and delights, asking God for needed grace; and (5) rest in God's amazing grace and live in hope for the new day.

Now Begin

An examen journal can be an invaluable record of daily struggle and progress. People who are verbally oriented often find the discipline of keeping a journal an especially effective means of spiritual growth (see the chapter "A Journal of Prayer"). Angry words, a failed civility, a missed opportunity to express care are all put down on paper. But there is also the good: a word bravely spoken, a kind act, a quiet prayer. Everything is recorded.

Stop, take up paper and pen, and ask the Spirit of God to guide your memory back over the past day (or week), step by step, right up to this present moment. If you are not a pen-and-paper kind of person, replay the time period in your mind like a rewound video on your personal television.

These five points are called "movements," and not steps, because one flows naturally into the next without distinction.

First, begin by quieting yourself. In the first movement, become aware of God's goodness. Give thanks to God for the gift of life and the opportunity to serve. Welcome spontaneous memories of the day's events in this initial stage of examen prayer. Be thankful. Recall that without faith—the eye of love—the human world seems too evil for a good God to exist. If you are using a journal, record activities and encounters for which you are grateful and give thanks.

Second, pray for the grace to see clearly, to understand accurately, and to respond generously to the guidance God gives you in your daily history. Ask God to illuminate your reflection time and give you clear insight as you enter this time of examination. Appreciate how God has been present to you throughout your day, working in your midst. Pray in your own words or those of Anselm, an eleventh-century pastor of Normandy, who reminds you that God is present even if you walk through your day numb to your surroundings:

O Lord my God,
Teach my heart where and how to seek you,
Where and how to find you.
Lord, if you are not here but absent,
Where shall I seek you?

But you are everywhere, so you must be here,
Why then do I not seek you?

Third, take an inventory of your day (or whatever stretch of time you are contemplating) as if sitting with God and watching a video playback. If you are reviewing today, begin with when you first opened your eyes and continue until the present moment. Allow God to show you concrete instances of God's presence and guidance—and perhaps of the activity and influence of evil. These instances can be detected by paying attention to strong feelings that may accompany (or arise from) a situation or encounter. Do not judge anything as good or bad. Simply note how you respond to God's presence in your life. The question does not focus on you ("What did I do or not do?") but instead centers on God ("How did God work within me?"). This examination of conscience is God's means to make you more aware of the people and creation around you so you can live with more purpose and compassion. God wants you to be present and fully conscious moment to moment, in all your relationships. If you travel through your days fully awake and alert, you are better able to discern the footprints of the Holy—where God is present in your life. As you write your examen, pinpoint the moments when God's presence and reality were especially apparent.

The fourth movement gives you the opportunity to lay your brokenness down before God. Once your reflection and writing is complete, enter into a determined time of prayerful repentance: "So when you are offering your gift at the altar, if you remember your brother or sister has something against you, leave your gift there before the altar and go; first be reconciled to your brother or sister, and then come and offer your gift" (Matt. 5:23–24).

Review your spiritual health to uncover those areas that need cleansing, forgiveness, holiness, and healing. Invite God to search your heart's depth with the scrutiny of divine love. Pray the words of the psalmist: "Search me, O God, and know my heart; test me and know my thoughts. See if there is any wicked way in me, and lead me in the way everlasting" (Ps. 139:23–24). Open your life to God's full examination. Because God is beside you in your search, there is no need for defensiveness or apology. God comforts and protects, and God shows you what you need to see when you need to see it.

Note in your journal any failings or sins that need God's forgiveness and your own resolve to change. As you review your writings, ask yourself when you experienced *consolation,* times when you felt drawn to God; or *desolation,* times when you were drained away from God and wrapped in selfish concerns.

In the fifth and final movement of the examen prayer lives God's grace: "For by grace you have been saved through faith, and this is not your own doing; it is the gift of God" (Eph. 2:8). Give thanks to God for those events that evoke your gratitude, and ask God's forgiveness for any failings and sins. This too can be done in writing, which is helpful. Set aside your meticulous perfectionism, recognize that you are human—and that God is perfect—and live in the resolve that tomorrow is another day, with fresh opportunities to love and serve. Set aside self-blame and accept forgiveness. Accede to your human limitations and step into divine power. The prayer of Catherine of Siena (1347–1380, Italy) names the light at the end of examen. It is grace; it is God's self.

> You, O Eternal Trinity, are a deep sea into which,
> the more I enter,
> the more I find,
> and the more I find,
> the more I seek.
> O abyss,

O eternal Godhead,

O sea profound,

What more could you give me than yourself?

God's grace, unsought and unearned, blows through my life, and all I

need to do is raise my sails to catch the full wind.

Conclude your prayer of examen with an Our Father (see the chapter "Lord's Prayer").

Some Things to Think About

This introspection of the examen prayer leads us to the priceless gift of self-knowledge, not as a way to personal peace but so that we can resolve to be more open to God's will in our relationships and particular daily situations. It is not a journey *into* ourselves but a journey *through* ourselves so that we can emerge from the deepest level of the self into God. In this total, unvarnished self-knowledge, we see our weaknesses and strengths, our brokenness and gifts. As John Chrysostom wrote, "Find the door of your heart, you will discover it is the door of the kingdom of God."

You may choose to attend worship and the Eucharist after your prayer of examen, so that your experience concludes with Holy Communion. In this way, you are reminded of God's gifts, as well as your place in the community of faith. God offers blessings to you; accept them. Theresa of Lisieux, Normandy (1873–1897) wrote: "The daring ambition of aspiring to great sanctity has never left me. I don't rely on my own merits, because I haven't any; I put all my confidence in him who is virtue, who is holiness itself." It is not by our own means that we reconcile our life; instead, "by grace you have been saved" (Eph. 2:8).

What follows is another way to practice, the "daily examen of conscience" (adapted from the *Spiritual Exercises* of Ignatius of Loyola). It can be helpful in daily use. This shorter examen of conscience, a version adapted from Kent Ira Groff, can be carried on a card in your wallet; it helps you pay attention at the beginning and the end of the day. Invite Christ, the light of the world, to walk with you as you rehearse the past twenty-four hours, or any recent time period, gently sifting through events and encounters.

Gift: Consider any gifts of the day, both those received, and those given. Celebrate God's empowering love at a time or times when you gave or received love.

Struggle: Notice times when you struggled to feel loved or to act in a loving way. Pay attention to any anxiousness or unrest in your soul or to any issues that are unresolved. Celebrate God's undefeated love, and hear "I know you and I love you; you are my beloved."

Invitation: Ask God, "What grace do I need to name and claim to be more whole in this new day?" Allow a word, phrase, image, or metaphor to come to mind. Begin to repeat it slowly, with the rhythm of your breath, or if it is an image then visualize it. Sit in silence for at least a few minutes. Finish by reading a short poem or scripture (such as the Lord's Prayer) or singing a song.

Questions for Reflection

1. "Search me, O God, and know my heart; test me and know my thoughts" (Ps. 139:23–24). Do you believe that God knows the real you? What does God think about you?

2. Did you gain self-knowledge during this time of introspective prayer? What did you learn? Do you pray to get to know yourself better or to get rid of some discomfort you are feeling?

3. What was your experience of the examination of grace? Which method worked best for you, and why?

Other Resources to Continue Your Journey

Jim Forest, *Confession: Doorway to Forgiveness* (Maryknoll, N.Y.: Orbis, 2002). This work is also listed as a resource in the chapter "Prayers of Confession." It is an excellent resource for deepening your prayer of examen. Here are a few others that are helpful.

Margaret Silf, *Inner Compass: An Invitation to Ignatian Spirituality* (Chicago: Loyola Press, 1999). This practical and experience-based guide is helpful to both newcomers and those already familiar with Ignatian spirituality.

Con O'Connell, O.F.M., *Making a Better Confession: A Deeper Examination of Conscience* (Liguori, Mo.: Liguori, n.d.). This extremely short (sixteen-page) book helps you unmask deep attitudes, and through soul searching and the help of the Holy Spirit begin a process of self-discovery and reconciling your life with God.

Dennis Linn, Sheila Fabricant Linn, and Matthew Linn, *Sleeping with Bread: Holding What Gives You Life* (New York: Paulist Press, 1995). This simple book gives you a process to hear God's voice and allow it to guide you. Through focusing each day on the examen questions posed in this book, you discover how to resolve your problems.

The Daily Office

O most merciful redeemer, friend, and brother,
may we know Thee more clearly,
love Thee more dearly,
and follow Thee more nearly,
day by day.

—RICHARD OF CHICHESTER, THIRTEENTH CENTURY

Thoughts Before You Begin

The daily office, divine office, breviary, liturgy of the hours, canonical hours, diurnal and nocturnal office, common prayer, cathedral office, ecclesiastical office, cursus ecclesiasticus, or simply cursus—called by many names through the years, this tradition is a time when certain prayers are to be prayed, at fixed hours of the day or night. The two most common times of prayer are morning and evening, traditionally called lauds (morning prayer) and vespers (evening prayer). In this prayer practice, the psalms are read, scripture lessons heard, prayers offered, and silence kept. These highly structured and unchanging daily prayer services include praise, thanksgiving, adoration, and worship.

Their beauty is in their simplicity, for once the ins and outs of the practice are learned you'll begin to notice the powerful sequence of readings, the mood of the psalms, and the presence of God more readily, not just in that moment but throughout your day. As you leave the office, you carry some bit of truth gleamed from the scripture reading, psalms, or prayers. For the ten to fifteen minutes that it takes to do morning or evening prayer—either privately or, in the best circumstances, in community, so that the call-and-response nature of the prayers is maintained—the time soon becomes a welcome part and texture of your life. This brief, intimate daily conversation with God is a way of saying "Good evening" and "Good morning, I'm just checking in." Some days it may feel like a formal conversation of pleasantries, but on some occasions it becomes a serious dialogue.

Like me, you will probably find yourself in the frequent situation of praying the divine office alone. To pray it alone—I pray morning prayer—means I have to hold myself accountable and resist the temptation to skip a day . . . or two. But these stable personal prayer times also allow great flexibility and bring an ease to prayer that I enjoy. Praying morning and evening daily has substantially improved my "holy habit" of prayer, encouraged meditation, and educated me in listening for God's voice in the scriptures. Above all, the prayers have strengthened my relationship with God as an everyday reality. When left without prayers that can be learned and recited, I tend to pray infrequently. Some of my friends tell me that when they pray they tend to do so briefly, on the fly, without discipline or organization. Their prayer is made up as they go, according to their mood, and certainly not in tune with the Christian calendar or lectionary readings.

From the earliest of days, the Church has followed an order of prayer that saw the rising of the sun and the lighting of the early evening lamps as symbols of God's power over death. Later they were known as the *officium* prayers, from the Latin for "duty" or "responsibility." For a time in Church history, these daily prayers became primarily the private prayers of the clerics. Today these prayers serve as bookends to the day, reminding us who we are, and whose we are, as we end and begin our daily rounds.

In the psalms, we find such expressions as "I will meditate on thee in the morning"; "I rose at midnight to give praise to thee"; "Evening and morning, and at noon I will speak and declare: and he shall hear my voice"; "Seven times a day I have given praise to thee" (KJV). The first Christians continued to attend the temple at the set hours of prayer (Acts 10:3, 9; and 16:25). Christian prayer consisted of almost the same elements as Jewish prayer: chanting psalms, reading the scriptures, and at times newly composed canticles. With time the custom of going to the temple disappeared and the Church developed its own distinct worship. The development of the daily office into what we know today was completed at the close of the sixth century.

During the early Middle Ages (specifically, the sixth century), one form of the hourly prayers, called the "cathedral office," was used extensively in churches as a regular part of community devotional life. It was a daily affair for the whole congregation. The cathedral-based service used the same prayer patterns, psalms, and hymns over and over, allowing full participation of old and young alike. Light and incense were also part of the prayer, thereby engaging all the senses.

As the Middle Ages wore on, the services, sung or said in Latin, fell into disuse in local congregations of average working people. Another form of the prayers, called the divine office, was practiced in monasteries and religious houses and became the domain of the clergy and of monks and nuns in the monasteries. Pastors and other professional religious individuals could be seen reading from their breviary, the official daily prayer book, when not engaged in other activities.

The daily office we have today is a telescoping of the eight offices that structure days of work and prayer. Matins (night office, joining with lauds) and lauds (morning, joining matins in the first canonical hour) were observed in community with the monks and nuns rising for these prayers at midnight. *Prime* (sunrise, or the second of the canonical hours) was added in the fourth century, establishing noon prayer. The next three—*terce* (the third canonical hour), *sext* (the sixth hour, or fourth canonical hour), and *none* (noon, or the fifth canonical hour)—were times of private prayer. *Compline* (night prayer) was added in the fourth century to precede the later hour of vespers (evening prayer), also identified as *vigils* (midnight), which kept watch through the night.

Just as for our Jewish ancestors before us, the psalms are an integral part of daily prayer with the early church reinterpreting the psalms to be about Christ, the Messiah. The language of the psalms and prayers is one of praising God directly, not talking to each other about God's greatness.

Now Begin

Here I introduce a practical way to implement this form of prayer into your life. Morning and evening prayer are deeply rooted in the Jewish faith tradition, and al-

though language and cultural adaptations have changed it over time, their essence remains the same. Accordingly, I have ordered the offices in their proper rotation, with
evening prayer first followed by morning prayer, since the day begins at the setting of
the sun, just as the Jewish community still begins the Sabbath at sunset. Upon learning this, one young exhausted mother of three told me it was such a relief to hear
that the first thing she gets to do at the beginning of each day is go to bed and sleep.

EVENING PRAYER

The evening hours are a good time for prayer. The approaching darkness quietly
raises questions: "What have I done today?" "Did I accomplish what I wanted?"
"Was it worth it?" We sit in the quiet and review our day—the hurts and hugs, dis-
appointments and enlightenments. Sleep, the sister of death, reminds us this life is
transient.

Sadly, many times we miss the opportunity for prayer as we continue to work,
watch TV, or surf the Web. We miss the God of the evensong, a wise mentor who,
like a mother holding her child, calms our fears and offers us hope: "O Lord, my
heart is not lifted up, my eyes are not raised too high; I do not occupy myself with
things too great and too marvelous for me. But I have calmed and quieted my soul,
like a weaned child with its mother; my soul is like the weaned child that is with
me" (Ps. 131:1–2).

Evening prayer, also known as nocturnal office and vigils, reminds us to place
ourselves in God's care as we go to sleep. The common evening hymn is the Tallis
Canon. The common canticle (a song found in the Bible) reading is that of Mary's
exhortation found in Luke 1:46–55. Incense is historically used in the evening
prayers in keeping with Psalm 141:2 ("Let my prayer be counted as incense before
you, and the lifting up of my hands an evening sacrifice").

194   *An Order of Evening Prayer*

These prayers and praises are to be read aloud:

Lifting the Light
(Light a candle.)

Light and peace in Jesus Christ. Thanks be to God.

Evening Praise
This can be sung to the tune of Tallis's Canon.

Melody of the Tallis Canon ("All Praise to Thee, My God, This Night")

THOMAS TALLIS, 1505–1585

All praise to thee, my God, this night, for all the blessings of the light!
Keep me, O keep me, King of kings, beneath thine own almighty wings.

Forgive me, Lord, for thy dear son, the ill that I this day have done,
that with the world, myself, and thee, I, ere I sleep, at peace may be.

Teach me to live, that I may dread the grave as little as my bed;
Teach me to die, that so I may rise glorious at the judgment day.

O may my soul on thee repose; and with sweet sleep my eyelids close,
sleep, that may me more vigorous make to serve my God when I awake.

Praise God, from whom all blessings flow; praise God, all creatures here
  below;
praise God above, ye heavenly host; praise Father, Son, and Holy Ghost.

Prayer of Thanksgiving

We praise you, O God
for you made the day for the works of light
and the night for the refreshment of our minds and bodies.
Keep us now in Christ; grant us a peaceful evening, a night free from sin,
and bring us at last to eternal life. Amen

Scripture (Also see "Suggested Lectionary Readings" in the back of the book.)

I lift up my eyes to the hills. From where does my help come?
My help comes from the Lord, who made heaven and earth.
The Lord will not let your foot be moved,
the Lord who keeps you will not slumber . . . nor sleep. . . .
The Lord will keep your going out and your coming in
from this time forth and for evermore. (Ps. 121)

Silence

Silence follows for meditation on the scripture that was just read.

Canticle of Praise

My soul magnifies the Lord, and my spirit rejoices in God my Savior, for
he has looked with favor on the lowliness of his servant. Surely, from now
on all generations will call me blessed; for the Mighty One has done great
things for me, and holy is his name. His mercy is for those who fear him
from generation to generation. He has shown strength with his arm; he
has scattered the proud in the thoughts of their hearts. He has brought
down the powerful from their thrones, and lifted up the lowly; he has

filled the hungry with good things, and sent the rich away empty. He has
helped his servant Israel, in remembrance of his mercy, according to the
promise he made to our ancestors, to Abraham and to his descendants
forever. (Canticle of Mary, Luke 1:46b–55)

Incense

An incense stick may be lit as this psalm is recited.

Let my prayer be counted as incense before you, and the lifting up of my
hands an evening sacrifice. (Ps. 141:2)

Prayers

After each prayer is said aloud or contemplated in silence, conclude with "Lord, in
your mercy hear our prayer."

This day I (we) pray for:
the people in my (our) life . . .
those who suffer and are in trouble . . .
the concerns of my (our) community . . .
the world, its people and its leaders . . .
the Church universal—its leaders, members, and mission . . .
the communion of saints. . . .

The Lord's Prayer

See the chapter "Lord's Prayer."

Blessing

The grace of Jesus Christ enfold us this night.
I (we) go in peace. Amen. (Extinguish candle.)

○ ○ ○

The service ends as the worshipper departs into the quiet of the night. I love the serene tranquility of evening prayer. My feelings are best summed up in this lyric by one of my favorite poets:

Wild Nights—Wild Nights!
Were I with thee
Wild Nights should be
Our luxury!
Futile—the Winds—
To a heart in port—
Done with the Compass—
Done with the Chart!
Rowing in Eden—
Ah, the Sea!
Might I but moor—tonight—
In thee!

EMILY DICKINSON, MASSACHUSETTS, 1830–1886

MORNING PRAYER

Morning prayer prepares us for the day ahead as we seek God's blessing and advice: "Lord, teach us to number our days aright, that we may gain wisdom of heart" (Ps. 90:12). We enter the new day, not groaning but hoping in God. We need wisdom in our words and thoughts, and in the choices we make, so we ask for the guidance of God.

Sadly, many of us miss the opportunity to speak with God first thing in the morning. As soon as our eyes open, we're off in a rush. Get ready! Get set! Go! We're running to work or school or the chores of the day. What about pausing long enough to consider living the day ahead wisely, with compassion and gentleness?

God meets us in morning prayer not as a taskmaster but as a loving presence who gives us strength and joy for the day. Basil, a wise fourth-century pastor from Asia Minor, said: "We pray in the morning to give the first stirrings of our minds to God. Before anything else, let the thought of God gladden you."

Before going into this day, let's pray. I find it best to pray the entire order aloud to God, who hears.

An Order for Morning Prayer

Call to Prayer

O Lord, open our lips and we shall declare your praise (drawn from
Ps. 51:15).

Morning Praise

A candle, representing Christ, the light of the world, may be lit as the first line is recited.

New every morning is your love, great God of light,
and all day long you are working for good in the world.
Stir up in us a desire to serve you,
to live peacefully with our neighbors,
and to devote each day to your son
our Savior Jesus Christ the Lord. Amen.

What follows can be sung to the tune of the Tallis Canon.

Awake, my soul, and with the sun thy daily stage of duty run;

shake off dull sloth and joyful rise, to pay thy morning sacrifice!

Lord, I my vows to thee renew; disperse my sins as morning dew,
guard my first spring of thought and will, and with thyself my spirit fill.

Direct, control, suggest this day; all I design, or do, or say.
That all my powers, with all their might, in thy sole glory may unite.

Praise God from whom all blessings flow; praise God, all creatures here below;
praise God above, ye heavenly host, praise Father, Son, and Holy Ghost.
(Thomas Ken, 1637–1711)

Scripture (Also see "Suggested Lectionary Readings" in the back of the book.)
Hear my prayer, O Lord; . . . I stretch out my hands to you; my soul
thirsts for you like a parched land. . . . Let me hear of your steadfast love
in the morning for in you I put my trust (Ps. 143:1, 6, and 8).

Silence
Silence follows for meditation on the scripture that was just read.

Canticle of Praise
Blessed be the Lord God of Israel, for he has looked favorably on his
people and redeemed them. He has raised up a mighty savior for us in the
house of his servant David, as he spoke through the mouth of his holy
prophets from of old, that we would be saved from our enemies and from
the hand of all who hate us. Thus he has shown the mercy promised to
our ancestors, and has remembered his holy covenant, the oath that he
swore to our ancestor Abraham, to grant us that we, being rescued from
the hands of our enemies, might serve him without fear, in holiness and

righteousness before him all our days. And you, child, will be called the prophet of the Most High; for you will go before the Lord to prepare his ways, to give knowledge of salvation to his people by the forgiveness of their sins. By the tender mercy of our God, the dawn from on high will break upon us, to give light to those who sit in darkness and in the shadow of death, to guide our feet into the way of peace. (Canticle of Zechariah, Luke 1:68–79)

Prayers

After each prayer is said aloud or contemplated in silence, conclude with "Lord, in your mercy hear our prayer."

This day I (we) pray for:
the people in my (our) life . . .
those who suffer and are in trouble . . .
the concerns of my (our) community . . .
the world, its people and its leaders . . .
the Church universal—its leaders, members, and mission . . .
the communion of saints. . . .

The Lord's Prayer

See the chapter "Lord's Prayer."

Blessing

The grace of the Lord Jesus Christ
and the love of God
and the communion of the Holy Spirit
be with us (you) all. Amen.

What a wonderful way to vanquish the darkness and begin our days! We leave morning prayer and walk into the light of a new day.

We bless you now, O my Christ, word of God,
light of light without beginning, bestower of the Spirit.
We bless you, threefold light of undivided glory.
You have vanquished the darkness
and brought forth the light, to create everything in it. (St. Gregory
Nazianzus, the Theologian, 329–389)

Some Things to Think About

I recently traveled to Taizé, France, as a pilgrim among other pilgrims. More than a
hundred thousand pilgrims, mostly young adults, from many denominations and
from sixty nations make pilgrimages to Taizé each year. To say that Taizé is off the
beaten track is not an exaggeration; what attracts so many to this place of faith? The
reason many people (I include myself) travel to Taizé is the prayer and worship. Yes,
it is the daily office that you have just experienced. This type of prayer brings people of all Christian traditions not only to France but also to increasingly popular
prayer communities, in Celtic Lindisfarne, Great Britain; Iona, Scotland; and
Northumbria, England, communities that structure their life together around the
ancient tradition of common prayer.

In Taizé simplicity, each day is organized around morning, noon, and evening
prayer—each lasting an hour. I entered the church and walked down some stairs to
sit on the floor in a room of flickering candles and icons evoking mystery and reverence. The robed brothers led a series of Taizé chants, short psalms and Gospel
readings, prayers that were spoken and translated into four languages, and a long silence that lasted about ten minutes. I had to leave almost immediately after the
service ended to catch my bus, but I learned later that others stayed in worship well
past midnight.

Although you will often pray the daily office alone, my hope is that the time comes when every church offers opportunities for daily morning and evening prayer (except when communion is being celebrated). I also pray you have the opportunity to participate in a community morning or evening prayer service. This prayer is based on the firm belief that prayer has power and that there is a greater power in prayer when we do it together.

The office represents daily bread, and it continues to be a mainstay of Christian prayer life. It invites you to participate in a practical spirituality by employing formal daily prayer. Theophan the Recluse, from the Eastern tradition, offers us our final words of advice: "Some Godly thoughts come nearer the heart than others. Should this be so, after you have finished your prayers, continue to dwell on such a thought and remain feeding on it. This is the way to unceasing prayer."

Questions for Reflection

1. Daily prayer—even if not in a shared space—is important for holding the dispersed community together. How do you understand your prayer alone as part of the community?

2. The office helps us pray when life is hard; when we have no words to say to God. Name a time when life was so overwhelming that you could not pray. Do you think that having the office would have helped you pray then?

Other Resources to Continue Your Journey

There are many new books out in the last few years that you can use for daily prayer.

Phyllis Tickle (ed.), *The Divine Hours* (New York: Doubleday, 2000). Of all the new books, this is a most noteworthy three-volume office. Tickle's manual encompasses the liturgical and calendar year with the offices of every day.

Robert Webber, *The Prymer: The Prayer Book of the Medieval Era Adapted for Contemporary Use* (Brewster, Mass.: Paraclete, 2000). This spiritual classic can be used for personal or communal use in a one-day retreat, a weekly cycle, or a thirty-day cycle of prayer.

Look at www.missionstclare.com/english on the Web to read morning, evening, and noonday prayers, as well as the compline from the *Book of Common Prayer of the Episcopal Church, USA.*

Tongsung Kido

How very good and pleasant it is when kindred live together in unity!
For there the Lord ordained his blessing, life forevermore.

—PSALM 133:1 AND 3B

Thoughts Before You Begin

The words *tongsung kido* mean "praying aloud." In Korea, and among Korean congregations around the world, tongsung kido is an important part of the prayer life of the worshipping congregation. The members are given a specific amount of time for the prayer and a common concern that everyone is instructed to pray about. The prayer might be general, a petition for patience or more love; or a very specific one, for a favorite aunt who is sick, or for a family left homeless after a house fire, or for a government leader. Then everyone present prays aloud at the same time, and in his or her own words.

Entering a room where this prayer is being practiced is like walking into a turbulent ocean and being overtaken by a massive wave. In the large assembly I attended, it was bold, with people praying *very* loudly, at the top of their voices. It reminded me of the Bible story in Acts 2:1–13, when the celebration of Pentecost "had come, they were all together in one place," and the Holy Spirit came upon the disciples "like the rush of a violent wind, and it filled the entire house. . . ." All "began to speak in other languages, as the Spirit gave the ability." The funny part of the story is when it says that "all were amazed and perplexed, saying to one another, 'What does this mean?' But others sneered and said, 'They are filled with new wine'" (meaning drunk). In that room I might have been watching a second Pentecost, or perhaps this group of Christians was tipsy. In truth, they were praying in the Korean fashion of tongsung kido.

Now Begin

Turn around and kneel on the floor facing your seat; use the chair, which is now in front of you, as a prayer altar. Set yourself a signal so you'll know when the time has expired, perhaps with the use of an alarm. When praying in a group, one individual can be responsible to ring a bell. Once settled, begin to pray aloud your needs and concerns, allowing five to ten minutes. Or you may choose one of these concerns to pray about:

> those who suffer and those in trouble . . .
> the concerns of this local community . . .
> the world, its peoples, and its leaders . . .
> the Church universal—its leaders, members, and mission . . .
> the communion of saints. . . .

Pray in a boisterous voice. If you are with a group, pray together aloud at the same time.

To close, rise from your knees and stand. Raise your arms skyward, palms up, and pray the Lord's Prayer (see the chapter "Lord's Prayer") in a loud and firm voice. Pray with the boldness of a person who wants, and is not afraid to ask for, God's grace.

Some Things to Think About

People sang psalms to God in their trials for themselves, as well as their sisters and brothers, and they were saved: "Then they cried to the Lord in their trouble, and he delivered them from their distress; . . . Let them thank the Lord for his steadfast love, for his wonderful works to humankind. For he satisfies the thirsty, and the hungry he fills with good things" (Ps. 107:6, 8–9).

There is power when we pray together in faith with one accord, and strong conviction. In this strong stance, our prayers are heard and answered. In collective prayer, Christ's presence is firmly assured: "Again, truly I tell you, if two of you agree on earth about anything you ask, it will be done for you by my Father in heaven. For where two or three are gathered in my name, I am there among them" (Matt. 18:19–20).

Tongsung kido is what I'd label "structured spontaneity," a sufficient, but not overbearing, framework in which people feel free to express their individual prayers as they see fit.

I was surprised that the voices of other pray-ers, even those sitting very close, didn't bother me. I was concentrating on my own earnest prayers, longing and waiting for the empowerment of the Holy Spirit. Romans 8:26 rang true: "Likewise the Spirit helps us with our weakness; for we do not know how to pray as we ought, but that very Spirit intercedes with sighs too deep for words."

Questions for Reflection

1. Some people feel self-conscious praying aloud, especially if it is in a very loud voice that might be heard by others. Were you able to overcome any self-consciousness in order to speak your prayers freely? How were you able to do it?
2. What need or concern did you choose to pray about?
3. What did this practice of prayer teach you about life in community with other pray-ers?

Other Resources to Continue Your Journey

New ways of praying, from our own as well as other cultures, enhance our prayer lives and help us envision God afresh.

Janet Morley (ed.), *Bread for Tomorrow, Prayers for the Church Year* (Maryknoll, N.Y.: Orbis, 1992). This book contains 175 prayers that follow the Church calendar. Themes center on ministry to the poor from voices around the world.

Philip Dunn, *Prayer, Language of the Soul* (New York: Dell, 1997). This paperback provides more than three hundred prayers, modern and ancient, from many cultures.

Owen Collins (ed.), *2000 Years of Classic Christian Prayers: A Collection for Public and Personal Use* (Maryknoll, N.Y.: Orbis, 1999). This is a treasury of prayers from the rich heritage of the Christian faith.

Michael Counsell (ed.), *2000 Years of Prayer* (Harrisburg, Pa.: Morehouse, 1999). This book comes highly recommended by one of my teachers, Diedra Kriewald.

Prayer Walks

Before us it is blessed, behind us it is blessed,
Below us it is blessed, above us it is blessed,
Around us it is blessed as we set out with Christ.
Our speech is blessed as we set out for God.
With beauty before us, with beauty behind us,
With beauty below us, with beauty above us,
With beauty around us, we set out for a holy place indeed.

—TRADITIONAL NAVAHO PRAYER

Thoughts Before You Begin

In this section, there are three prayer walks. The first simple prayer walk sets you on the Way with a walking meditation. It is a simple procession of contemplative peace and hope. On the path, wherever you go—around the block greeting neighbors, to a cemetery in remembrance, or in the natural surroundings of a nearby park—you will meet God. As Monica of Africa (323–387) said, "Nothing is far from God."

The Emmaus walk, the second prayer practice, takes you and a spiritual friend on an encounter with the Jesus of long ago.

Our third prayer walk, the stations of the cross, was originally performed by Christian pilgrims who dramatized the events at the supposed sites of Jesus' passion. Later the prayer walk was supported by the Franciscans, who were given custody of the holy places in Jerusalem in the 1300s.

Some of the practices here are for solitary praying, and others require a partner. All of them have their foundation in the scriptures and come from the oldest traditions of the Church. One is formally structured, and the others call for additional extemporaneous personal expression. Even a simple prayer walk through your backyard can be a rich experience because of the significance to the sacred that it holds for you.

Now Begin

Through my own experience, I have found a few helpful pointers. First, decide where and when to walk. You can walk around the block or in your own backyard. Perhaps your prayer walk is a trip home from the market or from dropping your child off at school. Even the parking lot at your work site at lunch time suits the purpose. It is not so much a matter of where and when you walk as the open and receiving attitude in which you walk.

Breathing is an important part of walking prayer. When we breathe in thanks-giving, we unite our breath with an invocation to the Holy Spirit, willing God to awaken our own spirit. Remember to breathe deeply. As you begin your walk, give God thanks for your breath and the ability to move your body. Moving further into your walk, unite the rhythm of your gait with the rhythm of your breath. As the Taoists say, "breathe from the heels" as you receive the blessings from all those who have walked this way before you. I find it helpful to inhale with the first three or four steps, and exhale with the following three or four steps. It may feel more natu-ral to take two steps between inhaling and exhaling.

Next, remember that you walk with an attitude of respect for the hand of the Divine in life and all of creation. A friend of mine takes prayer walks using her walker; she tells me it is more a matter of attitude than how you get around. So often we rush from one place to another, never noticing God's work is all around us. Take notice of all the beauty and wonder around you as you walk. What color is the sky? Are there clouds? Do you feel any wind, or is the air still? Look on the ground at the plants and stones and sand. What do you see that is jubilant and flourishing, or delicate or dying? What is the air temperature—hot or cold? Is it humid or dry? What do you hear? Are there sounds of chirping birds or rustling leaves? Do you hear the rush of cars or the roar of airplanes overhead? Do you see traffic signals and stop signs that have been installed for your safety? Are you alone, or do you see other people in the buildings or on the street? Who are they? A child, a postal worker, a truck driver? Knowing that everyone has at least one story that would break your heart, what do you think each individual's story may be?

Remember, with all that you see and feel and hear, there are no distractions. All is of God and worthy of prayer.

Walk the path of the Christ who is the Way, the Truth, and the Life. Ask the God of Abraham and Sarah, Mary and Joseph, Lydia and Paul, Francis and Clare, and of all who traveled the journey before you, to bless each and every step of your prayer walk.

As you near the end of your prayer walk, consciously release your own agenda and choose to accept the will of God. Only when you let go of your own plans and desires with every breath and consequently step out in faith, embracing God's peace and hope will you know the wealth of both giving and receiving. You may wish to pause and end this prayer time with formal thanks to the Creator for all that you have experienced on your walk. You can finish with the prayer given at the beginning of this chapter, or the Lord's Prayer, or another prayer of your choice.

Some Things to Think About

An account of the first Christians, in Acts 9:2, talks about the men and women "who belonged to *Halcha*," which translates from Hebrew to "the Way." The Way (or the Journey) was what some early Christians called their religion. Additional references to the Way are also found in Acts 19:23 and 22:4. In the Gospel of John, Jesus uses the term to identify himself: "I am *the way*, and the truth, and the life" (John 14:6, adapted).

As you are on the Way, making your journey and taking your prayer walk, I hope you find yourself transformed. Saint Francis said that he sought not so much to pray as to make his whole life a prayer. Through your prayer walks, may your whole life become a walking meditation of peace and hope.

Questions for Reflection

1. Were you able to use breathing to center yourself for the prayer walk? Which pattern of rhythmic breathing worked best for you?

2. Where did you decide to walk, and why there? What agenda did you release so that your walk could be one of faith?

3. If you felt distracted during your walk, how did you incorporate these distractions into your prayer?

Other Resources to Continue Your Journey

Peace Pilgrim: Her Life and Work in Her Own Words (Santa Fe, N.Mex.: Ocean Tree, 1994). She walked more than twenty-five thousand miles over three decades to demonstrate the ways of peace. Her writings, collected by her friends after her death, will inspire you to take to the road.

Douglas C. Vest, *On Pilgrimage* (Boston: Cowley, 1998). Vest explores the difference between taking a walk or hike and making of those steps a pilgrimage. He draws on his experiences and insights from his travels to Iona, St. Croix, Holywell, Lourdes, and Wales.

An Emmaus Walk

Thoughts Before You Begin

The Emmaus walk is a practice based on Luke 24:13–16. In the story, two people are walking to a village called Emmaus, a few miles from Jerusalem. It is shortly after the crucifixion of Jesus. As they walk, they discuss the events of the past days; their hearts are saddened by Jesus' death. Jesus (already risen, unbeknownst to them) approaches them on the road. He walks with them, but they don't recognize him.

An abridged version is printed here, but if this story is new to you, you'll find it in its entirety in Luke 24:13–49. If you are familiar with the sacred text, I invite you to be open to hear it again with a new ear. Either way, my hope is that you will enjoy the inward searching and relational aspects of this companionable time of prayer.

This prayer walk, which requires a partner, combines the simple joy of walking with the sometimes complex action of spiritual conversation and prayer. In your walk, you have the opportunity to express compassion in word (what you share with your partner) and deed (the valuable gift in spending time with your companion). In some way, this expression of compassion has the opportunity to change the world—at least the world where our lives touch those of other people. Praying with another means that we are giving our full attention to that immediate moment on the Way, sharing God's love and opening our life to transformation.

Now Begin

In this time of prayer, two people walk together for ten or more minutes. Before you begin your walk (or as you are walking), read aloud the complete Emmaus story (Luke 24:13–49). The version printed here is abridged to strategic verses: 13–18, 27–32, and 36. The Emmaus walk can also be prayed substituting other biblical scriptures or inspirational Christian readings.

Now on that same day two of them were going to a village called Emmaus, about seven miles from Jerusalem, and talking with each other about all these things that had happened. While they were talking and discussing, Jesus himself came near and went with them, but their eyes were kept from recognizing him. And he said to them, "What are you discussing with each other while you walk along?" They stood still, looking sad. Then one of them, whose name was Cleopas, answered him, "Are you the only stranger in Jerusalem who does not know the things that have taken place there in these days?" . . . Then beginning with Moses and all the prophets, he (Jesus) interpreted to them the things about himself in all the scriptures.

As they came near the village to which they were going, he walked ahead as if he were going on. But they urged him strongly, saying, "Stay with us, because it is almost evening and the day is now nearly over." So he went in to stay with them. When he was at the table with them, he took bread, blessed and broke it, and gave it to them. Then their eyes were opened, and they recognized him; and he vanished from their sight. They said to each other, "Were not our hearts burning within us while he was talking to us on the road, while he was opening the scriptures to us?"

While they were talking about this, Jesus himself stood among them and said to them, "Peace be with you."

Begin by taking a slow, meandering walk with your partner. Walk outside if the weather permits (you can remain inside if necessary). Later you may wish to stop and find a quiet spot to sit and talk. Reflect upon the scripture, each sharing the insights and wisdom the Spirit gives you. Or consider these thoughts and reflections: the two disciples say that their hearts were burning within them. Share a time when God spoke to you and set your heart on fire. When and where have you experienced God's presence in your life? Who are your closest companions and friends on the Way? How do you encourage and sustain one another?

When you finish, thank one another and pray for each other.

Some Things to Think About

In my experience, praying in the light of scripture creates an intimacy that is authentic, not superficial. Honesty breeds honesty. What you see is what you get. It is hard to hide when walking with the Word.

Remember to let silence be the rule for the walk, except when reading the scripture or sharing your spiritual reflections of the passage. This is not a time to analyze the story or to discuss geography or other incidentals to the story line. Instead, it is a time to reflect on what God is saying to you for your life and the life of your community.

Some people are afraid of silence, mistakenly believing that if they are not talking then nothing is happening. Be comfortable with silence. Leave a space for God to speak and your partner to think. You may hear God's word to you through your sister or brother.

Questions for Reflection

1. How is the walk of companionship different from a walk in solitude?
2. How did the scripture lead your thoughts and holy conversation? Where did it take you?
3. What did you pray for your partner at the end of your time together? What did he or she pray for you?

Other Resources to Continue Your Journey

Linus Mundy, *The Complete Guide to Prayer-Walking: A Simple Path to Body-and-Soul Fitness* (New York: Crossroad, 1996). This book explains all the whats, whens, and hows of prayer walks. It also offers meditations, prayers, and prayer starters as well as four first-person accounts by walkers.

Janet Holm McHenry, *Prayerwalk: Becoming a Woman of Prayer, Strength, and Discipline* (Cincinnati: Waterbrook Press, 2000). This book creates possibilities of combining your faith and spirituality with the exercise of walking.

J. Lynne Hinton, *Meditations for Walking* (Macon, Ga.: Smyth and Kelwys, 1999). Hinton wrote fifty-two entries that include scriptures, meditations, and prayers— all during a year when she was clearing a path in the woods behind her house.

Stations of the Cross

Thoughts Before You Begin

Since medieval times, the stations of the cross (also known as the way of the cross) has been the most widely practiced method of prayer on the theme of the passion—Christ's journey to the cross and his death and burial. The classic version of this popular prayer walk consists of a series of fourteen meditations on Jesus' final hours. A person or group "makes the stations" by walking to each sequential station for prayer and meditation about the event that the station symbolizes. The stations can be found on walls of churches, landscaped into quiet church yards, or observed in your own living room.

Each meditation is represented in a physical way by a marker or artwork depicting one of the fourteen events. The artistic rendition can be a picture or statue from a variety of media portraying Jesus' journey, starting with the Garden of Gethsemane (or, depending on the artist and the time in church history, his condemnation in the Sanhedrin) and continuing to his burial (or in some more modern instances, his resurrection). A cross is always incorporated in the artwork.

The foundations of pilgrimage behind the stations of the cross originated in our Jewish heritage. For Jesus and the Jewish people, Jerusalem has always been a special place of pilgrimage. Whole families traveled there each year for Passover and other major religious feasts. Jews who lived far away held in their hearts the hope that they would visit the holy city at least once in their lifetime.

The early Christian community was composed largely of Jews who continued to worship in the synagogues and make the pilgrimage to Jerusalem, although the focus of their pilgrimage shifted more and more to Jesus. Christians traveling from all over the known world had a deep desire to walk where Jesus walked, commemorating in this way his life and teachings. Locations in the city came to be identified with specific events in Jesus' life. Pilgrims visited the ruins of the temple; the fortress Antonia, where Pilate condemned Jesus; the garden of Gethsemane; the pool of Siloam; the burial tomb; and other sites.

In the following centuries, although interrupted by the Crusades, pilgrims continued to travel to the Holy Land visiting the sites associated with Jesus' death and resurrection. The *New Westminster Dictionary of Liturgy and Worship* states that the stations began very early by pilgrims on their way to Jerusalem walking from Pilate's house to Calvary. The Franciscans, popularizing the stations around 1342, became the guardians of the holy places and erected a series of tableaux for devotional purposes. Once home, pilgrims represented the Holy Land sites in their own church as "stations," or the way of the cross. The stations helped them meditate on the passion of Jesus, allowing those who could not go to Jerusalem to participate in remembering Christ's sacrifice.

During this time, the popularity of the Way (referring to Jesus' way toward death, the "way of the cross" or "the way of sorrows") resulted in artwork depicting stories of Jesus' death and resurrection and early Church tradition, such as his falling three times and being laid in the arms of his mother after his crucifixion. This folk telling, which originated with the biblical account, became a romanticized version of the drama, taking on additional stations that do not appear in the Bible. At least one, in which a woman named Veronica wipes the face of Jesus, may be fictitious. My guess is that as with Simon, a man in the crowd who helped carry the cross, there were other specific stories of women and men who acted with compassion toward Jesus on the Way. Like many of our church Christmas pageants of today, which always include *three* wise men although the Bible does not give the number of individuals, and other additions not in the Gospel accounts, this medieval drama is meant more as a vehicle for spiritual formation than as a history lesson.

Although the classic practice of the stations of the cross includes fourteen meditations, there is a growing custom of employing an additional image, the resurrection of Jesus, for a total of fifteen stations. Some churches add a sixteenth, "arrested in the garden," to keep symmetry: eight stations on each side of the church that lead you through the drama of the passion.

Bonaventure, a bishop of the Church from 1273 until his death in 1274, taught his members with these words: "The true disciple of Christ, who desires to conform himself to the Savior who was crucified for our sake, must strive above all to carry about in his soul and body at all times the cross of Jesus Christ until he experiences within himself the truth of the apostle's words, 'With Jesus I am nailed to the cross.'"

The way of the cross remains the simplest and easiest means of learning the lesson of sacrifice by studying the divine model of sacrifice. It is an expression of our acceptance of Jesus' invitation to "take up the cross and follow me" (Matt. 16:24).

Now Begin

In the stations of the cross, the pilgrim is invited to walk from one station to the next rather than sit down and meditate on the topics. This is called "making the stations." The two versions here hold fourteen and twelve stations respectively. To try the classic version, visit a local Roman Catholic or Episcopal church that has the stations on the interior walls. You can find pictures on the Web to accompany the texts.

The stations of the cross can be done anywhere, with a group or alone, aloud or silently. There are no specific prayers that are mandatory, although I've included here a wealth of beautiful and profound prayers that were written by various individuals and communities throughout the centuries. Many preprinted guides are available. You can also write your own personal prayers to pray and meditate at each stop.

To try the biblical version that I've created here, you can create your own set of ministations. Make copies of the pictures from the Web or some other source. Cut them out and place them on the walls of a room, equal distance apart. They can also be mounted on wood or sturdy cardboard and placed outside, or in any space conducive to prayer. In the written prayers corresponding to selected events, you will find the basic teachings of Jesus applied to our lives. Pause to contemplate and pray the scene depicted at each station.

Stations of the Cross: A Classic Version

Pray this opening prayer before beginning each station:

We adore you, O Christ, and we bless you,
because by your holy cross you have redeemed the world.

As you conclude each station, and before proceeding to the next station, pray these petitions in order:

1. The Lord's Prayer or Our Father (see the chapter "Prayer Beads")
2. The Hail Mary (see the chapter "Prayer Beads")
3. The Gloria Patri or Glory Be (see the chapter "Prayer Beads")

First Station: Jesus Is Condemned to Death

My Jesus, often have I signed your death warrant by my sins; save me by your death from that eternal death that I often deserve.

Second Station: Jesus Bears His Cross

My Jesus, who by your own will took on the heavy cross that I helped make for you by my sins. Make me feel their heavy weight, and weep for them for as long as I live.

Third Station: Jesus Falls the First Time Beneath the Cross

My Jesus, the heavy burden of my sins is on you and bears you down beneath the cross. I loathe them, I detest them; I call on you to forgive them; by your grace, help me never to commit them again.

Fourth Station: Jesus Meets His Mother

Suffering Jesus, Mary Mother most sorrowful, if, by my sins, I have caused you pain and anguish in the past, by God's assisting grace I will sin no more; rather, be my love from now on until death.

Fifth Station: Simon of Cyrene Helps Jesus Carry the Cross

My Jesus, blessed, three times Simon aided you to bear the cross. I too will be blessed if I aid you to bear the cross, by patiently bowing my head to the crosses you send me during life. My Jesus, give me grace to do so.

Sixth Station: Jesus and Veronica

My tender Jesus, you printed your sacred face upon the cloth that Veronica used to wipe the sweat from your brow. Print deeply in my soul, I pray, a lasting memory of your bitter pains.

Seventh Station: Jesus Falls a Second Time

My Jesus, I have sinned often and, by sin, beaten you on the ground beneath the cross. Help me to use the means of grace so that I may never fall again.

Eighth Station: Jesus Comforts the Women of Jerusalem

My Jesus, you who did comfort the women of Jerusalem who wept to see you bruised and torn, comfort my soul with your tender pity, for in your compassion lies my trust. May my heart answer your heart forever.

Ninth Station: Jesus Falls a Third Time

My Jesus, through all the bitter woes you endured when the third time the heavy cross bowed you to the earth, never, I beg you, let me fall into sin again. Ah, my Jesus, let me die rather than ever offend you again.

Tenth Station: Jesus Is Stripped of His Garments and Given Gall to Drink

My Jesus, stripped of your garments and drenched with gall, strip me of love for things of earth, and make me loathe all that savors the world and sin.

Eleventh Station: Jesus Is Nailed to the Cross

My Jesus, by your agony when the nails pierced your hands and feet and fixed them to the cross, make me crucify my flesh by Christian penance.

Twelfth Station: Jesus Dies

My Jesus, for three hours you hung in agony, and then died for me. Let me die before I sin, and if I live, live to love and faithfully serve you.

Thirteenth Station: Jesus Is Taken from the Cross and Laid in Mary's Arms

O Mary, Mother most sorrowful, the sword of grief pierced your soul when you saw Jesus lying lifeless on your bosom; lead me to hate sin because sin killed your son and wounded your own heart. Give me grace to live a Christian life and save my soul.

Fourteenth Station: Jesus Is Laid in the Tomb

My Jesus, beside your body in the tomb I, too, would lie dead; but if I live, let it be for you, so as one day to enjoy with you in heaven the fruits of your passion and bitter death.

Closing Prayer

O God, who by the precious blood of your only-born Son did make the cross holy, we ask you to grant that we who rejoice in the glory of the same holy cross may feel everywhere the gladness of your sovereign protection. Through the same Christ our Lord. Amen.

THE WAY OF THE CROSS: A BIBLICAL VERSION

Station One

Jesus prays in the garden and is betrayed (Matt. 26:36–46).

"I have come down from heaven, not to do my will, but the will of him who sent me" [John 6:38]. Jesus, keep me awake with you in the garden to travel your way of the cross. Amen.

Station Two

Jesus is tried and condemned to death (Matt. 26:57–68 and 27:1–2 and 11–26).

"No one has greater love than this, to lay down one's life for one's friends" [John 15:13]. Jesus, you were scourged and crowned with thorns, and unjustly condemned by Pilate to die on the cross. Amen.

Station Three

Jesus takes up his cross (John 19:16–17).

"If any want to be my followers, let them deny themselves and take up his cross daily and follow me" [Luke 9:23]. I too carry burdens and trials. Teach me, Jesus, by your example, how to carry my daily crosses. Amen.

Station Four

The soldiers mock Jesus (Mark 15:16–20).

"Here is the lamb of God who takes away the sin of the world!" [John 1:29]. Jesus, all human dignity was stripped from you. The soldiers hit you and spit on you, and you had done nothing wrong. I get so caught up in my own humiliations that I give up in discouragement. Jesus, let me never become so weary that I lose hope. Amen.

Station Five

Simon helps Jesus carry his cross (Matt. 27:32).

"Truly I tell you, just as you did not do it to one of the least of these, you did not do it to me" [Matt. 25:45]. My beloved Jesus, Simon the Cyrene was constrained to carry your cross for you. I pray that I will never refuse to carry the cross, but to accept and embrace it. Amen.

Station Six

Jesus meets his mother (John 19:25–27).

> "So you have pain now; but I will see you again, and your hearts will rejoice, and no one will take your joy from you" [John 16:22]. Jesus, you and Mary may have looked at each other and your hearts were wounded. Mary remembers you as a child taking your first steps; now, like her, I long to reach out to stop your suffering. Help me, like Mary, to remain watchfully silent—for your will is my will. Amen.

Station Seven

Jesus consoles the women of Jerusalem (Luke 23:28).

> "Daughters of Jerusalem, do not weep for me; but weep for yourselves and for your children" [Luke 23:28]. Jesus, I think of how these women wept with compassion when they saw you. You realize that others suffer with you and reach out to comfort them. Jesus, it is your love that causes me to weep for my sins. Amen.

Station Eight

Jesus is offered gall and vinegar to drink (Matt. 27:33–34).

> "None of you can become my disciple if you do not give up all your possessions" [Luke 14:33]. Jesus, what a terrible beverage to be offered as your last on earth. I look forward to drinking wine with you someday at the eternal banquet as you promised. Amen.

Station Nine

Jesus is nailed to the cross (John 20:25).

"Whoever wishes to be first among you must be slave of all" [Mark 10:44]. Jesus, arms and hands that were once extended in love are now stretched and fastened to the wood of the cross. Nail my heart to your feet that I may always remain there to love you and never leave you again. Amen.

Station Ten

Jesus dies on the cross (John 19:31–37).

"Come to me, all you that art weary and are carrying heavy burdens, and I will give you rest" [Matt. 11:28]. Jesus, you bow your head and die. O my dying Jesus, your death is my hope. I yield my soul into your hands. Amen.

Station Eleven

Jesus is taken down from the cross and laid in the tomb (Matt. 27:57–61).

"So you have pain now; but I will see you again, and your hearts will rejoice, and no one will take your joy from you" [John 16:22]. Jesus, you lived simply and had no place to be buried, so they laid you in the tomb of a stranger. My Jesus, as the soldiers closed the door of the tomb and a new chapter opened, may my life be opened to your transforming power. Amen.

Station Twelve

Jesus is resurrected (Matt. 28:1–10).

"And I, when I am lifted up from the earth, will draw all people to myself" [John 12:32]. Jesus rose on the third day and chose to appear to his disciple, Mary Magdalene.

228   *Closing Prayer*

Now I turn my life over to God and am transformed into a new person. My hatred is turned to love, my sadness to joy, my despair to hope and my weakness to strength. My Lord Jesus Christ, you have made this journey for me and I love you with my whole heart. I seek your forgiveness for offending you and thank you for permitting me to accompany you on this journey so that I may live and die united to you. Jesus, with your Spirit I face life anew. By your resurrection, make me be always united with you and make me rise glorious with you at the last day. Amen.

Some Things to Think About

Walking the streets of Jerusalem today, even in the noise and the hurried pace of city life, the feeling of the walk to Calvary is still present; you can almost see Jesus shouldering the cross, struggling through the crowds on the way to Calvary. For it is among the people that Jesus continues to carry the cross today. He carries it in me, and that is why I am impelled to walk this way of the cross with him. If I want to carry my cross in the steps of Christ, then this is my opportunity to experience those steps and follow him.

Questions for Reflection

1.   What crosses do you carry? Do any of these burdens belong to someone else? What crosses do you need to lay down? Which crosses do you feel called to pick up?

2.   At which station did you most identify with Jesus? In what way?

3. What was most helpful in your journey: the prayers? the scriptures? the
    pictures? the active participation?

Other Resources to Continue Your Journey

Megan McKenna, *The New Stations of the Cross: The Way of the Cross According to Scripture* (New York: Image Books, Doubleday, 2003). All of McKenna's writings are terrific, and I think this one is also.

Henri J. M. Nouwen, *Walk with Jesus: Stations of the Cross,* with illustrations by Sister David Helen (Maryknoll, N.Y.: Orbis Books, 1990). Any book by the late Henry Nouwen is worth picking up, but it is the contemporary illustrations of children in need and women carrying wood that make this a walk you'll be glad you took.

There are a number of excellent Websites featuring variations on the stations of the cross, complete with illustrations. Three of the best are www.christusrex.org, www.cptryon.org, and www.stmarythevirgin.org.

Innovative Prayer

*N*ourish your optimistic outlook and hopeful spirit with these innovative ways of praying. Get ready to enjoy the imaginative, creative part of yourself. As you contemplate the mysteries of God through these practices of prayer, you are sure to find connections to the deeper meaning of life.

Praying with Our Bodies
    Palms Up, Palms Down Prayer
    Body Prayer
    Body Prayer with Music
Prayer Labyrinth
Home Prayer Altars
Ignatian Prayer: Guided Imagination
Prayer Beads
    Praying the Rosary
    Chaplet of Seven: Covenant Chaplet
Praying with Mandalas
Prayer Dance
    Dancing the Lord's Prayer
    Hava Nagila Circle Prayer Dance
    Dance of Jesus

Praying with
Our Bodies

I will imagine that my soul and body are like two hands of a compass, and that my soul, like the stationary hand, is fixed in Jesus, who is my center, and that my body, like the moving hand, is describing a circle of assignments and obligations.

—ANTHONY MARY CLARET, 1807–1870, SPAIN

Have you been rushing all day? Perhaps even your whole life? Take a moment now to relax; to slow your physical self; and to surrender to prayer with your body, heart, and soul. As you enter into this time of prayer, don't worry about doing it right, or knowing the deeper meaning of this prayer ritual. Often it is best to jump right in and "do" prayer—see how prayer works and feels for *you*. Sometimes, rather than *represent* something, the reality of the ritual works the other way, and the meaning develops out of the doing.

Body prayer can incorporate breathing and the movement of the body into our time with God. We consciously slow our movements and our thoughts to be attentive to the voice of God in our lives. Praying with our bodies allows us to bypass our busy and overanalyzing minds, express our need for intimacy and our spirit's yearning for deeper connection, and hear God's voice of reassurance through our attention to our bodies. Our outward posture often reflects our inward state. For instance, think of what your body language tells people before you even open your mouth to speak. The body, mind, and spirit are inseparable.

Palms Up, Palms Down Prayer

Thoughts Before You Begin

This body prayer is called "palms up, palms down." In time, you will be able to do it with your eyes closed. But for your first time, read through all the instructions before beginning, and look back at the book when necessary. Many people find that this particular prayer is a good first-time introduction to praying with your body, because each movement directly correlates to our interaction with God.

Now Begin

Sit in a comfortable position. Put aside anything in your hands and lap. Sit crosslegged on the floor, or if you are in a chair, place both feet flat on the floor. Close your eyes. Begin by placing your palms face down on your lap or in front of you, as a symbolic indication of your desire to turn over any concerns you may have to God. Whatever it is that weighs you down, release it. Pause one or two minutes as you release your cares to God.

Now, turn your palms face up on your lap or in front of you, as a symbol of your desire to receive from the Lord. Ask for what you need. Pause one or two minutes as you await the Holy Spirit, who performs the work of prayer and knows our needs, the condition of our heart, and how properly to express it. This is our invitation to the Spirit to come and express our needs in a way that is beyond our ability to put them into words.

Next, bring your hands together and intertwine your fingers into a prayer position. Spend time in silence. Do not relinquish anything or ask anything. Be still in your heart, and sit in God's presence, allowing the Lord to speak to you. Pause again, for another one or two minutes.

When you are ready, return your awareness to the room and open your eyes. If you are participating in a group, wait until everyone's eyes are open before moving to another activity.

Some Things to Think About

I attempt prayer when I feel lonely or hurt, embattled or betrayed. I utter prayers of petition when my burden is overwhelming or when my stress level peaks. I pray small breaths of thanksgiving after overcoming an obstacle. Finally, I pray most successfully when I'm ready to face the hard answers—and not before.

Why do we strive to keep on the way of prayer? Each one of us has a unique answer. What has increasingly made sense to me is that in prayer I somehow catch a glimpse of what I am looking for, be it answers, comfort, or strength.

A prayer ritual, an external expression that places us—our minds and our hearts—at the disposal of the Spirit, may have many layers of meaning. Because we all relate to God differently, some ways of being in the presence of God work for some individuals but not for others. Take a moment to think about what happened as you prayed and to better understand prayer's meaning for your life.

Questions for Reflection

1. What did you desire to receive from God in your prayer?
2. What did you turn over to God in your prayer?
3. How did your hand placements aid you? Did the placement of your hands help you settle your body and quiet your mind, or was it distracting?

Body Prayer

Thoughts Before You Begin

You can do this prayer practice alone by recording it for yourself beforehand on a tape player. You can then replay the tape and follow the directions of your voice.

If you are in a group and one person is facilitating, he or she may not be able to participate fully. The experience is most effective if the facilitator reads at a relaxed pace with a soft but strong voice, pausing after each instruction or where movement is required to allow participants to respond. Alone or with a group, you may wish to light a candle and place it on the floor in front of you to create a gentle light and a tranquil mood for prayer.

Now Begin

For this body prayer, I recommend that you sit cross-legged on the floor. If you are not seated on carpet, use a yoga mat or a folded blanket for comfort. If you prefer to sit in a chair, place your feet flat on the floor. Free your hands of all objects.

With your eyes open, focus on the candle as a way to relax. Place your hands in front of you in a prayer position. Make an effort to be slow and deliberate in your thoughts, your movements, your breaths. Take a deep breath in through your nose. Now blow it out through your nose.

Lift your chest and drop your shoulders. Slowly and deeply inhale as you extend your arms out in front of you, with palms up, to receive your Creator's blessing. Exhale as you bring your arms and hands back to the prayer position.

Slowly inhale and extend your arms outward in front of you again, with palms up, to accept the blessing of Christ. Exhale and come back to the prayer position.

Once again, slowly inhale and extend your arms to receive the blessing of the Holy Spirit. Now exhale and come back to the prayer position.

Stay for a moment in the prayer position. Think about the Hebrew word *ruah*, which means spirit or breath. Inhale and feel the breath, the Spirit, the ruah, deep within you. Exhale through your nose.

Place your hands palms down on your knees. Close your eyes and give yourself permission to move into God's space and time. Take another deep breath in. This time, breathe out one word that names something you mourn or fear. Release anger, judgment, or compulsiveness. Make this place and time safe and peaceful—a time of blessing.

Sitting up straight, with shoulders back, place your hands on your abdomen with fingers spread. Feel your body breathe in its own rhythm. Tell yourself that it is all right to feel whatever you are feeling and sense whatever you are sensing as you sit with God.

Move your hands up to your ribs. Feel your breath expand and contract your ribcage. Allow the unimportant to drift away. Place your hands back on your knees. Invite yourself to rest in the presence of God.

Relax your neck, bending it gently to one side and then the other. Return your head to the center. Feel the tension escape from the back of your head, and let the tightness release from your eyes, eyebrows, cheeks, mouth, and jaw.

With your hands still on your knees, hold onto your knees. Lift your head and chest up. Inhale and arch your back slightly. Exhale as you round your back, pulling your head and chin down. Return to a comfortable sitting posture. Imagine God's gentle presence flowing through you—through the back of your neck and down your spine to your buttocks, through your thighs and calves, through your heels and into your toes.

Again, still holding onto your knees, lift your head and chest up. Inhale and arch backward slightly. Exhale as you round your back, pulling your head and chin down. Return to a comfortable sitting posture.

Repeat one more time. Inhale and arch back. Exhale and round down. Return to a comfortable sitting posture.

Now interlace your fingers and place your hands palms-down on top of your head. Gently press your elbows back. Turn your hands upward, fingers still interlaced. Stretch your hands and arms over your head. Return your hands to your knees.

Again, interlace your fingers and place your hands palms down on top of your head. Press your elbows back. Turn your hands upward. Stretch your hands and arms over your head. This time arch back slightly. Return your hands to your knees.

Place your right hand on your left knee and your left hand behind your back, palm flat on the floor. (If you are in a chair, you might grip the back of the seat with your left hand.) Look to your left and let your upper body comfortably twist to your left, following the direction of your gaze. Increase your twist to the left as far as you are comfortable and hold briefly. On your left, place all that binds you— all that holds you back from being the blessed person that God intends. Return slowly and with care to the center.

Now place your left hand on your right knee and your right hand behind your back, palm flat on the floor. (Again, if you are in a chair you might grip the back of the seat with your left hand.) Look to your right and let your upper body comfortably twist to your right, following the direction of your gaze. Increase your twist to the right as far as you are comfortable and hold briefly. On your right, receive God's grace and blessings. Return slowly and with care to the center.

With your hands on your legs, place your feet straight out in front of you. (If you are in a chair, simply extend your feet in front of you on the floor.) Bend your knees slightly if this is more comfortable. With your hands on your legs, bend at the hips and stretch your upper body forward as far as is comfortable.

Now lie on your back with your head on the floor and knees bent. Perhaps you can remember the snow or sand angels you made as a child; this movement is similar. Extend your arms along your sides, with your hands palms up next to your thighs. Now bend your arms at the elbow and slide your forearms with your hands palms up, along the floor until your hands are touching your shoulders. Hold briefly, then slide your hands back to your sides. Slowly do this motion two more times.

Lower your knees and lie flat on the floor, completely relaxed. God invites you to be just as you are.

Relax your feet; completely relax. Relax your legs and hips; completely relax. Relax your buttocks and abdomen; completely relax. Relax your lower back; completely relax. Relax your middle torso; completely relax. You are wonderfully made, for you are a creation of God.

Relax your chest and upper back; completely relax. Relax your hands and wrists; completely, totally relax. Relax your forearms and elbows; completely relax. Relax your upper arms and shoulders. Trust this moment to God as you learn to *be* and not *do*.

Relax your neck, head, and face. Completely relax. Your entire body is relaxed; completely relaxed. Daughter or son of God, you are God's beloved. Repeat in your heart over and over: "I am God's beloved."

Inhale deeply through your nose. Allow God's Spirit to breathe into your heart. Accept and welcome the blessings of the Holy Spirit, who dwells within you. Invite the Spirit to be your guide and help you discern God's will for you. As you exhale through your nose, breathe out a word that affirms what you feel—perhaps "peace," "relaxed," or "love." Embrace this feeling as you embrace God. Notice all the feelings that are present. Welcome feelings that lie just below the surface. Breathe into your feelings with acceptance.

Continue breathing in and out through your nose for a couple more breaths.

Slowly open your eyes. Remain on your back as you wiggle your fingers and toes. If you are comfortable, raise your hands over your head and stretch, as you might do when waking. Bend your knees and slowly hug them to your chest. Roll onto your side and sit up. When you are ready, return your attention to the room, remaining rested and assured.

Some Things to Think About

Praying with your body means learning to be comfortable with your body and to like it, which is hard for many people. If enjoying and loving your body is difficult, I suggest you pray often for release from these judgments. Ask God to open your heart to your body. Ask God to teach you how to see your body as a friend and cherished companion. Ask for acceptance and tolerance of your own body. Then go ahead and live in your body as fully as you can.

In *Honoring the Body: Meditations on a Christian Practice*, Stephanie Paulsell writes: "Such is the mystery of the body. Sometimes we know that we are our bodies, that our capacity for life and death makes us who we are. At other times, we feel that we simply inhabit a vessel that is inadequate to contain all that we are. But at all times, it is the body that allows us to reach out for one another, to steady each other on our feet when we are weak, to embrace one another in joy and in despair. Thank God we don't have to know what something is in order to hold it." Thank goodness we are coming around to reclaiming our bodies in a sacred way!

Questions for Reflection

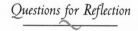

1. What kind of tension or stiffness did you feel released from your body during this prayer?
2. How important was controlling and slowing your breathing during the prayer?
3. What did it feel like to relax in God's care and feel the Divine's love? If you were unable to relax in this prayer, what blocked you from doing so?

Body Prayer with Music

Thoughts Before You Begin

During your prayer time, use soothing meditative music as a respite from the hectic pace of ordinary life. Gentle music playing in the background helps ease you into silence and cover up disturbances from outside. When choosing music for a time of prayer, stay away from familiar songs that might distract you from your deeper thoughts. At times, your prayer may call for music that invites stirring, energized movement, or even singing.

Don't be afraid to be creative and multicultural in your selection of music. Greek Byzantine chants, Irish melodies, American spirituals, and medieval Spanish *cantigas* are all rich, sacred resources available to you. Indulge in chants from Trappist monks or from France's Taizé community, Jewish songs, Tibetan chanting and drumming, or West African ceremonial dance rhythms.

Remember, the music is not an end in itself but a vehicle for renewing your heart in worship to God. The music is one more route to a deepened attentiveness to God.

If you are in a group and one person is facilitating, he or she may not be able to participate fully. The experience is most effective if the facilitator reads at a relaxed pace with a soft but strong voice, pausing after each instruction or where movement is required to allow participants to respond.

Now Begin

Start the music.

Stand comfortably with your feet slightly apart. Breathe deeply through your nose. Shake your arms. Let the energy flow down your arms and into your fingers. Wiggle your fingers. Continue to breathe deeply as you bend and straighten your legs, then move your shoulders up and down, and finally bend and straighten your arms. Stretch and move to loosen up your joints and to ease any tightness.

Now stand still, close your eyes, and let your facial muscles relax. Be aware of your body. Feel your own energy. Be awake to what your body tells you. Are you stiff, nimble, fatigued, or flexible? What about your mood? Are you feeling needy, satisfied, at ease, or pensive?

Remain standing or be seated in a chair or on the floor. Get comfortable, and then close your eyes. What is the best thing about your life right now? Take slow, deep breaths in and out and allow yourself to feel pleasure as you dwell on this best thing. Relish this pleasure as you slowly inhale and exhale. Continue breathing calmly and gently for approximately two minutes before proceeding.

What is most enjoyable about being who you are at this season in your life? Take a deep breath in and let yourself smile as you live in this present moment. Exhale as you take pleasure in being the person God created you to be. Continue breathing slowly and deeply for approximately two minutes before proceeding.

Slowly open your eyes and return your attention to the room.

Continue to breathe deeply as you stand up and begin to move around the room. Walk softly, swinging your arms. Flex your limbs and muscles. Walk in a way that reflects who you are as the beloved child of God. Forget how you carry yourself and focus totally on the moment.

Some Things to Think About

Inspirational music offers a gateway to spiritual feelings and ideas. Its impact is immediate and nonverbal, and more directly absorbed than complex systems of belief. An instrumental selection can take us to realms of joy or solemnity; a vocal can lead us to be reflective or frivolous. The power of music is a gift from above that brings together the sacred and the sensual. It connects the earthly and the divine. Music carries us beyond the everyday to something greater than ourselves.

Questions for Reflection

1. What feelings and ideas came to light? What music did you choose, and why? How did it enhance your prayer? To what gateway did the music take you in prayer?
2. What is most enjoyable about being who you are right now? What was the best thing that you named in this prayer?

Other Resources to Continue Your Journey

B.K.S. Iyengar, *Light on Yoga* (New York: Random House, 1994). This book has more than six hundred practical illustrations for both the novice and those more experienced, to help you put together your own body prayers. My yoga teacher, René, tells me that this is the definitive source for people who practice yoga daily for exercise, meditation, or relaxation.

Jane E. Vennard, *Praying with Body and Soul: A Way to Intimacy with God* (Minneapolis: Augsburg Press, 1998). You'll find this to be a most helpful book as you grow in your relationship with your bodily-emotional self and your relationships. Practical and biblically grounded.

Stephanie Paulsell, *Honoring the Body: Meditations on a Christian Practice,* (San Francisco: Jossey-Bass, 2002). How can we view and live in our bodies as a practice of faith? This book is very helpful for those who struggle with weight or body image.

# Prayer Labyrinth

All shall be well, and all shall be well, and all manner of things shall be well.

—JULIAN OF NORWICH, 1342–1416, ENGLAND

tion with circular constructions. Various forms of
many ancient cultures and civilizations: classical
ope, the Near East, Africa, New Zealand, North

geria used the labyrinth as early as A.D. 350; the
at the center confirm its sacred use. The labyrinth
he most famous today is in the inlaid floor of the
grims traveled to the labyrinths as a substitute for
"holy obligation," to walk where Jesus walked.
going to the Holy Land. These medieval pilgrims
reciting prayers.

ircles teach us to pray and meditate? We usually
th being lost, or going nowhere. However, the cir-
ted in ancient tradition, is making a comeback as
yrinths are showing up in parking lots, on sandy
t retreat centers. They are constructed of canvas,
er the appeal of the labyrinth for yourself, all you
ont of another. It invites and encourages you to per-
saying goes, the longest journey begins with a single

ght think the labyrinth is a maze, a route that confuses
rs and dead ends. But the type of labyrinth that I'm talk-
nding course of concentric circles that leads to a center
ks and nothing to figure out. After you reach the center, you
the same winding path out again.

Labyrinth

The religious community, as well as the medical community, is hailing its bene-fits. Walking this ancient design while praying or meditating is beneficial to spirit and body. In addition to the spiritual benefit of praying, the process of walking the labyrinth calms the mind, relaxes the body, and reduces stress. Using this tool, indi-viduals profoundly yet playfully experience the mystery of God's presence in a tan-gible way. As a work of the Spirit, the labyrinth is more about the journey than the destination, more about being than doing. By incorporating a physical journey into this time of prayer, the labyrinth integrates body and mind, reason and imagina-tion, thought and feeling into one harmonious whole. Simply put, the labyrinth is a space that guides the mind and heart.

The labyrinth offers a chance to take time out from busy lives and to leave schedules and stress behind. Prayerfully contemplating how the labyrinth journey mirrors our own spiritual journey can richly bless our lives and lead us to discovery, insight, peace, solace, and direction. It reminds us that no time or effort is ever wasted; no matter how circuitous the course of our lives, every step takes us toward the center and moves us closer to God. As we walk the labyrinth with others, we are reminded that each of us is at our own place on the discipleship journey, just as each is at a particular place on this labyrinth—not further ahead or lagging behind, not higher or lower, not faster or slower, just different.

Now Begin

Some people are anxious about their first walk. Be assured that there is no wrong way to walk the labyrinth. Your way is the right way. The ideas here have been sug-gested by other walkers, but remember that they are only possibilities. Walk the prayer labyrinth your way.

Prior to your walk, you may find it helpful to sit and relax. You may wish to say a beginning prayer or read some sacred text. Spend a few minutes in transition from the business of the outside world to a place of quiet and a feeling of calm.

From the ancients of the Middle Ages, we are told that there are three stages to walking the labyrinth:

1. Entering, or *purgation.* Walking toward the center, we release cares and concerns, emptying and quieting ourselves before God. As we surrender to the winding path, we seek wholeness and healing.

2. The center, or *illumination.* We pray and meditate within the circle, seeking clarity for our lives. We remain as long as we wish, receiving whatever is there for us.

3. Returning, or *union.* As we walk out on the same path, we are empowered by the Spirit to be more authentic in ourselves and in our service to the world.

Here are a few other suggestions to make the most out of your walk:

♦ *Walk in prayer.* Walk the labyrinth in thoughtful prayer, giving thanks and praise and seeking guidance. Empty yourself, shedding the confusion and busyness of your mind, and opening yourself to God's insight and grace.

♦ *Walk in focused reflection.* This is an excellent space to meditate on a specific care, a verse of sacred text, a question, or a joy.

♦ *Walk in silent reflection.* Let go of all thoughts, feelings, and emotions that bog you down and limit you. In doing so, you create inner space where God can enter. Gregory the Great of the sixth century talked about "resting in God." In this stillness, the mind and heart begin to experience and taste the interior peace you have been seeking. Enter a sacred space of silence and solitude. As distracting thoughts spring up, focus on a sacred word or special image to dispel them and return to the inner silence. Be at peace in the silence.

◆ *Walk as a body prayer.* The walk on the path can be a prayer in itself. Be spontaneous. Dance. Carry a flower, a shell, or some symbol of significance to you. Be free. Be playful and joyous. In the center, kneel and seek God's guidance before beginning the outward walk.

◆ *Walk in community.* You do not walk alone. You will meet people coming in, going out, facing you, and joining you in the middle. You may want to share your experience with others afterward. When you encounter another walker in your path, do not worry about doing anything wrong—one of you will simply step aside to let the other pass.

Some Things to Think About

My hope is that you will search out and find an opportunity to walk a labyrinth, whether it be a permanent one in your community or a portable labyrinth used for a group event (these are usually made of canvas and are approximately forty feet in diameter).

If you do not have access to a labyrinth, you can construct your own. Begin by drawing the classical labyrinth pattern shown on the next page. This pattern is the oldest and most popular design. After you try it a few times, you'll be able to draw it with ease. Simply connect the dots and solid lines, from right to left if you are right-handed or left to right if you are left-handed.

Once you master this freehand labyrinth, you can create a labyrinth anywhere. Mow the pattern in your grass. Use rocks or sticks to construct it. Sketch one in the sand on your next trip to the beach, and invite people to join you. You can also construct a labyrinth with duct tape on a smooth floor or with ropes and pegs in the backyard. Draw a labyrinth on a sheet of paper, and contemplatively trace it with your finger or the tip of a pencil. Enjoy!

254

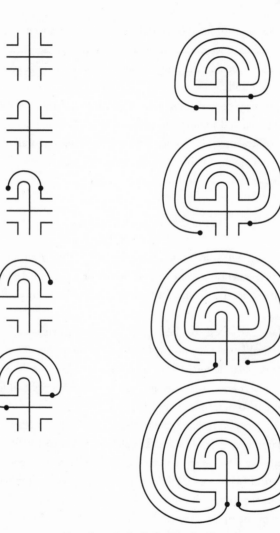

Drawing a Labyrinth, Step by Step

Questions for Reflection

1. What did you discover about prayer during your labyrinth walk? About yourself? About God?

2. What worked for you in this form of prayer? The first time I walked a labyrinth, I got turned around and lost. This was a wonderful analogy of my life. I often have to begin more than once when I strike out in a new direction. What analogies can you draw from your walk?

3. How was walking the labyrinth different from the way you usually pray or understand prayer? How was it the same?

Other Resources to Continue Your Journey

Lauren Artress, *Walking a Sacred Path: Rediscovering the Labyrinth as a Spiritual Tool* (New York: Riverhead Books, 1995). An excellent foundational book for beginners and novices alike. Includes a more detailed history of the labyrinth.

At www.spiritworks.org, a prayer labyrinth is available to congregations, fellowships, retreats, online seminar participants, and interested groups. It is on a circular painted canvas measuring approximately forty feet across. Spiritworks also offers training for labyrinth leaders.

Visit www.labyrinthproject.com if you are interested in owning your own labyrinth. Contact Robert Ferre, at the St. Louis Labyrinth Project. They cut, seam, and paint twelve-to-thirty-six-foot designs on either canvas or nylon. You can also purchase labyrinth-making instructions for a do-it-yourself project or have Robert consult and design one uniquely for you. Lots of possibilities.

Home
Prayer Altars

Then I will go to the altar of God, to God my exceeding joy.

—PSALM 43:4

Thoughts Before You Begin

Constructing a prayer altar at home creates a physical space where we can express the spiritual part of ourselves, a special place where we can pray, read, and reflect—as an individual, a couple, or a family. A home prayer altar points our attention to the Greater Being who exists beyond our own limited lives and creates a physical space where we can glimpse and experience the Divine. Setting aside this sacred space in your own home for family or personal use can reaffirm your spiritual strength and enhance your relationship with God.

The idea of the home altar draws upon a tradition from biblical times, when women and men constructed altars to acknowledge God's presence. Noah's family members built an altar in gratitude to God for saving them from the great flood. Early Christians, like those of the Jewish faith in which they were raised, met in homes and sat around a wooden table to break bread; this table was, in effect, their altar. Eventually people of faith met less frequently within the domestic realm and moved into buildings outside the home.

Personal altars and focus centers that remind us of the sacred may be new to some of us, but in the cultures of Latin America and Asia they have been fixtures in homes for centuries. A typical home altar at a friend's home in Mexico City consisted of religious symbols such as a cross, candle, and picture of Jesus as well as a family photo of deceased parents and an infant's rattle. The baby's toy, I learned, was the reminder of prayers for a longed-for child. One couple I know sit at the kitchen table—always in the same chairs—and read the Bible and offer daily devotion. It is their altar.

Now Begin

Make your own home altar. To get into the mood, light a candle or put on some music. Gather some items that you love, items that remind you of an answered prayer or a yearned-for request, items that make you feel close to God. Then, on a cloth or a scarf, arrange the items in a place in your home that feels right, perhaps on a mantle, table, ledge, or shelf. As you spend time with your altar, you develop a sense of what works for you, and what else you might add.

On my own altar, I presently have a pinecone and twig from a California redwood, reminding me of God in nature. There is a candle in a very pretty stained-glass cylinder that was a present from my sister-in-law. Swinging overhead is a whimsical woman flying by on a feather—a holiday present from my grown son. These items remind me of God's love, since they hold both the cherished memory of the giver and the fond reminiscence of the joyous occasion for the gift. The altar sits inconspicuously in a quiet spot by the living room fireplace. My Bible and prayer book sit on a table close by. When I sit there, my family knows that it is Mom's uninterrupted prayer time.

One friend built her altar out of mountain stones by the creek near her home. A secretary has one on her desk at work: a simple fountain and oil lamp. The glow of the light and sounds of the water remind her of God's constant love. One smart young dad with toddlers keeps his on top of the refrigerator. In disquieting times, he literally looks up to remind himself of God's love and blessings. It feeds his soul and spirit. Whether simple or elaborate, make your altar a reflection of God's Spirit within you.

Some Things to Think About

I like what author Peg Streep has to say about home altars. She found North Americans to be unusual in their separation of the sacred from everyday life. She believes people are looking for a vision of life that is not chopped into a million pieces. They are trying, she says, to break down the distinction between their spiritual selves and their mundane selves.

I'm glad that the home altar is making a comeback into spiritual groups and homes, to break down these separations. It makes sense to me in light of the growing emphasis on the home as central to the faith community and family values. My home altar gives me a physical place within the home to pray and meditate, read sacred texts, and be with God.

Questions for Reflection

1. Where might you place an altar within your home or work space?
2. What items and objects would you include on your altar?
3. Draw a simple pencil rendition of the prayer altar you wish to create. Share your idea with someone else.

Other Resources to Continue Your Journey

Marie Romero Cash, Siegfried Halus, and Lucy R. Lippard, *Living Shrines: Home Altars of New Mexico* (Santa Fe, N.Mex.: Museum of New Mexico Press, 1998). Here, Hispanic families pray for healing, guidance, and even miracles. Beautiful photography.

Jean McMann, *Altars and Icons: Sacred Spaces in Everyday Life* (San Francisco: Chronicle Books, 1998). This book has colorful pictures of more than forty eclectic personal shrines, both formal and casual, that will inspire you to create your own. You'll enjoy reading the interviews with the creators of these remarkable altars.

Peg Streep, *Altars Made Easy: A Complete Guide to Creating Your Own Sacred Space* (San Francisco: HarperSanFrancisco, 1997). Beautifully illustrated, this volume contains examples to help you create your own unique sacred space.

Ignatian Prayer

GUIDED IMAGINATION

*In making a choice or in coming to a decision, only one thing is really important—
to seek and to find what God calls me to at this time of my life.*

—IGNATIUS OF LOYOLA, 1491–1556, SPAIN

Thoughts Before You Begin

Using your God-given imagination is an especially good way to pray if you have a busy schedule or harried nerves or are easily distracted. It takes seriously the power of our memory and imagination in influencing how we perceive and act in the world. Ignatius believed that the process of contemplation meant bringing all our senses to bear on the images, events, and stories that mediate God to us. This form of guided prayer does not ask you to put on the brakes and stop at the end of a busy day, but to keep your mind active and agile. It uses your memory and imagination to lend you a serene alertness that is helpful in this method of prayer.

Ignatius of Loyola used the term *contemplation* when he talked about using the imagination in praying. Ignatius had an orderly mind, so his contemplation was structured. In his own words, he introduced carefully planned exercises or a "method of examination of conscience, of meditation, of vocal and mental prayer and of other spiritual activities." Using the imagination while praying the scriptures was a major part of his contemplative exercises.

What is the purpose of this style of contemplation? Ignatius tells us that it is a "way of preparing and disposing the soul to rid itself of all inordinate attachments and, after their removal, of seeking and finding the will of God in the disposition of our life for the salvation of our soul." We rid ourselves of attachments so as to be fully with God.

Ignatian exercise is a school of prayer that continues to be taught by the community of the Society of Jesus. The exercises, as practiced by the society, initiate a three-way dialogue among an individual, a spiritual director, and God. Organized into four parts, called "weeks," the Ignatian exercises use scriptures from the Bible to contemplate Christ's life, death, and resurrection. These are interlaced with specific spiritual teachings and down-to-earth practices on topics such as discerning the actions of God (incidents that are of God and those that are not God's work), bodily postures in prayer, and diet and health issues.

There are many Ignatian exercises that we could learn for praying, but in this case let us center on one. This prayer practice invites you to enter the narrative, picture the situation, and identify with the characters of the story. Although you can use any biblical story, some passages are better suited to this process than others. The stories told of and by Jesus are especially rich and will engage your imagination as a way to enter into prayer.

Ignatius was powerfully attracted to the life and teachings of Jesus and therefore used the stories of Jesus' life to form much of his subject matter. He believed that the Gospels were an avenue through which God addressed each individual in the circumstances of his or her life. Through the scriptures we are able to open our hearts and minds to hear the word of God as fully as possible.

Now Begin

Begin by reading this short story about Jesus from Matthew, chapter 8.

> When Jesus had come down from the mountain, great crowds followed him; and there was a leper who came to him and knelt before him, saying, "Lord, if you choose, you can make me clean." He stretched out his hand and touched him, saying, "I do choose. Be made clean!" Immediately the leprosy was cleansed.

Read through the story again slowly. This time, pause after each phrase and imagine the scene. Close your eyes and open your imagination.

"When Jesus had come down from the mountain, great crowds followed him." Explore this scene fully. Enter into the action. What is the setting? What are the sounds, sights, and aromas? Who else is there? What do they look like? What do their faces tell you?

"...and there was a leper who came to him and knelt before him, saying, 'Lord, if you choose, you can make me clean.'" Where are you in the story? What is your role in this drama? Where are you in the crowd? Let the story unfold in your imagination. Does anyone speak to you? What do you say? Is there other action of which you are a part? What are you feeling?

"He stretched out his hand and touched him, saying, 'I do choose. Be made clean!' Immediately the leprosy was cleansed." Now the story is concluded. Do you stay there? Do you go elsewhere? Whom do you tell about what you have witnessed?

What is the story's meaning for you now? Spend the next few minutes looking back at your time of prayer and noting what happened during that time. Note the moments when you felt consoled, desolate, happy, or other feelings. Paying attention to your responses may help you better attune yourself to the leading of the Spirit, not only now but later, when you return to the demands of your daily life.

Some Things to Think About

This approach to prayer is fruitful for those who can readily exercise their imagination. Ignatius was particularly concerned that our imagination should be drawn to God in love, surrender, and commitment. Thus he recommends that the contemplation include a "colloquy," a conversation in which you freely and confidently express any feelings that have been stirred in the fullness or emptiness of your heart. The next time you use this method you may find it helpful to write down the basic outline of your imaginative encounter with the text, any dialogue with God or the other characters in the story, and any insights you drew from your prayer.

Ignatius believed in the progressive integration of life and prayer. God wants us to be people who are holy in heart and life. This means we seek to live a life of justice, mercy, truth, and above all else love. Our holiness is cultivated by our spiritual disciplines and our life of service. The real challenge is to sustain this holiness and love in our daily lives. With God's grace and the support of sisters and brothers, we can join together to express God's love.

Questions for Reflection

1. How did you experience the Gospel through Ignatius's exercise? What did you think and feel? How did your prayer change as you read the story a second or third time?
2. Where did you connect with this short-but-powerful story? What insight into yourself, God, or your relationships came through praying the story in this way?
3. What other Jesus story might you choose for this form of prayer?

Other Resources to Continue Your Journey

John A. Hardon, S.J., *Retreat with the Lord: A Popular Guide to the Spiritual Exercises of Ignatius of Loyola* (Ann Arbor, Mich.: Charis Servant, 1993). Father Hardon presents an up-to-date guide of the sixteenth-century exercises for you to do with a spiritual director.

David Lonsdale, *Eyes to See, Ears to Hear: An Introduction to Ignatian Spirituality* (Maryknoll, N.Y.: Orbis Books, 2000). This is an excellent introduction, written in a clear and easy style.

André Ravier, S.J., *A Do It at Home Retreat: The Spiritual Exercises of St. Ignatius of Loyola* (San Francisco: Ignatius Press, 1989). This book is a careful guide for anyone who cannot make it to a retreat center and wants to participate in an Ignatian retreat at home.

Prayer Beads

Grant me, O merciful God, that I might ardently love,

Prudently ponder,

Rightly acknowledge,

And perfectly fulfill all that is pleasing to you,

For the praise and glory of your name.

—THOMAS AQUINAS, 1225–1274, FRANCE

Like our ancient ancestors of faith, we can use beads to assist us in our prayer. Fingering and moving the beads can calm our spirit, help us concentrate, and integrate our senses of touch and sight into our experience of prayer. With our fingers busy, our minds are open to ponder the deeper mysteries of God. In times of crisis, simply holding the string of beads can be a prayer, especially when our minds are unable to formulate any helpful thoughts.

Praying with beads has been a beautiful and inspiring Christian prayer practice since the early centuries of the Church. Numbered beads were made of cord, pebbles, or seeds and worn as necklaces or wrapped around the waist, wrist, or fingers. They were used to count prayers and mantras (repeated phrases or sayings) and even to aid memorization of the 150 psalms.

During the Middle Ages, prayer beads became common in every part of Christian Europe. Depending on the owner's place in society, they could be made from sea shells or semiprecious stones, or even strings of rare jewels. Olive wood, taken from the trees of the garden of Gethsemane and carved into beads, was (and still is) a special prize. Christians in the tenth century used a string of knots, either tied into a circle or in a straight strand, to pray the Lord's Prayer and other repetitive prayers. These beads were often carried in a pocket or tied around one's wrist or neck for easy access. Monks, taking seriously the mandate to pray always, wore a prayer cord around their waists so that the beads were in easy reach whenever a hand was free. Even making the beads was a holy ritual. The weaver wove the prayer into each knot upon which a bead was placed.

Thoughts Before You Begin

For the most part, the Protestant tradition hasn't relied on beads, so you may not have any experience with them. If beads are new to you, here are some simple guidelines. Start with any string of beads, or craft your own string specifically for this purpose. A single bead held in your hand, like a "worry stone," would also work.

There are any number of factors that might influence your decision about what beads to use and how you design your strand. As for size, make sure the beads are large enough that you can hold them between your fingers one at a time. Spacers between the larger beads, usually in the form of seed beads, also help with handling. You'll want a bead that feels soothing to the touch; not too heavy or too lightweight. Choose beads that have a pleasing appearance or texture. Be open to using all kinds of materials, such as pearl, crystal, clay, wood, or bone.

You can choose from a variety of beads whose shapes or colors hold special meaning or significance. For example, to pray for your family you might want shapes that remind you of their personalities or colors that bring to mind each individual's particular favorite. You may have a preference for a bead that summons you to a prayer of gratitude. Another bead on your string could prompt you to refresh a promise made to God.

Fingering the beads in their designated order can become a discipline that keeps you faithful in your prayer life. Their presence in your hand encourages you to continue praying, even though you may not feel like it. They also connect your experience of prayer to the physical world, so that you acknowledge God's presence in a tactile way.

Now Begin

For this prayer, you will need a bead or string of beads and a partner. Begin with one or two minutes of silence, encouraging yourself to develop a listening heart. Theophan the Recluse advises us to "let your mind descend into your heart." As we bring our conscious attention to the depth of our hearts, we enter into communion with God.

Sit calmly with a pure heart. When Jesus told his followers "Blessed are the pure in heart, for they will see God" (Matt. 5:8), he was asking people to allow their souls to be transparent to God, and to adopt an attitude of genuine trust and goodness. Of course, a pure heart doesn't come naturally for most of us but is instead created by some sudden transformation, or by years of discipline and struggle. Either way, it is ultimately the work of the Holy Spirit in our lives. So, as best you can, ready yourself to listen to your heart, growing keenly aware of God's presence surrounding you.

Hold your bead or string of beads in your hands in whatever way is comfortable for you. Quiet yourself inside and out. Remain in this position for a minute or longer. Once you are ready to proceed, close your eyes. Place an empty hand on your stomach and the other (the one holding the beads) on your chest. Take three deep breaths, pausing between breaths. Inhale slowly so your diaphragm expands. Exhale slowly, so your stomach contracts, imagining that your belly button is touching your spine. Deep, slow breathing helps you calm down and focus on this time with God.

Then ask yourself, *Since I last prayed, when did I feel my heart awakening?* Pause in stillness for one more minute to answer the question. If you are praying alone, adapt the instructions in the next paragraphs as needed.

Open your eyes, and with your partner take two minutes per person to describe when and how you felt your heart awakening. Remember—1-2-2-1: you'll share one minute of silence, then allow two minutes for the first person to talk, then two minutes for the second person to talk. When you finish, sit together in silence. After the quiet settles between you again, continue.

Now, exchange beads and hold your partner's bead or string of beads to your heart. If you are alone, hold your own beads to your heart. Spend one more minute in prayer for your partner (or for yourself if you are alone). Close your eyes and picture your heart fully awakened. What does it look like to be fully alive? In this time of prayer with another, picture your prayer partner's face. Hold hands if you wish. Silently lift up a prayer of thanksgiving.

When you are ready, return the bead or string of beads to your partner and give him or her some sign of appreciation and care, such as a hug or a kind word. If you are praying alone, give yourself a hug.

Some Things to Think About

There are many other ways you can use beads as a tool for prayer. I have prayed with both the Celtic rosary and Anglican prayer beads. Make a string of seven and pray the seven fruits of the Spirit: love, joy, peace, patience, kindness, gentleness, and self-control. Hold the first bead while you pray for love, the second while you pay for joy, and so forth. As a variation, you can contemplate the nature of each fruit of the spirit.

Make a string of ten beads and pray the Ten Commandments. Use the same string each evening as a sign of gratitude, naming ten things for which you are thankful. Or use them to pray for ten people or needs, one for each bead.

Repetitio mater studiorum . . . that is, "Repetition is the mother of learning." It can also be the way into a deeper relationship with God. As these prayers are repeated and the beads are moved through your fingers, may the prayers ignite the embers of contemplation and mystical union in your soul.

Questions for Reflection

1.   Have you ever used beads in your prayer practices? If so, how and when?

2.   Imagine you are making a set of beads for yourself. What kinds and colors would you choose? What or who would each bead represent? How and when would you use them?

Other Resources to Continue Your Journey

Janet Coles and Robert Budwig, *The Book of Beads* (New York: Simon and Schuster, 1990). This text is for serious bead people. You'll learn about the making and history of beads from around the globe. The volume is beautifully done and very educational.

Anglican prayer beads are available from Our Lady of New Glastonbury, P.O. Box 1017, Anacortes, WA 98221–1017. Composed of thirty-three beads (the number of years Jesus walked this earth), this form of prayer combines a sense of Christ's physical presence with a Celtic view of the sacredness of all creation. You can order the beads along with the instructional book from the hermitage of Our Lady of New Glastonbury.

You can order beads and supplies to create your own unique set from www.shipwreck-beads.com. To begin, I suggest using 8mm glass beads and Rocaille seed beads. You can also order a cross or heart pendant for the tail. Silk thread packets, with the needle already attached, are available from www.rings-things.com.

Praying the Rosary

The three major variations of the Western Christian bead prayers of the rosary are the Franciscan Crown; the Bridgettine; and the Rosary of the Joyful, Sorrowful and Glorious Mysteries. This last is also called the Rosary of the Seven Sorrows and continues to be the most popular today.

How did this string of beads we call the rosary get its name? Thomas of Contimpre of the Western Church seems to be the first, around 1250, to call this a rosary—*rosarium maning,* or rose garden. Perhaps he felt that we most truly enter into the spirit of the prayer beads when we enter it as a rose garden, with its white roses of joy, red roses of sorrow, and yellow roses of glory. We contemplate the thorns and the red blood and find peace in the joy of the garden. The moments we spend with a rosary are moments spent in a garden of love.

The form of the rosary, as we know it today, dates back to the late fifteenth century, when a version attributed to Saint Dominic was popularized by the Dominican teacher Alan de La Roche. The standard rosary holds fifty beads (five sets of ten, called *decades*), as well as five story beads, called *mysteries,* placed between sets. Praying the rosary involves cycling around the string of beads, repeating specific prayers and contemplating a new mystery at each set of beads. If you wish to pray the entire rosary in one sitting, you will need to travel around the necklace of beads three times (which takes thirty to forty-five minutes). It is more common to pray five mysteries on any given day (which takes about ten to fifteen minutes). General practice is to meditate on the "glorious mysteries" on Sundays and Wednesdays; the "joyful mysteries" on Mondays and Saturdays; the "sorrowful mysteries" on Tuesdays and Fridays; and the "mysteries of light" on Thursdays..

It was on my way home from Rome in 2002 that I read in the paper that there were five new decades being added to the rosary. I was excited to find that they broadened contemplation on Christ's public ministry between his baptism and his passion. Set between the first joyful mysteries and the second sorrowful mysteries, they are the "mysteries of light." The title for these "luminous" mysteries is drawn from Jesus' words, "As long as I am in the world, I am the light of the world" (John 9:5).

THE FOUR TYPES OF MYSTERY

1. Joyful mysteries (Mondays and Saturdays)
   - The Annunciation: The archangel Gabriel tells Mary she is to give birth to Jesus. (Luke 1:26–38)
   - The Visitation: Mary visits her cousin Elizabeth, pregnant with John the Baptist. (Luke 1:39–56)
   - The Nativity: Jesus is born. (Luke 2:1–20)
   - The Presentation: Jesus is taken to the temple. (Luke 2:22–38)
   - The finding of the Child: Jesus in the temple. (Luke 2:41–52)
2. Mysteries of light (Thursdays)
   - Jesus' baptism in the Jordan. (Matt. 3:13–17)
   - Jesus' self-manifestation at the wedding of Cana. (John 2:1–11)

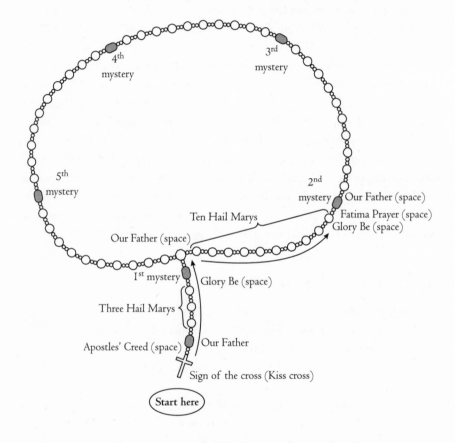

4th
mystery

3rd
mystery

5th
mystery

2nd
mystery

Our Father (space)

Ten Hail Marys

Fatima Prayer (space)
Glory Be (space)

Our Father (space)

1st mystery

Glory Be (space)

Three Hail Marys

Our Father

Apostles' Creed (space)

Sign of the cross (Kiss cross)

Start here

The Rosary

- Jesus' proclamation of the Kingdom of God. (Mark 1:14–15)
- Jesus' transfiguration. (Luke 9:28–36)
- Jesus' institution of the Eucharist. (Matt. 26:26–30)

3. Sorrowful mysteries (Tuesdays and Fridays)

- The Agony in the Garden: Jesus prays in the garden of Gethsemane. (Matt. 26:36–56)
- The Scourging: The scourging at the pillar. (Matt. 27:15–26)
- The Crowning with Thorns. (Matt. 27:27–31)
- The Carrying of the Cross: Jesus carries the cross. (Matt. 27:32)
- The Crucifixion: The crucifixion and death of Jesus. (Matt. 27:33–61)

4. Glorious mysteries (Sundays and Wednesdays)

- The Resurrection: Jesus rises from the dead on the third day. (Matt. 28:1–15)
- The Ascension: The ascension of Jesus into heaven. (Matt. 28:16–20).
- The Descent of the Holy Spirit: The Spirit descends at the observance of Pentecost. (Acts 2:1–41).
- The Assumption: Mary is taken into heaven (this is an ancient church tradition, but there is no reference to it in the Bible).
- The Coronation: The crowning of Mary as queen of heaven (again, this is an ancient tradition, believed to be drawn from Rev. 12:1).

Remember, when you pray the rosary, to meditate on the mysteries of the story of Jesus instead of focusing your attention on reciting the Hail Marys. Repeating the Hail Marys serves to ensure that you take time to contemplate the mysteries remembered. It's as if you were taking the hand of Christ and walking through his final days with him and his mother, Mary. She, so close to him, had a privileged view.

These are the recited prayers you use in the rosary:

276 *The Sign of the Cross*

In the name of the Father and of the Son and of the Holy Spirit. Amen.
(Kissing the cross is optional.)

The Apostles' Creed

I believe in God, the Father almighty, creator of heaven and earth

I believe in Jesus Christ, his only Son, our Lord. He was conceived by the
power of the Holy Spirit and born of the Virgin Mary. He suffered
under Pontius Pilate, was crucified, died, and was buried. He descended
to the dead. On the third day he rose again. He ascended into heaven, and
is seated at the right hand of the Father. He will come again to judge the
living and the dead.

I believe in the Holy Spirit, the holy catholic Church, the communion of
saints, the forgiveness of sins, the resurrection of the body, and the life
everlasting. Amen.

The Our Father (Lord's Prayer)

Our Father who art in heaven
hallowed be thy name;
thy kingdom come;
thy will be done on earth as it is in heaven.
Give us this day our daily bread,
and forgive us our trespasses
as we forgive those who trespass against us;
and lead us not into temptation,
but deliver us from evil. Amen.

The Hail Mary

Hail Mary, full of grace; the Lord is with you: blessed are you among women, and blessed is the fruit of your womb, Jesus. Holy Mary, Mother of God, pray for us sinners, now and at the hour of our death. Amen.

The Glory Be (Also known as the Gloria Patri)

Glory be to the Father and to the Son and to the Holy Spirit, as it was in the beginning, is now, and ever shall be, world without end. Amen.

The Fatima Prayer (This prayer can be included or not.)

This addition comes from the nineteenth century, when the community felt Mary's presence and heard her voice reminding them to "do whatever he tells you" (John 2:5).

O Jesus, forgive us our sins, save us from the fires of hell. Lead all souls to heaven, especially those who are most in need of your mercy.

The Hail, Holy Queen

Hail, holy Queen, Mother of Mercy! Our life, our sweetness, and our hope! To you do we cry, poor banished children of Eve; to you do we send up our sighs, mourning and weeping in this valley of tears. Turn, then, most gracious Advocate, your eyes of mercy toward us; and after this our exile show unto us the blessed fruit of your womb, Jesus; O clement, O loving, O sweet Virgin Mary. Pray for us, O holy Mother of God. That we may be made worthy of the promises of Christ.

If you do not already own a rosary, you can purchase one at your local Catholic church or liturgical/bible bookstore. For beginners, or those who have difficulty remembering all the mysteries, see the list of resources for information on buying a beginner's rosary.

Now Begin

~

Beads are labeled in the illustration earlier in this chapter, to help you navigate your way around the rosary.

STEP ONE: To signal the beginning of this time for prayer, pray and make the sign of the cross while holding the crucifix pendant that hangs at the end of the tail in your dominant hand. As your hand moves from forehead to breast, from left shoulder to right, you acknowledge that you belong completely to God. You may pause and kiss the cross as an expression of your gratitude and love.

STEP TWO: Next, move your way up the tail of beads, using the first space, knot, or bead, depending on the design of your rosary, to express your faith by reciting the Apostles' Creed and the Our Father, followed on the next three beads by a trinity of Hail Marys as you petition God for faith, hope, and charity or love (one time for each bead). You can also use the prayer of the Eastern Christian tradition and easily substitute the Hail Marys with the Jesus Prayer: "Lord Jesus Christ, Son of the living God, have mercy on me a sinner." Another choice can be drawn from the reading of your daily scripture. You might choose Jesus' words to the woman who was healed in Matthew 9:22, "Take Heart, daughter; your faith has made you well"; or his words to his followers during a storm at sea, "Take Heart, it is I; do not be afraid." For a longer verse you could use Matthew 16:24: "If any want to become my followers, let them deny themselves and take up their cross and follow me."

STEP THREE: On the next space or knot before the last bead, sing or recite the Glory Be in praise of the Trinity.

STEP FOUR: The last bead of the tail, almost on the circle, is the first of the mystery beads (referring to the joyful, luminous, sorrowful, and glorious mysteries listed earlier), which tell the story of Christ beginning with the angel's appearance to Mary, as detailed in Luke 1:26–38, and ending with Mary's enthronement in heaven, as recorded in Revelation 12:1. Decide if you want to pray a complete rosary (four full times around the circle, including a new set of mysteries on each cycle), or select one set of mysteries to proceed once around the circle of beads. Meditate on the mystery that corresponds to the category you have chosen.

STEP FIVE: After the mystery bead, moving on to the circle, recite the Our Father, which forms in us the heart and mind of Christ.

STEP SIX: Now begin around the circle of beads. Each set of ten consecutive, usually identical beads is called a decade. Hold each bead in the first decade one by one as you recite ten Hail Marys, one for each bead.

STEP SEVEN: End each decade with the Glory Be and the Fatima Prayer. In summary, each phase of the rosary begins with a mystery bead, the Our Father, ten Hail Marys, the Glory Be, and the Fatima prayer. You circle one time to four times around the circle. If you are circling around the beads more than once, remember that the first mystery bead of the new cycle is at the base of the tail.

HAIL MARY!

We Protestants are only now beginning to regain an understanding and appreciation of the rosary, in part because we don't have an understanding of or appreciation for the concept of the enthronement of Mary. Indeed, the accepted scriptures of both Catholic and Protestant Christians are silent, except for the Revelation 12 text that speaks of "a woman clothed with the sun and moon under her feet, and on her head a crown of twelve stars," who gives birth to a son who is to be the ruler of all nations. Mostly, the belief in Mary's presence in heaven with Jesus is based on very old literature. It is believed that John, the friend to whom Jesus had entrusted his mother at his death, kept a home with Mary in Ephesus until her death and then recorded the story of Mary's ascension. In 431, the Church leaders in Ephesus recognized these writings as valid and declared Mary the *Theotokos*, the Mother of God.

I overcame my hesitation about Mary by thinking of it this way. If I were in a room and wanted to say something to the president of the United States, I would probably be pretty intimidated. But I would feel much more at ease telling his mother, who is present, what is on my mind and asking her to relay it to him for me. So too, asking Mary's favor is an act of humility. Besides, it worked for the wedding party in Cana, when Jesus changed the water into wine because his mother asked him to. If you still feel uneasy about using Mary in the prayer, that's OK. Simply substitute that prayer with the Jesus Prayer or another.

STEP EIGHT: Pray a Hail, Holy Queen as you conclude. The end of your prayer time may come after you have made one circle of the beads, praying one set of the mysteries, or after praying all four circles of the beads with all four sets of mysteries.

Some Things to Think About

In the Western Church, the beads were first introduced as a formal act of devotional prayer in the sixth century by Benedict of Nursia. The 150 beads were employed to keep track of the memorization process of the 150 psalms that the community prayed each week. For some, committing the psalms to memory was too hard, and so these individuals substituted the psalms with 150 recitations of the Lord's Prayer, called *Paters,* instead. The beads, in that early time, became known as the *Pater noster* (Latin: *pater* = father; *noster* = our), and the individual prayed ten recitations of the Lord's Prayer with each decade.

Some Christians started saying the Gloria Patri in the third century, but it wasn't until the sixth century that it was officially adopted for the rosary. In the seventh century, the "Psalter of Mary" (now designated the Hail Mary), replaced the Our Father for each of the 150 beads. The incorporation of this prayer with Mary served the same purpose as the Lord's Prayer before it, offering the person memorizing the 150 psalms a break. Taken from the gospel of Luke, chapter 1, the welcomed interruption began: "(Hail) Mary full of grace. The Lord is with you." In the eighth century, the phrase "Blessed are you among women and blessed is the fruit of your womb" was added; in the sixteenth century came the addition of "Holy Mary, Mother of God, pray for us sinners now and at the hour of our death." A more recent addition to the ever-evolving beads came in 1917, when three children in Spain claimed that Mary appeared to them. The Church's response was to add the Fatima Prayer. In 2002 the Mysteries of Light were added. From this long evolution, with a few other twists and turns not mentioned here, the beads come to Christians today.

Questions for Reflection

1. Reflect on your experience of the rosary. When and where might you employ its use?
2. If this was your first time praying the rosary, what surprised, delighted, or hampered you?

Other Resources to Continue Your Journey

Basil M. Pennington, *Praying by Hand: Rediscovering the Rosary as a Way of Prayer,* (New York: HarperCollins, 1985). Wisdom from a Trappist monk who knows his stuff; you'll learn about the history and use of the rosary and it will add meaning to your prayers.

Wayne Weible, narrator, *Pray the Rosary,* VHS videocassette (Orleans, Mass.: Paraclete Press, n.d.). Here is a video that tells you about the rosary and then invites you to participate with the congregation to pray it. It is a bit dry but helps you visualize the community process.

Our Lady's Rosary Makers, 4611 Poplar Level Rd., Louisville, KY 40213. You can become a member of Our Lady's Rosary Makers. Visit their Website, www.ourladysrosarymakers.org, and you can help make and distribute rosaries affordably.

For beginners, I heartily recommend the "How to Pray the Rosary" rosary from Autom. Each mystery bead is labeled with three remembrances (one for each category). In addition, the rosary comes with a wallet-size card of simple directions and a pamphlet of full instructions. Contact (800) 521–2914 or automonline.com.

Chaplet of Seven: Covenant Chaplet

Thoughts Before You Begin

Numerous forms of prayer beads developing today are variations on the rosary prayer. These beads are called *chaplets,* and the primary prayer we use is the covenant prayer. The term *chaplet*—drawn from the word *chapel,* which means a place of worship or house of God—designates the beads themselves but also the prayers that accompany them. I designed the covenant chaplet for myself, and I share it here with you.

It is a chaplet of seven sevens; the circular string holds seven consecutive petition beads (like the Hail Mary beads in the rosary) in between seven "covenant" beads (like the rosary's mystery beads), in this case scallop shell beads; or you can use a larger oblong bead. The scallop is an ancient symbol for the grace of baptism and is also the symbol for Saint James the Greater, evangelist, first martyred apostle, and the patron saint of pilgrimage. This symbol holds special personal and spiritual significance for me, but if you choose you may replace the scallop with another meaningful symbol, such as an ichthys (fish).

Here are the prayers and petitions you recite in the chaplet:

The Lord's Prayer (presented earlier in this chapter)
The Apostles' Creed (presented earlier in this chapter)
The Gloria Patri (also earlier in this chapter)
The Petition

> O Lord, forgive what I have been,
> sanctify what I am,
> and order what I shall be. Amen.

CHAPLET COVENANT PRAYER

The covenant prayer was originally published in 1663 by Richard Alleine, a Puritan. In 1753, John Wesley popularized it among Methodists, who used it yearly at the New Year's Eve Watchnight Covenant Service, to renew their commitment to God's will and work in their lives. For our use, here I've adapted the version from the 1780 worship book.

First Covenant

Kneel or be seated, head bowed:

> Jesus, I am on my knees to say
> that I accept you as the way to new life
> and that I am ready to make a covenant with you.

Second Covenant

> I come just as I am. Now, with all that is within me.

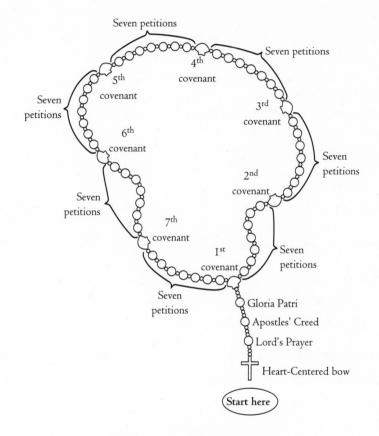

Seven petitions

Seven petitions

4th covenant

5th covenant

Seven petitions

3rd covenant

6th covenant

Seven petitions

2nd covenant

Seven petitions

Seven petitions

7th covenant

1st covenant

Seven petitions

Gloria Patri

Apostles' Creed

Lord's Prayer

Heart-Centered bow

Start here

Chaplet of Seven: Covenant Chaplet

Third Covenant

I accept you as the driving force in my life.
I stop trying to do it on my own, and count on your power.

Fourth Covenant

I stop living as though I have all the answers, and allow you to guide me.
I stop doing what I want to do, and begin living your will for my life.
I am no longer my own, but yours.

Fifth Covenant

Put me to what you will, rank me with whom you will.
Put me to doing, put me to suffering.
Let me be employed by you, or laid aside for you.

Sixth Covenant

Let me be full, let me be empty.
Let me have all things, let me have nothing.

Seventh Covenant

I freely and heartily yield all things to your pleasure and disposal.

Now Begin

Holding the cross at the end of the tail in your hand, begin by holding it to your chest and making a heart-centered bow in the name of the Trinity: "Father, Son, and Holy Spirit" or "Creator, Redeemer, and Sustainer." Follow the next three beads to pray the Lord's Prayer, the Apostles' Creed, and the Gloria Patri. Move up to the first covenant bead and pray the first prayer of the covenant prayer. Finger the next seven smaller beads, moving individually from one bead to the next in sequence, while repeating the petition. At the second covenant bead, pray the second prayer of the covenant. Again, pray the petition on the following seven beads. Continue in this manner until you arrive back at the tail.

When you reach the tail, work your way down to the cross pendant, repeating the petition three times, once for each tail bead. At the cross pendant, say this closing prayer:

And now, O glorious and blessed God,
Father, Son, and Holy Spirit
    [hold the pendant to your heart center and bow],
You are mine, and I am yours. So be it.
And the covenant that I made on earth, let it be ratified in heaven. Amen.

For the chaplet, I chose the petition, "O Lord, forgive what I have been . . . ," whose source is unknown, because it expresses my heartfelt desire to grow into Christ. It is also easy to remember. Another repetitive phrase that you might use is, "O God, make speed to save us. O Lord, make haste to help us," or you might choose to change the language to a singular form if you are praying alone ("O God, make speed to save *me*. O Lord, make haste to help *me*"). Other choices are "Be still and know that I am God," or "My soul for God in silence waits." You can even replace it with the trinitarian doxology or Gloria Patri. Whatever petition you use, the repetition of the vocal prayers will begin to function as a powerful centering device, freeing your mind to reflect on the covenant. The purpose of this method is to get past the surface meaning of the words and penetrate to the heart of their deepest meaning—and to the heart of the person praying.

How to Make a Chaplet of Seven

Supplies:

1 cross or pendant
1 center pendant or covenant bead
6 covenant beads (these look and feel different from the 52 petition beads)
52 petition beads (6mm or 8mm)
68 seed beads

STEP ONE: Begin by making the tail. Measure four inches from the end of the cord and place a piece of tape over the thread.

STEP TWO: Thread the cord through the top of the center piece, in this instance a shell.

STEP THREE: String three seed beads and then one larger (6mm or 8mm) bead. Repeat this two more times to make a total of three sets. End with three seed beads.

STEP FOUR: Run the cord through the eye of the cross or pendant.

STEP FIVE: Run the cord back through all the beads just strung, back to the center piece.

STEP SIX: Now make the main loop of the chaplet. On the cord, place one seed bead and then one larger bead. Repeat this pattern until you have seven seed and larger beads. End with a seed bead.

STEP SEVEN: Place on the cord one covenant bead.

STEP EIGHT: Repeat step seven until you have seven sets of seven. The center pendant counts as one of the seven covenant beads.

The chaplet of seven can be prayed in a variety of ways. In place of the covenant prayer, you can pray any seven of the fruits of the spirit: love, joy, peace, patience, kindness, generosity, faithfulness, gentleness, and self-control (Gal. 5:22). Pray the beatitudes (Matt., chapter 5), or the seven last words of Christ (Luke, chapters 22 and 23).

You might pray the names and descriptions of Jesus:

1. Emmanuel, meaning "God is with us" (Matt. 1:23)
2. Child with Mary (Matt. 2:11)
3. Mother Hen (Matt. 23:37 and Luke 13:34)
4. Healer (Matt. 9:2–8)
5. Rabbi, meaning teacher (John 3:2)
6. The Way (John 14:6)
7. Light of the World (John 8:12)

You can also use the chaplet to pray a biblical version of the scenes of Jesus' life, much like the mysteries of the passion. As with the rosary, begin with the tail and on the three beads pray in sequence the Lord's Prayer, Apostles' Creed, and Gloria Patri.

Make your way around the beads *four* times, once for each category: joyful, luminous, sorrowful, and glorious moments. Recite or meditate on the twenty-eight biblical texts, one for each covenant bead, which tell the story of Christ beginning with the angel's appearance to Mary and ending with the Spirit on the Day of Pentecost. Use any scripture verse you choose to prayerfully repeat in place of the petition.

290 ## THE CHAPLET MOMENTS OF JESUS' LIFE

1. Joyful Moments
   - Jesus' birth is announced to Mary by the archangel Gabriel. (Luke 1:26–38)
   - Jesus' father, Joseph, is assured by an angel in a dream. (Matt. 1:18–25)
   - Jesus' mother, Mary, visits her cousin Elizabeth, pregnant with John the Baptist. (Luke 1:39–56)
   - Jesus is born. (Luke 2:1–7)
   - Jesus is announced by angels, and shepherds and wise men worship Jesus. (Luke 2:8–20 and Matt. 2:1–12)
   - Jesus is presented and blessed in the temple. (Luke 2:22–38)
   - Jesus is found in the temple. (Luke 2:41–52)

2. Luminous Moments
   - Jesus is baptized by John in the Jordan River. (Matt. 3:13–17)
   - Jesus is tempted in the wilderness. (Matt. 4:1–11)
   - Jesus' first miracle at the wedding of Cana. (John 2:1–12)
   - Jesus teaches, performs miracles, and heals the sick. (Matt. 5–7 and John 4:46–6:21)
   - Jesus' proclamation of the Kingdom of God. (Mark 1:14–15)
   - Jesus' transfiguration. (Luke 9:28–36)
   - Jesus' institution of the Eucharist. (Matt. 26:26–30)

3. Sorrowful Moments
   - Jesus prays in the garden of Gethsemane. (Mark 14:32–42)
   - Jesus receives a crown of thorns and is scourged at the pillar. (Matt. 27:15–31)

- Jesus is denied by Peter. (Mark 14:66-72; John 18:15–18, 25–27)
- Jesus carries the cross. (Matt. 27:32)
- Jesus delegates the care of Mary, his mother, to John. (John 19:25–27)
- Jesus is crucified and dies. (Matt. 27:33–61)
- Jesus is laid in the tomb. (John 19:38–42)

4. Glorious Moments
   - Jesus rises from the dead on the third day. (Matt. 28:1–15)
   - Jesus appears to Mary Magdalene. (John 20:11–18)
   - Jesus appears to the disciples. (John 20:19–23; Luke 24:36–49)
   - Jesus on the walk to Emmaus. (Luke 24:13–35)
   - Jesus ascends into heaven. (Acts 1:6–11)
   - The commissioning of the disciples. (Matt. 28:16–20)
   - The Spirit descends on the day of Pentecost. (Acts 2:1–41)

◇　◇　◇

The prayer beads (rosary, chaplet, or whatever form you use) are a time-tested spiritual tradition founded on solid rock. These paths to God are one more way to be in constant and intentional remembrance of the cross we are called to carry. The fifteenth-century author of the classic *The Imitation of Christ*, Thomas à Kempis (1380–1471), makes the point again: "We must . . . make diligent search, both within and without, to leave nothing inordinate unreinforced in us, as fully as our frailty permits. Jesus has many lovers of his kingdom of heaven, but he has few bearers of his cross."

The way to begin is to begin. Don't allow yourself to become distracted with such questions as "Am I accomplishing anything?" "Am I doing something meaningful?" When we pray with the beads, we come into God's presence in faith, and that is what we do with the beads. We don't pray to accomplish something, but to offer ourselves to God so that God might do something in us. As you continue to pray the rosary or chaplet, the reward is not your accomplishment, but a gift from God to you.

Questions for Reflection

1. What form of the chaplet did you employ? What petition did you use? Why did you make these particular choices?
2. The covenant prayer is powerful. What lines stood out in your reading? How were they meaningful to you?

Other Resources to Continue Your Journey

Order your own chaplet prayer beads containing seven strands of seven beads, either ready-made or in a kit for you to assemble prayerfully. Log onto www.spirit-works.org to request ordering information.

Joan Hutson, *Praying with Sacred Beads* (Liguori, Mo.: Liguori/Triumph, 2000). The prayers, visualizations, and meditations in this little book use a string of ten beads. You'll appreciate the many ways you can use beads in your prayers.

Praying with Mandalas

Just as the wheel encloses within itself what lies hidden within it, so also does the Holy Godhead enclose everything within itself without limitation, and it exceeds everything.

—HILDEGARD VON BINGEN, 1098–1179, GERMANY

Thoughts Before You Begin

Mandala is the Sanskrit word for center, wholeness, or circle. A mandala is a circular art form that encompasses a graphic and often symbolic pattern. The circle is one of the first shapes we learn to draw as children, and it continues to be a fundamental conceptual pattern of the mind throughout life. For instance, my wedding band represents my unity with my spouse. When I am in a circle with others, I sit facing them, thereby demonstrating equality and shared responsibility for the group. When we speak of "ever-widening circles," it indicates we are being welcoming and inclusive.

Contemplating the symbolism of the mandala with an artistic frame of mind can serve as a doorway to the creative part of ourselves by literally getting us out of our box. Think about it: most tables where we think and work, as well as the sheets of paper that cross our desks during the day, are rectangular. A circular pattern has a different flow and movement than square or angular patterns. The mandala helps us break through layers of meaning to awaken a deeper, mysterious connection to ourselves and therefore to God, in whose image we are made. So, when I studied mandalas and thought about circular artistic expressions, I began to see how this form of art could be a tool for prayer.

My use of mandalas to facilitate prayer began when I was directing a group retreat. We arranged ourselves to sit in a circle denoting a sacred action of equality among persons and equal commitment to the process. First, we individually wrote a prayer to God ("Dear God . . ."; see the chapter "A Journal of Prayer"). Then I gave each individual a paper plate along with squeeze bottles filled with colored sand— yellow, blue, green, red, orange—and invited them to create a design that expressed their prayer. In this prayer process, we worked from the verbal to the visual, allowing individuals to process information more completely by using both their spatial and visual capabilities.

I explained to them that the circle is universally supportive of meditation, healing, and prayer. In Christian art, the mandala has been a symbol of wholeness, encompassing eternity. This art form is more than an image created by our God-given imagination or seen with our eyes. As a symbol that represents eternity, it can be used as a road map to explore our relationships with ourselves, each other, and God. It can be prayer.

From her memoirs and voluminous correspondence, we know that Hildegard was the tenth child in her family and was dedicated to the Church as a tithe. At the age of eight, she entered a small convent near Bingen. Hildegard was a prophet, mystic, and genius of her day, a notable herbalist and healer, composer and poet, writer and artist. She created many beautiful mandalas to celebrate her visions and experiences, express her beliefs, and communicate her understanding of God to others. She declared herself and her inspired works to be a mere vessel for the Divine Word.

The most beautiful mandala I've seen was at "Mary's church," the Notre Dame Cathedral in Paris. I still remember the first time I saw it: the West Rose Window. I let my eyes adjust to the dim medieval lighting of the church as I stood in the back, pausing to take in the scene before me. The rosette consisted of an infinite number of small pieces of brilliantly fired glass, forming an exquisite whole. Radiating streams of light flowing through stained glass, glancing off the floor and pews. My eyes then followed the slender columns up to the window and there she was: the Virgin in her rich reds and blues. Her eyes settled upon mine and I caught my breath to take her in. Sitting in the cathedral's dimness, contemplating the light pouring through her inspired designs prompted a powerful experience—it was heavenly.

The West Rose Window of Notre Dame Cathedral

The architecture of Gothic cathedrals was designed during a terrible era of plagues and war. These great cathedrals gave people hope and stood as a reminder that God had not deserted them. Thirty minutes south of Paris is a second mandala that served people of the Middle Ages; this time it is not in the windows but upon the floor to be walked. By creating a labyrinth marked out on the floor of Chartres Cathedral, medieval Christians were able to take an on-the-spot pilgrimage to the Holy City of Jerusalem. (See the chapters "Prayer Labyrinth" and "Pilgrimage.")

The essence of a pilgrimage is evident: motion toward a center. Intoning prayers, these medieval pilgrims walked toward the center, symbolic of the dwelling of God.

Other mandalas also come to mind. Sand mandalas, created by Tibetan Buddhist monks, hold intricate patterns and illustrations of religious significance that are used for meditation. The design is ritually prepared over a period of days and then, when complete, blown away to represent the impermanence of life. The sand is blessed throughout the process. The sand mandala, as a prayer tool, aids the monks in achieving what they call enlightenment.

I was born and raised in Pennsylvania, where religious symbols of the Amish community are part of the scenery, popularly sewn into handmade quilts. These bright patterns and geometric forms, known as hex signs, were used by the ancestors of our Pennsylvania German settlers on birth certificates, furniture, pottery, textile, and so on. Many came originally from religious motif designs, the two main patterns being the sun and the tree of life.

The Amish Sun Pattern   **The Amish Tree of Life Pattern**

Powerful symbolism is seen in the sacred circles of Native American paintings, weavings, sand paintings, and even jewelry. I have one such necklace made by the men of the tribe of the Choctaw Indians during a United Methodist conference in Oklahoma. Hanging from its beaded chain is a meticulously designed and beaded circular pendant, which I wear in religious services over my alb as I would my cross. It continues to be one of the finest thank-you gifts I've ever received.

Prior to the Christian influence on the Celts, known Celtic artwork consisted of geometrical patterns such as spirals, key patterns, and step patterns called plaitwork. Plaitwork, which is a pattern of interwoven (but unknotted) cords, is the earliest form of knotwork. With the coming of the Christian era came the knotwork that we know today. By breaking the plait's cords and reattaching them, knotwork patterns were derived. The first examples of this practice came in the early 700s, during the appearance of the Book of Lindisfarne, the earliest illuminated manuscript featuring knotwork patterns. Besides knotwork, the Christian Celts also added human, plant, and animal forms to their decorations.

Celtic Knot

In *Brigit's Feast*, Frank Mills writes of the symbolism behind the Celtic circular knot designs: "The interlaced patterns with their unbroken lines symbolize humankind's pilgrimage, both as a quest to return to our divine source and our spiritual growth as we move along in the quest. The pattern is to be mentally unraveled, which, while occupying the mind with a repetitive task, creates a deeper concentration enabling us 'to see.' In this it is akin to the use of a mantra or rosary beads."

Now Begin

Creating a prayer mandala can be a rewarding prayer practice if you take the time to master a few simple guidelines. As Jung wrote, "When the self finds expression in such drawings, the unconscious reacts by enforcing an attitude of devotion to life." Creating a mandala is best performed with an attitude of reverence and respect. Honor your intuition and perception of your reality and your relationship with God.

The directions given here are not steps so much as guidelines to orient you to this prayer practice.

- *Decide how you want to do your mandala.* Will it be alone, or with others? A mandala can be created by an individual, a couple, or a group. Creating a group mandala can be a unifying experience in which individuals offer self-expression within a unified structure. Group mandalas take the form of quilts, rock and flower gardens, and even designs laid out on sandy beaches. For this mandala prayer, you can work alone.

- *Select your materials.* A mandala can be made with sand (as I have already described), as well as clay, paint, stones, charcoal, or cloth. The possibilities are limitless. Be spontaneous in your selection of color and form within the circle. To get started, I suggest you use a sheet of paper and colored pencils or crayons. Or make a copy of the mandala presented here and prayerfully color it as you feel called.

Mandala to Color

◆ *Give your mandala prayer attention and care.* Don't be afraid to create your own symbolic language. To enrich and clarify your prayer, make a list of your associations to shape, compass direction, texture, and number, as well as color. Your asso-

ciations are a reflection of who you are. They express your thoughts, feelings, intu-
itions, and even your physical sensations. Mindful of the symbols you select, you
learn to go deeper into your prayer and into the meaning of who you really are and
who God is within you. Decide what colors mean; does dark blue represent the
abyss and light blue tenderness? Do bird shapes represent freedom, and the sun
hope? Perhaps the spirals and circular motions depict your life's journey and a stair-
way or avenue to heaven.

  ◆ *Accept the mystery of the mandala.* You will never delve to the absolute bottom of
the meaning of your mandala prayer. This reflects our mysterious relationship with
God. Your prayer of colors and forms is a living process; it cannot be completely
understood or neatly categorized. But praying mandalas can give you contact with
the deeper wisdom and help you live out God's will for your life. Prayer with a mandala becomes a celebration of the gift of life itself, an opportunity and avenue to
grow in love with God.

Some Things to Think About

My first experience with a mandala was probably as a curious young girl looking
through a kaleidoscope. A later interest in mandalas developed out of a seminary
class where we were touching on the work of psychologist and Christian Carl Jung.
Jung became interested in the archetype while studying Eastern religion. He then
began to study the circular images that people created. At the age of thirty-eight,
Jung quit his academic university post and devoted his work to the inner life. He
kept a journal of his thoughts and dreams. Each morning he drew circular designs
in his journal.

  For Jung, the mandala was a "vessel" into which an individual could project
spontaneous expression of his or her inner spirit. Jung discovered that drawing

mandalas is spontaneous and untaught—an orderly natural pattern performed in much the same way in varied cultures. He used them to help individuals search for meaning, personal growth, and spiritual enrichment, thereby experiencing restoration. Jung saw the mandala as a symbol of hope, "a safe refuge of inner-reconciliation and wholeness."

Questions for Reflection

1. What mandalas are in your life? Can you find them in your children's refrigerator art, your jewelry, glassware, and home decorations? How about in your church sanctuary? Are they found in the architecture, the paintings, or the stained glass?
2. What colors, shapes, textures, numbers, or other symbolism did you choose for your mandala? What do the symbols represent for you?
3. How did your prayer grow or change as you created your mandala?

Other Resources to Continue Your Journey

Susanne F. Fincher, *Creating Mandalas, for Insight, Healing, and Self-Expression* (Boston and London: Shambhala, 1991). This book is a practical guide to creating a mandala. It introduces the history of mandalas in cultures all over the world.

Judith Cornell, *Mandala: Luminous Symbols for Healing* (Wheaton, Ill.: Quest Books, 1995). The author presents the art of the mandala as a dramatically empowering approach to well-being and self-knowledge. This book helps you understand mandalas and how to use them as a tool for exploring the meaning of your art work.

Monique Mandali (illustrator), *Everyone's Mandala Coloring Book, Vol. 1* (Santa Fe, N.Mex.: Mandalart Creations, 1991). Volumes 2 and 3 are just as intriguing. Each contains dozens of designed mandalas for you to pray, color, and paint to your heart's delight.

Hildegard Von Bingen, *11,000 Virgins: Chants for the Feast of St. Ursula* (music CD), France, harmonia mundi, performed by Anonymous 4. These four women, Johanna Maria Rose, Susan Hellauer, Ruth Cunningham, and Marsha Genensky, use their astonishing vocal blend and technical virtuosity to offer this rendition of Hildegard's musical compositions. I use this marvelous CD as background music to inspire the prayers of my mandalas.

Sheila Sturrock, *Celtic Spirals and Other Designs* (East Sussex, U.K.: Guild of Master Craftsman, 2000). The author leads you step-by-step in the process of creating your own two-, three-, and four-ribbon spirals.

Jacob Zook, *Legendary Hex Signs* (Marina, Calif.: German Corner, n.d.). Zook, who is Pennsylvania Dutch, explains history, colors, hex signs, and their meaning, as well as hex stories. Order through German Corner on their Website, www.amishmarket.com.

Prayer Dance

You have turned my mourning into dancing; you have taken off my sackcloth and clothed me with joy, so that my soul may praise you and not be silent.

—PSALM 30:11

Thoughts Before You Begin

When praying, it is good to be reminded that humor and celebration are important and that playfulness has its place. As we learn to give ourselves permission to dance and laugh and experience the wisdom of foolishness, we return unconsciously to the full, unburdened breath of childhood. Sacred dance involves the whole person with all the bodily senses; it is an opportunity for full physical and sensory involvement to express our deepest passions and ultimate delights.

The prayer dance is a beautiful, spontaneous form of prayer in which the audience is God. It is as if God is saying to you, "My child, nothing could be more beautiful than you praying with your whole being from within your heart and soul." You don't have to be a trained dancer—or even be coordinated—to dance your prayers. In dance, we let go of self-pride and focus on expressing ourselves to God, no matter what we think we look like. Carla DeSola, the mother of sacred dance, wrote in her book *The Spirit Moves*, "How you look isn't important, what is important is how you feel as if God were feeling your prayer, not looking at your movements."

Why dance our prayers? Because dance communicates a unique language. Dance uses movements and gestures that free us to feel the Spirit within and draws us into the mysteries of the faith. It is a bridge between the visible and invisible worlds of the spirit, making us better able to praise God spontaneously and lovingly. Perhaps prayer dance's most important gift to us lies in its ability to unify us and make us whole by uniting our inward life with our outward expression.

The music begins, and with the body as instrument we respond to the movement of the Spirit and express these stirrings through dance. Through movement we gain a "sense-ability"; that is, we develop a spiritual sensitivity and creative consciousness through our attention to our physical senses. We grow more awake and energized. We develop a new bodily awareness and learn from our senses.

Dance is an invitation and gift from the creative Christ. As we allow ourselves the freedom to dance in prayer, we can experience a deepening spiritual awareness that makes us more responsive to God's voice. Prayer dance can be an act of obedience. It is us giving ourselves to God, a prayer of total surrender. In the end, it is God who leads the dance, and we follow.

Now Begin

Find or create a space for exploration away from competition or judgment. We do not all move alike and therefore we cannot compare ourselves to anyone else. Wear clothes that are loose fitting and comfortable to move in.

It is always a challenge to write choreography notes and illustrations that can be understood and translated into movement. These instructions are specific, simple, and dignified movements that are well within most individuals' ability. Of course, what is more important than the physical movements are the heartfelt intentions you bring to the prayer.

DANCING AND THE LORD'S PRAYER

Begin with this blessing:

May peace be in my mind, on my lips, and in my heart.

Bring your hands together, palm to palm with fingers spread and touching each other. With hands still together, palm to palm, slowly touch your forehead, lips, and heart, saying the words in the blessing as you touch each place.

Then, cross your arms over your chest and fold in a reverent bow from the hips. Hold a moment and gradually unfold to again stand straight.

Now pray the Lord's Prayer, with verse or music, while using the dance movements described here and illustrated on the next page.

STEP ONE: Our Father, who art in heaven . . . [Raise arms upward in an
               arc or "V" position.]

STEP TWO: . . . holy is your name. [Kneel down; bow your head; bring
               arms with palms facing in, in front of your chest, and bow
               low.]

STEP THREE: Your kingdom come. [Sweep right hand boldly outward
               across body and upward, palm up.]

STEP FOUR: Your will be done. [Repeat motion with left hand.]

STEP FIVE: On earth as it is in heaven. [Turn palms down. With your
               arms extended and palms facing the earth, sweep your arms
               together in front of you; then uncross them and return them
               in front of you.]

STEP SIX: Give us this day our daily bread . . . [Cup your hands in front
               of you. Bring your hands up and touch your mouth.]

STEP SEVEN: . . . forgive us our sins . . . [Raise your hands over your head
               and let them flow down over your shoulders, as in a washing
               movement.]

STEP EIGHT: . . . as we forgive those who sin against us. [Open arms to
               your side and straighten your body.]

STEP NINE: Lead us not into temptation . . . [Place your right hand up in
               front of your head at eye level.]

STEP TEN: . . . but deliver us from evil . . . [Repeat motion with the left
               hand.]

STEP ELEVEN: . . . for yours is the kingdom . . . [Sweep the right arm, palm
               facing up, over your head.]

Step one

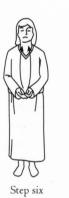

Step two

Steps three and four

Step five

Step six

Step seven

Fourteen-Step Dance

Step eight

Steps nine and ten

Steps eleven
and twelve

Step thirteen

Step fourteen

STEP TWELVE: . . . the power . . . [Repeat with the left arm.]

STEP THIRTEEN: . . . and the glory forever. [Swing both arms in a circular motion over your head.]

STEP FOURTEEN: Amen. [Bring your arms down and bend over from the hips.]

HAVA NAGILA CIRCLE PRAYER DANCE

Dance forms and rituals take on the context of the cultural group. For instance, the stylized hand and arm movements of the Japanese and Egyptians seem subtle compared to the more vigorous athletic maneuvers of European folk dances.

The ancient ecstatic circle prayer dance arises from deep, spirit-filled emotion. The dance usually begins slowly and rhythmically and gradually increases in tempo and intensity as the dancers become caught up in the energy of the sound and motion. Circling is an ancient ritual that symbolizes the prayer of protection against evil. Therefore this could be appropriately danced around the family during or after a service of baptism, where those baptized take the vow to "renounce the spiritual forces of wickedness" and "reject the evil powers of this world."

A circle step could also be danced around the bride and groom, a semblance of the eastern Orthodox Christian tradition where the newly married couple circle the altar three times in the marriage ceremony. The guest(s) of honor—in this instance, the bride and groom—are placed in the center of the dancers.

Hava nagila, meaning "wake up with joyful heart!" is a well-known Hebrew folk song. The circle dance, called the *hora,* is used for joyous community celebrations such as festivals, weddings, and anniversaries. It invites participants to reach out and touch others and feel a lively bond. The dance proves to be contagious as other people join in. Even I quickly learned the *hora* step, and so can you. Information on obtaining the music is in the resource list.

Begin by forming a circle. Hold hands and move counterclockwise.

STEP ONE: With the right foot, step right.

STEP TWO: Cross the left foot behind the right foot.

STEP THREE: The right foot steps right again.

STEP FOUR: Hop on the right foot and swing the left foot in front of the right foot in a low kicking motion.

STEP FIVE: The left foot steps left.

STEP SIX: Hop on the left foot and swing the right foot in front of the left foot in a low kicking motion.

STEP SEVEN: Jump on both feet twice. Then begin all over again.

DANCE OF JESUS

In the mystical "dance of Jesus," described in the apocryphal second-century Acts of St. John, Jesus invites the disciples to move into a circle dance. This wonderful hymn is one of the earliest Christian rituals known. The ritual dance, used from the first to the fourth centuries, was done as part of the initiation of new disciples.

The verses of the song describe Jesus gathering his disciples around him before his passion and death. In this dance of reenactment one member, representing Jesus, stands in the middle of the circle as twelve others, representing the disciples, rhythmically dance around him.

I have no trouble imagining Jesus leading such a dance when placed in the context of what the gospels tell us about his spirit and the Hebrew culture at that time. In Matthew 11:16–17 Jesus says, "But to what will I compare this generation? It is like children sitting in the marketplaces and calling to one another, 'We played the flute for you, and you did not dance; we wailed, and you did not mourn.'" Jesus urges those who will listen to respond to life as children, to respond as fully human persons. To children, dancing comes as naturally as breathing. Jesus invites us to become a dancing people.

A slowed version of the circular hora step can be used by the twelve dancers. Or, with the dancers in a circle holding hands, each participant can do a simple step sideways with the right foot and then slide the left foot over to meet it, and continue this step-slide throughout the song. The twelve dancers in the circle all sing together while the Jesus figure in the middle is silent. The dancers then stop and remain holding hands in the circle as the Jesus figure sings the lines of her refrain. Here is a hymn that can be done in the sing-song fashion found in such childhood chants as "Little Sally Saucer," "Rain, Rain Go Away," or "Ring Around the Rosie":

> He gathered all of us together and said:
> Before I am delivered up to them,
> let us sing a hymn to the Father,
> and so go forth to that which lies before us.
> He asked us therefore to make a ring,
> holding one another's hands.
> And himself, standing in the midst, said:
> Answer "Amen" to me.
> He began then to sing a hymn and to say:
> "Glory be to thee, Father."
> And we, going about in the ring, answered him,
> "Glory be to thee, Word: Glory be to thee, O Grace, Amen."
> I would be saved and I would save. Amen.

Grace dances. I will pipe; dance all of you.
I would mourn; lament all of you. Amen.
The whole world on high takes part in our dancing. Amen.
Whoever does not dance, does not know what will come to pass.
I will be united and I will unite. Amen.

Jesus sings in refrain:

I am a torch to you who behold me. Amen.
I am a mirror to you who perceive me. Amen.
I am a door to you who knocks to me. Amen.
I am a way to you who are a wayfarer. Amen.

At the completion of this dance, reenacting the mystical circle, the early Christian community held a "love feast," called an *agape*, and participated in the custom of sharing the "kiss of peace."

Some Things to Think About

The people of God have always danced: to express joy, sorrow, love, and fear; at sunrise and sunset; at birth and even death. The Bible's first reference to dance is in Exodus 15:20–21, when the prophet Miriam used her timbrel and did a dance of thanksgiving following the crossing of the Red Sea.

The Hebrews wrote psalms, prayer songs that were danced as people approached the temple on high holy days, celebrating their trust that they were God's chosen people: "Sing to the Lord a new song, in the assembly of the faithful. . . . Let them praise his name with dancing, making melody to him with tambourine and lyre!" (Ps. 149:1,3). Many of the psalms invite dance in praise to God: "You have turned my mourning into dancing" (Ps. 30:11); "Clap your hands, all you peoples; shout to God with loud songs of joy" (Ps. 47:1); "Singers and dancers alike say 'All my springs are in you'" (Ps. 87:7); "Praise him with tambourine and dance" (Ps. 150:4).

Although the best remembered instances of dance are by individuals such as the prophet Miriam leading the Israelites and King David dancing before the ark of the covenant, (2 Sam. 6:5), in general dance was a communal act of worship or celebration. Dancing expressed the collective well-being of the community and accompanied every joyous occasion in the Israelite's life as an expression of being moved by the transcendent power of God. References beyond the psalms are found in Judges 11:34, Ecclesiastes 3:4, Lamentations 5:15, and Jeremiah 31:13.

Historically, the Church has always prayed to God through movement in ritual gesture and expressive bodily moves. "In him (God) we live and move and have our being" (Acts 17:28). In Romans 12:1 and I Corinthians 6:19, Christians are reminded that they are to use their bodies to glorify God. Early Christians, believing in the afterlife, borrowed Greek and Roman rituals, gave them new interpretations, and wove them into the Christian story. Sacred dance employed rounds or processions to celebrate the anniversary of a martyr's death.

Perhaps it was because the dance became too boisterous, or because of Augustine's harsh teachings about the body, or the later ruling by Gregory the Great officially expelling dance from worship—for a combination of reasons, dance was eventually moved outside the Church proper to the margins of religious observance, much as the wedding dances today are no longer held as part of the more formal religious service but as part of a later informal reception. Yet the celebration after the formal service is an essential part of the total rite.

A most vivid example of the rich historical meaning of dance is found in the iconography of the Eastern Church. It may have been while gazing upon a picture of angels and blessed souls in paradise that Basil, the fourth-century bishop of Caesarea, wrote, "Could there be anything more blessed than to imitate on earth the ring-dance of the angels, and at dawn to raise our voices in prayer and by hymns and songs to glorify the rising Creator?"

It is not surprising to learn that eighth-century traditional Christmas carols were part of the folk art and were meant to be danced. By the eleventh century, as a design for worshipful movement and dance, the labyrinth was placed in the floor of many a great European cathedral. On Easter in France's Auxerre Cathedral, worshippers were led in a long chain dance by a senior leader of the congregation. In this three-step rhythm, they recalled the passion of Christ, his death, and his burial and resurrection. Simultaneously a ball, symbolizing Christ the Sun, was passed from dancer to dancer in a do-si-do fashion.

Once again, liturgical dance is being used in community worship. Its most recent revival began in 1960, with the first "Consultation on the Dance," sponsored by the National Council of Churches at the Riverside Church in New York City.

Questions for Reflection

1. Most of us have a history of dance in our own lives. I cringe remembering my first high school dance, and I still swoon when I think of Audrey Hepburn dancing with George Peppard in *Breakfast at Tiffany's.* Take some time to think back on your own experiences—for better or worse.

2. Through dance we can gain a new *sense*-ability. What did you sense about your relationship with God as you moved through the instructions in A Blessing and the Lord's Prayer?

3. Both ancient dances, the hora circle prayer dance and the dance of Jesus, call for a community of dancers. What do you feel draws people to these dances? Why are you drawn, or not drawn, to these dances?

Other Resources to Continue Your Journey

Celeste Snowber Schroeder, *Embodied Prayer* (Liguori, Mo.: Triumph Books, n.d.). This book has energizing and enjoyable exercises in embodied prayer for both individual and community prayer. Schroeder weaves together scripture, theology, and life experiences that will deepen your prayer life.

JoAnne Ticker and Susan Freeman, *Torah in Motion: Creating Dance Midrash* (Van Nuys, Calif.: Heaven Fire Productions, 1997). Both experienced in prayer, dance, and Judaic studies, the authors tell the historic stories from the Torah through dance. This is an e-book available on the Web. Read this book along with watching the instructional video *Minding the Temple of the Soul: Balancing Body, Mind and Spirit Through Traditional Jewish Prayer, Movement and Meditation* by Tamar Frankiel and Judy Greenfeld, and you'll be on your way to dancing your prayers.

Lu Bellamak, *Non-Judgmental Sacred Dance: Simple Ways to Pray Through Dance* (Austin, Tex.: Sharing Company, 1984). Printed in the 1980s but still available, this little book of thirty-one pages takes you right to the heart of employing dance in your own personal prayer life.

A Closing Benediction

Do not worry about anything, but in everything by prayer and supplication with thanksgiving let your requests be made known to God. And the peace of God, which surpasses all understanding, will guard your heart and your minds in Christ Jesus.

—PHILIPPIANS 4:6–7

Why do we pray? For two reasons. First, we need to seek, and we want to be found. In prayer, nothing is hidden—all we need to know is available to us. All the wisdom and guidance we seek is right before our eyes. Second, as we grow in our willingness to enter into prayer we become increasingly attentive and, I hope with time, fully alive. We stop to smell the roses and see the beauty of the blossoms and the fragility of the petal, and inhale its fragrance.

We become infinitely new in our acceptance and openness, wisdom and compassion. We are able to accept who we are. We are the created of God—good and holy. We belong here. We begin to see that the life of prayer does not lead us to another world but reveals the depth of this world. We begin to realize, to be habitually aware of, the depths in the everyday that were once hidden.

It begins to dawn on me: Prayer isn't to let God know things God's not aware of. Instead, prayer is God's way of making me aware of who I am and the divine depths of all that surrounds me and that in which I take up my being.

Writing a book on prayer is a presumptuous act; one sets oneself up as an expert. Perhaps one is even taken seriously and becomes raw material for footnotes! Yet I am still working on my understanding of prayer, and even more aware that as a pray-er I am not quite there yet. So I am thankful for my beginner's status and pray to God that I never lose it.

Annie Dillard writes about "your one necessary" in her book, *Teaching a Stone to Talk*, "I think it would be well, and proper, and obedient, and pure, to grasp your own necessary and not let it go, to dangle from it limp wherever it takes you. Then even death, where you're going no matter how you live, cannot you part."

This I know is true: the one thing necessary for me is prayer.

Suggested Lectionary
Readings

$\mathcal{T}$he lectionary for Sundays is arranged in a three-year cycle, in which Year A always begins on the first Sunday of Advent in years evenly divisible by three. The Church Year and the lectionary readings begin with Advent in November/December.

Year A: 2004–2005, 2007–2008
Year B: 2002–2003, 2005–2006
Year C: 2003–2004, 2006–2007

In this abbreviated lectionary from the *Book of Common Prayer* the principal service Gospel readings are listed. Not included are the psalms, Old Testament, or Epistle readings. If more than one text was listed, only the first was included here except for

Palm/Passion Sunday when two scriptures are listed. Christmas Day and Ash Wednesday, although not Sundays, are included because they mark a change in the liturgical season. Suggested expanded readings are also excluded. The Easter Vigil listing, identically used in Years A, B, and C, includes the entire sweep of the salvation story.

Use these scriptures to practice the daily office and lectio divina to pray the scriptures. One text is listed for each week. To access all Sunday and feast day scriptures go to "Revised Common Lectionary" of your favorite search engine. You can also access daily readings.

YEAR A

First Sunday of Advent	Matthew 24:37–44	Sixth Sunday after the Epiphany	Matthew 5:21–24, 27–30, 33–37
Second Sunday of Advent	Matthew 3:1–12		
Third Sunday of Advent	Matthew 11:2–11		
Fourth Sunday of Advent	Matthew 1:18–25	Seventh Sunday after the Epiphany	Matthew 5:38–48
Christmas Day	Luke 2:1–14		
First Sunday after Christmas	John 1:1–18	Eighth Sunday after the Epiphany	Matthew 6:24–34
Second Sunday after Christmas	Matthew 2:13–15, 19–23	Transfiguration Sunday, Last Sunday after the Epiphany	Matthew 17:1–9
Epiphany of the Lord	Matthew 2:1–12		
Baptism of the Lord, First Sunday after the Epiphany	Matthew 3:13–17	Ash Wednesday	Matthew 6:1–6, 16–21
		First Sunday in Lent	Matthew 4:1–11
Second Sunday after the Epiphany	John 1:29–41	Second Sunday in Lent	John 3:1–17
		Third Sunday in Lent	John 4:5–26, 39–42
Third Sunday after the Epiphany	Matthew 4:12–23	Fourth Sunday in Lent	John 9:1–13, 28–38
		Fifth Sunday in Lent	John 11:17–44
Fourth Sunday after the Epiphany	Matthew 5:1–12	Sixth Sunday in Lent, Passion/Palm Sunday	*Liturgy of the Palms:* Matthew 21:1–11
Fifth Sunday after the Epiphany	Matthew 5:13–20		*Liturgy of the Passion:* Matthew 27: 1–54

EASTER VIGIL (YEARS A, B, AND C)

(The number of readings may vary, but Exodus 14 and at least two other readings from the Old Testament should be used in addition to the New Testament readings.)

Old Testament Readings and Psalms (A, B, and C)

Genesis 1:1–2:4a

Isaiah 55:1–11; Psalm 136:1–9, 23–26 or Psalm 33 (UMH 767)

Isaiah 12:2–6; Genesis 7:1–5, 11–18; 8:6–18; 9:8–13

Ezekiel 36:24–28; Psalm 46 (UMH 780)

Psalm 42 (UMH 777); Genesis 22:1–18

Ezekiel 37:1–14; Psalm 16 (UMH 748)

Psalm 143 (UMH 856); Exodus 14:10–31; 15:20–21; Exodus 15:1b -13, 17–18 (UMH 135)

Second Reading and Psalm (A, B, and C)

Romans 6:3–11; Psalm 114 (UMH 835)

Gospel Readings

Matthew 28:1–10; Mark 16:1–8; Luke 24:1–12

Easter Day	John 20:1–10 or Matthew 28:1–10	Sixth Sunday of Easter	John 15:1–8
		Ascension of the Lord	Luke 24:49–53
Second Sunday of Easter	John 20:19–31	Seventh Sunday of Easter	John 17:1–11
Third Sunday of Easter	Luke 24:13–35	Day of Pentecost	John 20:19–23 and
Fourth Sunday of Easter	John 10:1–10		Acts 1:1–11
Fifth Sunday of Easter	John 14:1–14		

On the weekdays which follow, the numbered Proper which corresponds most closely to the date of Pentecost in that year is used.

Trinity Sunday	Matthew 28:16–20

Season of Pentecost

On the weekdays that follow, the numbered Proper which corresponds most closely to the date of Trinity Sunday in that year is used. This is the "Season of Pentecost" and these Sundays are numbered as "Sundays after Pentecost."

Proper 1 *closest to May 11*	Matthew 5:21–24, 27–30, 33–37
Proper 2 *closest to May 18*	Matthew 5:38–48
Proper 3 *closest to May 25*	Matthew 6:24–34
Proper 4 *closest to June 1*	Matthew 7:21–27
Proper 5 *closest to June 8*	Matthew 9:9–13
Proper 6 *closest to June 15*	Matthew 9:35–10:8
Proper 7 *closest to June 22*	Matthew 10:24–33
Proper 8 *closest to June 29*	Matthew 10:34–42
Proper 9 *closest to July 6*	Matthew 11:25–30
Proper 10 *closest to July 13*	Matthew 13:1–9, 18–23
Proper 11 *closest to July 20*	Matthew 13:24–30, 36–43
Proper 12 *closest to July 27*	Matthew 13:31–33, 44–49a
Proper 13 *closest to August 3*	Matthew 14:13–21
Proper 14 *closest to August 10*	Matthew: 14:22–33
Proper 15 *closest to August 17*	Matthew 15:21–28
Proper 16 *closest to August 24*	Matthew 16:13–20
Proper 17 *closest to August 31*	Matthew 16:21–27
Proper 18 *closest to September 7*	Matthew 18:15–20
Proper 19 *closest to September 14*	Matthew 18:21–35
Proper 20 *closest to September 21*	Matthew 20:1–16
Proper 21 *closest to September 28*	Matthew 21:28–32
Proper 22 *closest to October 5*	Matthew 21:33–43
Proper 23 *closest to October 12*	Matthew 22:1–14
Proper 24 *closest to October 19*	Matthew 25:1–13
Proper 25 *closest to October 26*	Matthew 25:14–30
Proper 26 *closest to November 2*	Matthew 25:31–46
Proper 27 *closest to November 9*	Matthew 10:24–39
Proper 28 *closest to November 16*	Matthew 10:40–42
Proper 29 *closest to November 23*	Matthew 11:16–19, 25–30

YEAR B

First Sunday of Advent	Mark 13:33–37
Second Sunday of Advent	Mark 1:1–8
Third Sunday of Advent	John 1:6–8, 19–28
Fourth Sunday of Advent	Luke 1:26–38
Christmas Day	Luke 2:1–14
First Sunday after Christmas	John 1:1–18
Second Sunday after Christmas	Matthew 2:1–12
Epiphany of the Lord, *January 6*	Matthew 2:1–12
First Sunday after the Epiphany	Mark 1:7–11
Second Sunday after the Epiphany	John 1:43–51
Third Sunday after the Epiphany	Mark 1:14–20
Fourth Sunday after the Epiphany	Mark 1:21–28
Fifth Sunday after the Epiphany	Mark 1:29–39
Sixth Sunday after the Epiphany	Mark 1:40–45
Seventh Sunday after the Epiphany	Mark 2:1–12
Eighth Sunday after the Epiphany	Mark 2:18–22
Last Sunday after the Epiphany, Transfiguration Sunday	Mark 9:2–9
Ash Wednesday	Matthew 6:1–6, 16–21
First Sunday in Lent	Mark 1:9–15
Second Sunday in Lent	Mark 8:31–38
Third Sunday in Lent	John 2:13–22
Fourth Sunday in Lent	John 6:4–15
Fifth Sunday in Lent	John 12:20–33
Sixth Sunday in Lent, Passion/Palm Sunday	*Liturgy of the Palms:* Mark 11:1–11a *Liturgy of the Passion:* Mark 15:1–39

EASTER VIGIL (SEE YEAR A)

Easter Day	Mark 16: 1–8	Fifth Sunday of Easter	John 14:15–21
Second Sunday of Easter	John 20:19–31	Sixth Sunday of Easter	John 15:9–17
Third Sunday of Easter	Luke 24:36b–48	Seventh Sunday of Easter	John 17:11b–19
Fourth Sunday of Easter	John 10:11–18	Day of Pentecost	John 15:26–27; 16:4b–15

On the weekdays that follow, the numbered Proper which corresponds most closely to the date of Pentecost in that year is used.

Trinity Sunday	John 3:1–17

Season of Pentecost

On the weekdays that follow, the numbered Proper which corresponds most closely to the date of Trinity Sunday in that year is used. This is the "Season of Pentecost" and these Sundays are numbered as "Sundays after Pentecost."

Proper 1 *closest to May 11*	Mark 1:40–45	Proper 15 *closest to August 17*	John 6:53–59
Proper 2 *closest to May 18*	Mark 2:10–12	Proper 16 *closest to August 24*	John 6:60–69
Proper 3 *closest to May 25*	Mark 2:18–22	Proper 17 *closest to August 31*	Mark 7:1–8, 14–15, 21–23
Proper 4 *closest to June 1*	Mark 2:23–28	Proper 18 *closest to September 7*	Mark 7:31–37
Proper 5 *closest to June 8*	Mark 3:20–35	Proper 19 *closest to September 14*	Mark 8:27–38
Proper 6 *closest to June 15*	Mark 4:26–34	Proper 20 *closest to September 21*	Mark 9:30–37
Proper 7 *closest to June 22*	Mark 4:35–41	Proper 21 *closest to September 28*	Mark 9:38–43, 45, 47–48
Proper 8 *closest to June 29*	Mark 5:22–24, 35b–43	Proper 22 *closest to October 5*	Mark 10:2–9
		Proper 23 *closest to October 12*	Mark 10:17–27
Proper 9 *closest to July 6*	Mark 6:1–6	Proper 24 *closest to October 19*	Mark 10:35–45
Proper 10 *closest to July 13*	Mark 6:7–13	Proper 25 *closest to October 26*	Mark 10:46–52
Proper 11 *closest to July 20*	Mark 6:30–44	Proper 26 *closest to November 2*	Mark 12:28–34
Proper 12 *closest to July 27*	Mark 6:45–52	Proper 27 *closest to November 9*	Mark 12:38–44
Proper 13 *closest to August 3*	John 6:24–35	Proper 28 *closest to November 16*	Mark 13:14–23
Proper 14 *closest to August 10*	John 6:37–51	Proper 29 *closest to November 23*	John 18:33–37

Year C

First Sunday of Advent	Luke 21:25–36	Last Sunday after the Epiphany,	
Second Sunday of Advent	Luke 3:1–6	Transfiguration Sunday	Luke 9:28–36
Third Sunday of Advent	Luke 3:7–18	Ash Wednesday	Matthew 6:1–6
Fourth Sunday of Advent	Luke 1:39–49	First Sunday in Lent	Luke 4:1–13
Christmas Day	Luke 2:1–14	Second Sunday in Lent	Luke 13:31–35
First Sunday after Christmas	John 1:1–18	Third Sunday in Lent	Luke 13:1–9
Second Sunday after Christmas	Matthew 2:13–15, 19–23	Fourth Sunday in Lent	Luke 15:11–32
		Fifth Sunday in Lent	Luke 20:9–19
Epiphany of the Lord, *January 6*	Matthew 2:1–12	Sixth Sunday in Lent, Passion/Palm Sunday	*Liturgy of the Palms:* Luke 19:29–40
First Sunday after the Epiphany	Luke 3:15–17, 21–22		*Liturgy of the Passion:* Luke 23:1–49
Second Sunday after the Epiphany	John 2:1–11	Easter Day	Luke 24:1–10
Third Sunday after the Epiphany	Luke 4:14–21	Second Sunday of Easter	John 20:19–31
		Third Sunday of Easter	John 21:1–14
Fourth Sunday after the Epiphany	Luke 4:21–32	Fourth Sunday of Easter	John 10:22–30
		Fifth Sunday of Easter	John 13:31–35
Fifth Sunday after the Epiphany	Luke 5:1–11	Sixth Sunday of Easter	John 14:23–29
Sixth Sunday after the Epiphany	Luke 6:17–26	Ascension of the Lord (A, B, and C)	Luke 24:49–53
		Seventh Sunday of Easter	John 17:20–26
Seventh Sunday after the Epiphany	Luke 6:27–38	Day of Pentecost	Acts 2:1–11 and John 20:19–23
Eighth Sunday after the Epiphany	Luke 6:39–49		

On the weekdays that follow, the numbered Proper which corresponds most closely to the date of Pentecost in that year is used.

Trinity Sunday   John 16:12–15

Season of Pentecost

On the weekdays that follow, the numbered Proper which corresponds most closely to the date of Trinity Sunday in that year is used. This is the "Season of Pentecost" and these Sundays are numbered as "Sundays after Pentecost."

Proper 1 *closest to May 11*	Luke 6:17–26		Proper 16 *closest to August 24*	Luke 13:22–30
Proper 2 *closest to May 18*	Luke 6:27–38		Proper 17 *closest to August 31*	Luke 14:1, 7–14
Proper 3 *closest to May 25*	Luke 6:39–49		Proper 18 *closest to September 7*	Luke 14:25–33
Proper 4 *closest to June 1*	Luke 7:1–10		Proper 19 *closest to September 14*	Luke 15:1–10
Proper 5 *closest to June 8*	Luke 7:11–17		Proper 20 *closest to September 21*	Luke 16:1–13
Proper 6 *closest to June 15*	Luke 7:36–50		Proper 21 *closest to September 28*	Luke 16:19–31
Proper 7 *closest to June 22*	Luke 9:18–24		Proper 22 *closest to October 5*	Luke 17:5–10
Proper 8 *closest to June 29*	Luke 9:51–62		Proper 23 *closest to October 12*	Luke 17:11–19
Proper 9 *closest to July 6*	Luke 10:1–12, 16–20		Proper 24 *closest to October 19*	Luke 18:1–8a
Proper 10 *closest to July 13*	Luke 10:25–37		Proper 25 *closest to October 26*	Luke 18:9–14
Proper 11 *closest to July 20*	Luke 10:38–42		Proper 26 *closest to November 2*	Luke 19:1–10
Proper 12 *closest to July 27*	Luke 11:1–13		Proper 27 *closest to November 9*	Luke 20:27, 34–38
Proper 13 *closest to August 3*	Luke 12:13–21		Proper 28 *closest to November 16*	Luke 21:5–19
Proper 14 *closest to August 10*	Luke 12:32–40		Proper 29 *closest to November 23*	Luke 23:35–43
Proper 15 *closest to August 17*	Luke 12:49–56			

References

*C*ountless sources helped to shape my chapters. Many are already listed for you in each chapter under the heading "Other Resources to Continue Your Journey." I have not repeated those resources and contacts here unless it seemed prudent for the reader. Many of the quotes used throughout this book were gathered for personal devotional use over the years, without noting their original source. A good-faith effort was made to uncover the original sources, and others will be noted in future editions as they are researched and supplied. These include quotes by Richard of Chichester, "O Most merciful Redeemer"; Thomas Aquinas, "Grant me, O merciful God"; Mother Teresa of Calcutta, "There are some people who . . ."; Monica of Africa, "Nothing is far from God"; Bonaventure, "The true disciple of

Christ"; St. Gregory of Nazianzus, "We bless you"; Catherine of Siena, "You, O Eternal Trinity"; John Chrysostom, "Find the door of your heart"; Theresa of Lisieux, "The daring ambition of aspiring to great sanctity has never left me . . ."; Ignatius, "In making a choice"; Hildegard Von Bingen, "Just as the wheel"; Theophan the Recluse, "Let your mind descend"; Isaac of Syria, "Endeavor to enter into your inner treasure house"; Douglas Steele, "The adoration of God" and "A first-hand feeling of being moved to the core"; Frank Mill, "The interlaced patterns with their unbroken lines"; and Dame Gertrude More, "O my God, let me walk in the way of love." The quotations of Teresa of Avila throughout the book are from her works. See *The Soul's Passion for God, Selected Writings of Teresa of Avila* (Nashville, Tenn.: Upper Room Books, 1997). Three books offer sweeping surveys of the current religious culture and influenced my opinions: *Spiritual Marketplace: Baby Boomers and the Remaking of American Religion,* by Wade Clark Roof (Princeton, N.J.: Princeton University Press, 1999); *The Restructuring of American Religion,* by Robert Wuthnow (Princeton, N.J.: Princeton University Press, 1988); and *After Heaven: Spirituality in America Since the 1950s,* also by Wuthnow (Berkeley: University of California Press, 1998). For a more expansive discussion on current spiritual trends, see Wayne Teasdale, *The Mystic Heart: Discovering a Universal Spirituality in the World's Religions* (Novato, Calif.: New World Library, 1999).

FOUNDATIONS OF PRAYER

The quote from Pat Collins is from *Prayer in Practice: A Biblical Approach,* (Maryknoll, N.Y.: Orbis Books, 2001). The quote from *The Cloud of Unknowing* is from *The Cloud of Unknowing and the Book of Privy Counseling,* edited by William Johnston (New York: Doubleday, 1973, p. 149). The quote from Joseph Driskill is from *Protestant Spiritual Exercises: Theology, History and Practice* (Harrisburg, Pa.: Morehouse, 1999, p. 9).

HOW DO YOU PRAY?

If you are interested in knowing more about personality type indicators, or other personality assessments, you can read individuals such as James Fowler and Carl Jung, who combined theology (the study of God) and psychology (the study of the mind) to write about the correlations and implications between spiritual and psychological development. Studying the social sciences of personality preferences and developmental stages can be helpful in understanding our personal spiritual growth. Examining psychology alongside religious experiences can explain how we develop spiritually. Through psychology we are reassured that most of our life experiences are a normal part of what it means to be a human being made in the image of God and that transitions as we grow in Christ are normal, predictable patterns for people of faith.

The personality and stage development sciences can enhance our knowledge of our relationship to God through prayer, but these social sciences are not a substitute for the Church's own Christian story and faith tradition. Spiritual formation is a different discipline from psychology's developmental perspective. Spiritual formation and spiritual direction are not substitutes for psychotherapy or counseling, but neither do psychotherapy or therapeutic counseling substitute for spiritual formation and direction. Each seeks a different kind of growth, yet each complements and contributes to the other's process.

Despite these precautionary warnings, self-revealing tools can help you to understand yourself better, bringing clarity as well as a new depth to your prayer life.

Knowing something about our own personality helps steer you toward spiritual practices you're more likely to be receptive to. At first you may feel hesitant to employ an assessment tool, such as the one used in this book, that may help reshape your self-understanding. You already have a self-identity that is familiar and with which you are at some level of comfort. To re-look at your self-concept is hard work. But this refection can be important in helping you clarify your beliefs and to examine which beliefs pull you towards God and which ones push you away. This reinterpretation of yourself may even help you to reconsider your relationship to your faith tradition.

André Ravier's book *A Do It at Home Retreat: The Spiritual Exercises of St. Ignatius of Loyola* (San Francisco: Ignatius Press, 1991) was important in my reflections on prayer influenced by this sixteenth-century saint. Quotations of Evelyn Underhill are from *Mysticism: A Study of the Nature and Development of Man's Spiritual Consciousness* (London: Methuen, 1911). The confessional prayer from Kenya is from *Bread of Tomorrow: Prayers for the Church Year*, edited by Janey Morley (Maryknoll, N.Y.: Orbis Books, 1992), p. 37.

LORD'S PRAYER

St. Gregory Palamas's quote is found in Robert Ellsberg, *All Saints: Daily Reflections on Saints, Prophets, and Witnesses for Our Time* (New York: Crossroads, 1997), p. 496.

PRAYING THE SCRIPTURES

Madame Guyon's directions can be found in *Gracious Voices, Shouts and Whispers for God Seekers*, by William P. McDonald, Discipleship Resources, Nashville, 1996. Although there are numerous variations, I first used this general description of the lectio divina process in my book *Spiritgifts: One Spirit, Many Gifts*, Abingdon Press, Nashville, 1996. Learnings concerning "I" statements and importance of listening were forged while working with various prayer groups.

A Journal of Prayer

Instructions on how to journal were first drafted while working with women's groups on what would later become the *Heart to Heart Guidebook: A Spiritual Journey for Women,* and *From the Heart Journal: A Personal Prayer Journal for Women,* Abingdon Press, 1999.

Pilgrimage

The opening prayer "Sancti Colombani Opera" comes from Philip Sheldrake's *Living Between Worlds: Place and Journey in Celtic Spirituality* (Cambridge, Mass.: Cowley, 1995), p. 61. Basic information on pilgrimage came from *Catholic Shrines of Western Europe: A Pilgrim Travel Guide,* by Kevin J. Wright (Liguori, Mo.: Liguori, 1997). Origen's quote is from the text *Origen: Selected Writings, Classics of Western Spirituality Series,* translated by Rowan A. Greer (New York/Mahwah, N.J.: Paulist Press, 1979), p. 250. Simon Coleman and John Elsner's book *Pilgrimages Past and Present in the World Religions* (Cambridge, Mass.: Harvard University Press, 1995), excerpt from p. 104, was important in my understandings on pilgrimage as well as George Henderson's *Chartres* (Baltimore, Md.: Penguin Books, 1968), excerpt from p. 53.

Praying with Icons

Quote by Joan Chittister from *A Passion for Life: Fragments of the Face of God* (Maryknoll, N.Y.: Orbis, 1996). For a thumbnail history of icons and iconography, go to *The New Dictionary of Catholic Spirituality,* edited by Michael Downey (Collegeville, Minn.: Liturgical Press), pp. 519–521. Icons by Robert Lentz are found in the book *A Pas-*

sion for Life, Fragments of the Face of God (Maryknoll, N.Y.: Orbis Books, 1996). *Praying with Icons,* by Jim Forest (Maryknoll, N.Y.: Orbis Books, 1997), offers a readable text with special emphasis on the practical use.

NOVENAS

The quote from Saint Augustine comes from *Prayer: Language of the Soul,* by Philip Dunn (New York: Dell, 1997), p. 154. A modern-day source used to study novenas was *Novena: The Power of Prayer,* by Barbara Calamari and Sandra Di Pasqua (New York: Penguin Putnam, 1999). My professional colleague Sister Angela Hibbard, IHM, also lent her knowledge to understanding this practice.

PRAYERS FOR THE DEAD

To read more of Henri J. M. Nouwen's *Reflections on Death and Life,* read his book *Beyond the Mirror* (New York: Crossroads, 1990). In this chapter, I also draw on my years as a hospital and hospice chaplain as well as on Dom Gregory Dix's 1945 *The Shape of the Liturgy* (London, N.Y.: Continuum, reprint 2000) and *The Liturgy of Christian Burial: An Introductory Survey of the Historical Development of Christian Burial Rites,* by Geoffrey Rowell (Lincolnshire, U.K.: Alcvin Club/S.P.C.K., 1977). The prayer at the burial of an adult is from the 1979 edition of *The Book of Common Prayer According to the Use of the Episcopal Church,* Burial I (New York: Seabury Press, 1979, pp. 469–489). The song for eventide by Henry F. Lyte can be found in most hymn books, including the one I used: *The United Methodist Hymnal* (Nashville: United Methodist Publishing House, 1989), p. 700. The end quote is by Sarah York in her book *Remembering Well: Rituals for Celebrating Life and Mourning Death* (San Francisco: Jossey-Bass, 2000).

332   FASTING

The opening quote and other words of wisdom by Megan McKenna can be found in *Rites of Justice* (Maryknoll, N.Y.: Orbis Books, 1997). John Wesley's quote is found in "Causes of Inefficacy of Christianity," *Sermons on Several Occasions*, ed. Thomas Jackson, vol. 2 (New York: T. Mason and G. Lane, 1840), p. 440. The quote by Seraphim of Sarov is found in *Prayer and Fasting: A Study in the Devotional Life of the Early Church* (New York: Carlton Press, 1971). *A Hunger for God, Desiring God Through Fasting and Prayer*, by John Piper (Wheaton, Ill.: Crossway Books, 1997), is a comprehensive study of fasting and was influential in my thinking.

BREATH PRAYER

Several sources helped to shape this chapter: Ron DelBene's book with Herb Montgomery *The Breath of Life: A Simple Way to Pray* (Minneapolis: Winston Press, 1981); *The Art of Prayer: An Orthodox Anthology*, compiled by Igumen Chariton of Valamo and translated by E. Kadloubovsky and E. M. Palmer (London: Faber and Faber, 1966); and *The Way of the Pilgrim and the Pilgrim Continues His Way*, Helen Bacovcin (trans.) (New York, Doubleday, 1978). The writings of Simeon the New Theologian can be found in *Writings from the Philokalia on Prayer of the Heart*, translated by E. Kadloubovsky and G.E.H. Palmer (London: Faber and Faber, 1975).

BENEDICTION AND BLESSING

The opening Celtic prayer comes from *200 Years of Classic Christian Prayers: A Collection for Public and Personal Use*, edited by Owen Collins (Maryknoll, N.Y.: Orbis Books, 1999), p. 281. Although the cross blessing used here is from *Come to the Wa-*

ters: Baptism and Our Ministry of Welcoming Seekers and Making Disciples, by Daniel T. Bene-

dict (Nashville, Tenn.: Discipleship Resources, 1996), another worthy source is *The Awe-Inspiring Rites of Initiation: The Origins of the R.C.I.A.* by Edward Yarnold, S.J. (Collegeville, Minn.: Liturgical Press, 1971).

TALLITH: THE PRAYER SHAWL

Judy Petsonk's book is *Taking Judaism Personally: Creating a Meaningful Spiritual Life* (Free Press, 1996). Material basic to Jewish prayer I found on various Websites, as well as in *To Pray as a Jew: A Guide to the Prayer Book and the Synagogue Service* by Hayim Halevy Donin (Cambridge, Mass.: Basic Books, 1980). Mentoring by Rabbi Eliezer Havivi was invaluable.

CENTERING PRAYER

In this prayer practice, I drew together the contemplative methods of a number of teachers of contemplation into a coherent whole, among them John Main and Thomas Keating. I also relied on the wisdom of practitioners Brother Wayne Teasdale and Rev. Kent Groff.

MEDITATION

Julian's words "God showed me" came from *Revelations of Divine Love,* edited by Clifton Wolters (London: Penguin Books, 1966), p. 68. I confess that I do not narrowly delineate "meditation" (strictly regarded as the mental consideration of something) from "contemplative prayer" (placing oneself in a disposition of resting in God's presence), for my essential goal is to still the constant movement of the mind and open myself to deeper union with Christ's indwelling and guiding presence. John Main ideas come from *Moment of Christ: The Path of Meditation* (New York: Continuum, 1998).

ANOINTING FOR HEALING

The opening quote comes from *Stretch Out Your Hand, Exploring Healing Prayer* by Rev. Tilda Norberg and Robert D. Webber (Nashville, Tenn.: Upper Room Books, 1998). My use of the term "sign act" comes from the teachings of Laurence Hull Stookey and his text *Baptism: Christ's Act in the Church* (Nashville, Tenn.: Abingdon, 1982). The prayer to bless the oil is from *The United Methodist Book of Worship* (Nashville, Tenn.: United Methodist Publishing House, 1989).

ADORATION PRAYER

I gathered an understanding of the French school of spirituality from a number of sources, including the *New Dictionary of Catholic Spirituality,* edited by Michael Downey (Collegeville, Minn.: Liturgical Press, 1993), pp. 420–423. For more on Rahner's thoughts on prayer, see *The Need and the Blessing of Prayer* by Karl Rahner (Collegeville, Minn.: Liturgical Press, 1997). The reflective prayer of Mechtild of Magdeburg comes from *Prayer: Language of the Soul,* by Philip Dunn (New York: Dell, 1997), p. 173.

PRAYERS OF CONFESSION

"The work of purging," by Francis de Sales, comes from *Introduction to the Devout Life,* edited by John K. Ryan (New York: Doubleday Press, 1950), p. 48. The complete questions of John Wesley can be found in *The United Methodist Book of Worship*

(Nashville, Tenn.: United Methodist Publishing House, 1989). Jim Forest's book *Confession: Doorway to Forgiveness* (Maryknoll, N.Y.: Orbis Books, 2002) and subsequent e-mails with Jim were important in my reflections on confession, for both its theological depth and emotional intensity; quotation from p. 103.

PRAYER OF EXAMEN

The quote of Florence Nightingale comes from Barbara Montgomery Dossey's book *Florence Nightingale: Mystic, Visionary, Healer* (Springhouse, Pa.: Springhouse, 2000). The words of Anselm of Normandy can be found in "The Proslogion," in *The Prayers and Meditations of St. Amselm,* translated by Sr. Benedicta Ward, SLG (Middlesex, England: Penguin Books, 1973), pp. 239–240. Normandy's "the daring ambition" is found in *Story of a Soul,* translated in *The Wisdom of the Saints,* edited by Jill Haak Adels (New York: Oxford Press, 1987), p. 4. Kent Ira Groff is the author of "A Daily Examen of Conscience." My thoughts on consolation and desolation come from the works of Ignatius and the book *Inner Compass: An Invitation to Ignatian Spirituality,* by Margaret Silf (Chicago: Loyola Press, 1999), pp. 38–61.

THE DAILY OFFICE

To learn more about the Jewish pattern of prayer, see *The Way into Jewish Prayer,* by Lawrence A. Hoffman (Woodstock, Vt.: Jewish Light, 2000), pp. 20–28. As a member of the Order of St. Luke, I use *The Book of Offices and Services* of our order (edited by Timothy J. Crouch, O.S.L., 1994) as my understanding of morning and evening prayer featured here. You can order the paperback: P.O. Box 22279, Akron, OH 44302–0079. The complete works of Emily Dickinson can be had at http://members.aol.com/GivenRandy/r_emily.htm. Theologian Theophan the

Recluse's word on the way to unceasing prayer is found in *The Art of Prayer: An Orthodox Anthology,* compiled by Igumen Chariton of Valamo and translated by E. Kadloubovsky and E. M. Palmer (London, Faber and Faber, 1966), p. 80.

TONGSUNG KIDO

This prayer practice was introduced to many through *The United Methodist Book of Worship* (Nashville, Tenn.: United Methodist Publishing House, 1989).

PRAYER WALKS

The traditional Navaho prayer is found in *The United Methodist Book of Worship* (Nashville, Tenn.: United Methodist Publishing House, 1989), p. 562.

PRAYING WITH OUR BODIES

"I will imagine," by Anthony Mary Claret, is found in the Prologue to "The Temple and Palace of Our Master" in *San Antonio Maria Claret* (Madrid: B.A.C., 1985), p. 147. The body prayer segment was composed with the help of yoga instructor René Graney.

PRAYER LABYRINTH

Julian of Norwich's famous quote was found in *All the Saints: Daily Reflections on Saints, Prophets, and Witnesses for Our Time,* by Robert Ellsberg (New York: Crossroads, 1997), p. 212. The most comprehensive book I used was *Through the Labyrinth,* by Hermann Kern (New York: Prestel, 2000).

Home Prayer Altars

A more extended account of the themes developed in this chapter is found in *Altars Made Easy: A Complete Guide to Creating Your Own Sacred Space*, by Peg Streep (San Francisco: HarperSanFrancisco, 1997).

Ignatian Prayer

Works that I have found useful in thinking about Ignatian spirituality are *Retreat with the Lord: A Popular Guide to the Spiritual Exercises of Ignatius of Loyola*, by John A Hardon, S.J. (Ann Arbor, Mich.: Charis Servant, 1993); *Eyes to See, Ears to Hear: An Introduction to Ignatian Spirituality*, by David Lonsdale (Maryknoll, N.Y.: Orbis Books, 2000); and *A Do It at Home Retreat: The Spiritual Exercises of St. Ignatius of Loyola*, by André Ravier, S.J. (San Francisco: Ignatius Press, 1989).

Prayer Beads

Many sources were used to study prayer beads, but an important and up-to-date resource continues to be the Vatican Website.

Praying with Mandalas

More information on Celtic plaitwork can be found in *Celtic Spirals and Other Designs*, by Sheila Sturrock (East Sussex, U.K.: Guild of Master Craftsmen, 2000). See *Man and His Symbols*, edited with an introduction by Carl G. Jung (New York: Bell, reprint 1997, pp. 266–285) for his quote used in this chapter as well as more information on his work with mandalas. Many of his works can be downloaded from the Web.

PRAYER DANCE

"How you look isn't important" is by Carla DeSola, who is called the mother of sacred dance, from her now out-of-print book *The Spirit Moves*. The dance of Jesus is described in the *Apocryphal New Testament*, M. R. James translation and notes (Oxford: Clarendon Press, 1924), Acts of St. John, verses 94–96. To read it for yourself, see www.earlychristianwritings.com/text/actsjohn.html.

A CLOSING BENEDICTION

Annie Dillard writes about "your one necessary" in her book *Teaching a Stone to Talk*, revised edition (San Francisco: HarperSanFrancisco, 1999).

 *Acknowledgments*

*T*he writing of this book spans many years, and I am thankful for all the people who have supported me in its various stages. Thanks to Rev. Adele Wilcox and Bette Sohm-Johnson, who read the earliest drafts. I thank my doctoral committee, who were most generous in their contribution, doctors all: Carol Barrett, my core faculty adviser; Edna Kovacs, for her keen Jewish edge; Barbara Dossey, my Episcopal friend and wondrous healer, and her spouse, Dr. Larry Dossey; Rev. Kent Groff, for his United Church of Christ sensibilities; Judith Berling, of the Graduate Theological Union in Berkeley; Brother Wayne Teasdale, our committee mystic; and Kevin Sharpe and Susan Amussen, of the Union Institute and University. I am also

grateful for those who gave their time as doctoral consultants: Rev. Linda Brond-
sted, Rev. Danielle Morris, Lea Barbato Gaydos, Rev. Sue Haupert-Johnson, and
William Burrows (managing editor of Orbis Books). In addition, I thank doctoral
classmates who participated in an online course on prayer.

Special thanks to Rabbi Eliezer Havivi for his help with the tallith, and to Jim
Forest for his help with icons; Robert Ferre for expertise concerning labyrinths;
Our Lady's Rosary Makers; Christian Gloddy and the Conchis Media Group for
other computer assistance; and Rev. Keith Beasley-Topliffe of The Upper Room.

Special mention must be made of the many congregations and church groups
who prayed the practices with me and offered generous feedback that contributed
to making this book true to life and down to earth. Special thanks to Rev. James
Jennings and Donna Maynard and the First UMC, Sarasota; my Sunday school
class, the Parent's Forum Class of First United Methodist Church, Orlando; the
Christ Path Community, especially Ken Cowles; the Institute for Christian Studies
Formation Program in Spiritual Direction; Judy Gober and the Christian Educa-
tion Fellowship of the Florida Conference of the United Methodist Church; Rev.
John W. Harrington, Anita Randolph, and Rev. Jennifer Stiles Williams and the
Mandarin United Methodist Church; the pilgrimage group who accompanied me
to France in May 2001; Ann Williams and the Titusville United Methodist
Women; Rev. Sami Wilson and her church in Miami; Mollie Clark and the Univer-
sity Hospital Department of Pastoral Care in Birmingham, Alabama; Rev. George
Buie, Amy and Rev. Brian Fowlers, and the First United Methodist Church, Fort
Myers, Florida; Joyce Estes and the St. George Island United Methodist Church;
Rev. Tom Otto and the Flagler Beach United Methodist Church; Rev. Kendall Tay-
lor and the Palm Beach District pastors; Rev. Jeannette Burton of Largo, Florida;
and Rev. Lindsay Orr, Rev. Joyce Crawford, and the ministers of the Lackawanna
Presbyterian churches. Thanks also to the General Board of Higher Education of

the United Methodist Church gathering of Campus Ministers in Atlanta, along with Cynthia Blankenship, who taught us how to make our first prayer beads.

I gratefully acknowledge the host of groups who offered feedback via e-mail and letters: Fred H. Bowen of Bradley Beach, New Jersey; Marietta H. Snedaker of Endicott, New York; Rev. Ralph Reynolds and the Chenango Bridge UMC; Rev. Evelyn Lintern of Otego, New York; Barbara Newman and CCUMC; Doris Biddix; Tom Hoffman; Rev. Fairy Caroland; and Rev. Lois Kitto.

I also express my appreciation to professional colleagues: Sister Angela Hibbard, IHM, for her invaluable guidance in things Roman Catholic; Diane Noble; Andrew Dreitcer of Claremont School of Theology; Diedra Kriewald of Wesley Theological Seminary, and René Graney, my Yoga teacher par excellence, who graciously taught me to pray with my body.

Of course, this book would not be a reality without my friends at Jossey-Bass and my excellent editor, Julianna Gustafson, who took the risk to believe in this project. Big hugs go to my husband, Dale, for his support; my younger son, Stephen, for his music and laughter; and to my elder son, Christian, for his encouragement. Most of all, this book is a creation of Divine energy and inspiration, a gift from God who allows me to work and serve, and I offer forever my gratitude.

The Author

Patricia D. Brown is an ordained minister with the United Methodist Church and is associate professor of educational ministries and Christian formation at Seattle Pacific University. In her twenty-five years in ministry, she has served as a pastor of seven congregations, both rural and urban, and as a chaplain to two major medical centers. The author of nine published books, Brown is a popular speaker and workshop leader, and her ongoing ministries are specifically formulated to help individuals and communities become alive in Christ.